SAINT THOMAS AQUINAS

SUMMA CONTRA GENTILES

BOOK ONE: GOD

University
of
Notre Dame Press
Notre Dame
London

Translated,
with an Introduction
and Notes,
by
ANTON C. PEGIS,
F.R.S.C.

University of Notre Dame Press edition 1975

Copyright © 1955 by Doubleday & Company, Inc.

First published in 1955 by Hanover House as

On the Truth of the Catholic Faith

First paperback edition 1955 by Image Books

Published by arrangement with Doubleday & Company, Inc.

Printed in the United States of America

Library of Congress Cataloging in Publication Data

Thomas Aquinas, Saint, 1225?-1274.
    Summa contra gentiles.

    Reprint of the ed. published by Hanover House,
Garden City, N.Y., under title: On the truth of
the Catholic faith.
    Includes bibliographies.
    CONTENTS: book 1. God, translated, with an
introd. and notes, by A. C. Pegis. —book 2. Crea-
tion, translated, with an introd. and notes, by
J. F. Anderson. [etc.]
    1. Apologetics—Middle Ages, 600-1500. I. Ti-
tle.
[BX1749.T4 1975]   239   75-19883
ISBN 0-268-01675-5
ISBN 0-268-01676-3 pbk.

FOR MY CHILDREN

The pursuit of wisdom especially joins man to God in friendship

—SAINT THOMAS AQUINAS

Contents.

General Introduction.

I. ST. THOMAS AND HIS WRITINGS

St. Thomas Aquinas was born in Italy in the castle of Roccasecca, near Aquino, early in 1225. Until 1239 he remained an oblate in the Benedictine Monastery of Monte Cassino where he had been entered by his parents in 1231. He studied the liberal arts at the newly established University of Naples, and in 1244 decided to become a Dominican. He set out for Paris, arriving there in the summer of 1245. It is uncertain whether he remained in Paris or went on for his studies to Cologne. In 1248 Albert the Great was sent to Cologne to found a House of Studies. Thomas was Albert's pupil in Cologne from 1248 until 1252 when he returned to Paris. After commenting on the Gospels (1252–1254) and on the *Sentences* of Peter Lombard, he received his license to teach from the University of Paris in 1256. For the next three years he taught in Paris at the Dominican convent of St. James. The years 1259 to 1268 Thomas spent in Italy, lecturing at the Papal Curia. In 1261 to 1265 he was in Orvieto. Here he met his fellow Dominican William of Moerbeke. It was at this time (1263) that Pope Urban IV renewed the efforts of Pope Gregory IX to receive the writings of Aristotle into the Christian world in a manner that would insure a maximum of benefit to Christianity as well as a minimum of harm. William of Moerbeke embarked upon his long and famous series of translations of the writings of Aristotle from the original Greek. Thomas himself undertook his no less famous series of minute commentaries on these translations. At a time when an Arabianized Aristotle was being hardened into an enemy of Christianity in Paris and elsewhere, the work begun by St. Thomas in Orvieto was destined to become a constructive contribution to the emergence of an enduring Christian Aristotelianism. That all St. Thomas' contemporaries did not appreciate or understand this contribution is a fact, and a sad one. That contribution remains, however, a great monument in the history of the 13th century.

St. Thomas was back in Paris by 1269. There he entered into the two struggles that were agitating the University, namely, the attack of the secular clergy on the mendicant orders and the emergence of what has been traditionally called Latin Averroism in the Faculty of Arts of the University. In 1272 St. Thomas was given the task of founding a new House of Studies in Naples for his Order. In 1274 he was summoned by Pope Gregory X to the Council of Lyons. He died on the way at the Cistercian Monastery of Fossanuova, March 7, 1274.

He was canonized by Pope John XXII on July 18, 1323, and in 1567 Pope Pius V declared him the Angelic Doctor. Both by tradition and by Papal authority St. Thomas holds a unique place as a teacher within the Church.

The writing career of St. Thomas was not very long. But in the short span of twenty years he dictated and wrote an enormous number of works, including theological and philosophical commentaries, many doctrinal discussions commonly known as *Disputed Questions*, two famous summaries of Christian doctrine, and several short treatises. It is extremely difficult for the historian to determine the chronology of these writings, and even to know how St. Thomas had the time to accomplish as much as he did.

In addition to commentaries on different parts of Scripture, St. Thomas composed a commentary (1254–1256) on the then current textbook in theology, the *Four Books of Sentences*, written by Peter Lombard in the 12th century. He wrote commentaries on two theological tracts of Boethius (*De Trinitate, De Hebdomadibus*, 1257–1258); on the famous treatise *On the Divine Names* (*De*

Divinis Nominibus) of the no less famous Dionysius the
Pseudo-Areopagite (about 1261); and on the anonymous
and most influential Neoplatonic Book of Causes (Liber
de Causis, 1272). But the most important of St. Thomas'
commentaries are those that he wrote on almost all the
works of Aristotle, beginning with the psychological writings and including the Aristotelian treatises in ethics, poli-
tics, physics, metaphysics, and logic (1266–1272).

The Disputed Questions of St. Thomas, which are the
product of his teaching, cover many problems: On Truth
(De Veritate, 1256–1259), On the Power of God (De
Potentia Dei, 1265–1267), On Evil (De Malo, 1269–
1272), On Spiritual Creatures (De Spiritualibus Creaturis,
1268), On the Soul (De Anima, 1269–1270). To the
Disputed Questions are to be added the more infrequent
and varied Quodlibetal Questions.

Among the theological treatises we must note in particular three in addition to the Commentary on the Sentences
(which, though a commentary in its intention, is yet a
highly original theological work). The Summa Contra Gentiles (1259–1264) is a classic manual of Christian doctrine
intended for the use of Christian missionaries in Spain.
Though St. Thomas himself did not give this work a title,
there are sufficient indications in it to justify the old tradition according to which the work is to be called On the
Truth of the Catholic Faith (De Veritate Fidei Catho-
licae). The famous work called by tradition the Summa
Theologica, whose correct title is either Summa or Summa
Theologiae, belongs to the years 1265 to 1272 and was left
unfinished. To these two large theological syntheses we
must add the much smaller Compendium of Theology
(Compendium Theologiae, 1273).

It has proved difficult for historians to discover the man
behind the author of these works. Unlike St. Augustine,
who can be seen and felt as a man across the pages of his
writings, St. Thomas remains in his work a mind entirely

devoted to the intellectual task of being a disciple and a student of the truth contained in the Christian Revelation. One might say that this discipleship *is* the St. Thomas Aquinas who faces us in his writings with unfailing calmness, with total devotion to the cause of Christian truth, with an unbounded confidence in reason, with a zealous admiration for Aristotle, and yet with an awareness of the errors and failings to which men are subject. In his pages, St. Thomas stands before us as the voice of the Christian reason living and teaching within faith, working to save and to purify the thought of the Greeks and the Arabs in the higher light of the Christian Revelation, confident that all that had been rational in the ancient philosophers and their followers would become more rational within Christianity, just as man himself came to know the secret of his own destiny with certainty and finality from God Himself. In the only personal reflection that St. Thomas Aquinas has ever set down, he has said this of himself in the *Summa Contra Gentiles*:

> "And so, in the name of the divine mercy, I have the confidence to embark upon the work of a wise man, even though this may surpass my powers, and I have set myself the task of making known, as far as my limited powers will allow, the truth that the Catholic faith professes, and of setting aside the errors that are opposed to it. To use the words of Hilary: *I am aware that I owe this to God as the chief duty of my life, that my every word and sense may speak of Him.*"[1]

These words are the spiritual signature of St. Thomas the Dominican monk, dedicating his intelligence to the Truth Who became man for the salvation and perfection of mankind. These words are also a fitting introduction to the SCG, which is not merely the only complete *summa* of Christian doctrine that St. Thomas has written, but

---

1. *Summa Contra Gentiles*, I, ch. 2, ¶2 (below, p. 62). The abbreviation SCG will hereafter be used in the present work to refer to the *Summa Contra Gentiles*.

also a creative and even revolutionary work of Christian apologetics composed at the precise moment when Christian thought needed to be intellectually creative in order to master and assimilate the intelligence and the wisdom of the Greeks and the Arabs.

II.   ARISTOTELIANISM AND THE OCCASION OF THE
Summa Contra Gentiles

The modern student of St. Thomas Aquinas does not always face the task of interpreting his larger treatises as wholes. It is much easier to cite individual texts from the *Summa Theologiae* on specific problems or points of doctrine than to interpret the *Summa* as a whole. For the unity of context that the *Summa* as a whole contains we have tended to substitute the notion of an abstract philosophical system called "Thomism." This Thomism, we sometimes imagine, was inspired by St. Thomas Aquinas and transmitted to the modern world by his great commentators. In the process of transmission it has become developed, and especially it has acquired a systematic character and autonomy that it did not have in St. Thomas himself. But the relation of St. Thomas to this general Thomism is often as tenuous as the relation of Plato to the many Platonisms that have been inspired by his writings. Hence, just as the students of Plato have had to return to his writings in order to determine what Plato himself said and thought, so the students of St. Thomas Aquinas need to return to his writings in order to see within the framework of his express intentions the meaning of the many isolated passages of his writings that are frequently quoted out of context.

The *SCG* is a good example of the present issue. This work is one of the great expressions of the thought of St. Thomas Aquinas. It is, in many ways, the most personal of his doctrinal writings. Strangely enough, however, the *SCG* finds no unanimity of opinion among the historians and students of St. Thomas. There is disagreement as to the nature and purpose of the work. There is disagreement as to its general organization and the articulation of its doctrine. Supposing for a moment that the SCG is one of the two or three truly classic expressions of the mind of their author, these disagreements bear on nothing less than the interpretation of the Thomism of St. Thomas himself in its most fundamental aspects. In the presence of the SCG, the issue is not one of maintaining a coherent interpretation of particular texts on a particular problem, but of seeing the SCG in the unity that inspired it.

In the main, the SCG has posed two problems for its interpreters. One concerns the fundamental purpose of the work with reference to the historical situation that occasioned it. The second problem concerns the internal organization of the SCG. This is a far-reaching problem and certainly the more serious of the two. The question asked is this. How are the four books of the SCG related to one another? Are they parts of a theological work? Is the SCG wholly theological or also partly philosophical? In St. Thomas' own intention, how is the SCG organized and articulated?

As to the occasion and the purpose of the work, there is an old tradition that goes back to the beginning of the 14th century. In an often quoted passage from the chronicle by Peter Marsilio completed in 1313, there occurs the following paragraph on St. Raymond of Penafort and St. Thomas Aquinas:

"Furthermore, strongly desiring the conversion of unbelievers, Raymond asked an outstanding Doctor of Sacred Scripture, a Master in Theology, Brother Thomas of Aquino of the same Order, who among all the clerics of the world was considered in philosophy to be, next to Brother Albert, the greatest, to compose a work against the errors of unbelievers, by which both the cloud of darkness might be dispelled and the teaching of the true Sun might be made manifest to those who refuse to believe. The renowned Master accomplished what the humility of so great a Father asked, and composed a work called the *Summa Contra Gentiles*, held to be without equal in its field."[2]

There are no serious historical reasons for refusing to accept this testimony. The objection that the SCG is too intellectual in character to be a manual of apologetics for missionaries is not a very strong one. St. Thomas himself may very well have thought that the SCG was precisely the sort of work needed by Christian missionaries in Spain face to face with the high intellectual culture of the Moslem world. Seen from this point of view, the SCG is a manual of apologetics against the intellectual picture of the universe created for the Western world by the translation of the writings of Aristotle and his followers into Latin in the course of the 12th and 13th centuries. This is a perfectly understandable objective. In a large sense, therefore, the SCG is part of the Christian intellectual reaction against Arabian intellectual culture, and especially against Arabian Aristotelianism. To the Arabs, and especially to Averroes, Aristotle was philosophy, and therefore the cause of Aristotle was the cause of philosophy itself. To Christian thinkers, consequently, who were reading Aristotle across Arabian commentaries, the cause of Aristotle concentrated within itself the basic conflict between Christianity and the Arabs on the nature of philosophy and the philosophical picture of the universe. To Arabs and Christians alike, Aristotle was the master of those who know. St. Thomas did not create this situation. But the situation did pose for him the great issue of the interpretation of Aristotle, just as it gave him the opportunity to formulate a Christian Aristotelianism that could solve the problem agitating the Christian world since the beginning of the century and especially since the time of Pope Gregory IX.

2. The text is cited in *Sancti Thomae Aquinatis . . . Opera iussu impensaque Leonis XIII P. M. edita* (Romae: ex Typographia Polyglotta), vol. XII, 1918, p. VI.

St. Thomas' attitude towards Aristotle is a particular instance of his attitude towards philosophy, and this in turn is one of the major themes in the over-all plan and purpose of the SCG. Two issues merge in this question. One concerns the attitude of 13th century Christian theologians and philosophers towards Aristotle and his writings. The other concerns their attitude towards philosophy itself. For Christians thinkers to learn philosophy from Aristotle was, in the circumstances, a dangerous complication. To learn it from Aristotle as commented upon by Averroes was to suppose, as Averroes supposed, that philosophy was exactly what Aristotle had taught in the 4th century before Christ. Now Aristotle had in fact taught many doctrines that were untrue and unacceptable to Christian thinkers. To follow Averroes' estimate of Aristotle would consequently lead not only to accepting these errors as philosophically necessary, but also to destroying the very possibility of the unity of truth. How, then, could Christianity assimilate philosophy—the philosophy of Aristotle—without destroying either itself or philosophy?

The situation could not be more complicated or more dangerous. In fact, both the Parisian condemnation of 1277 and the general direction of mediaeval philosophy after it indicate that the Christian thinkers of the Middle Ages were not completely successful in the problem of assimilating Aristotle. As for St. Thomas, from the beginning of his career he took a position on Aristotle and philosophy that, were it followed, would have proved a successful diagnosis of the problem. He did not believe that Aristotle or any other philosopher was errorless; yet he did believe that, within its own domain, philosophy was not necessarily subject to error; in other words, that as the work of the human reason philosophy could be errorless. He believed that truth was one and came from God. He therefore believed that nothing that was philosophically demonstrable could ever contradict or be contradicted by anything taught to man by the Christian Revelation. Even more, he believed that, in the divine plan of creation, reason was a sort of preamble to faith, leading man by its light towards a God Who, out of His infinite love and generosity, had created man in order to raise him to a participation in His life. Not only, therefore, was truth one, but the human reason was at home in revelation as in a transcending truth that answered to its deepest needs and fulfilled it in a way that man could not know or expect. The Christian Aristotelianism of St. Thomas Aquinas, therefore, is a witness to his belief in the unity of truth, in the completion of reason by faith, indeed in the purification and growth of the very rationality of reason through faith, and in the service of reason to faith as its preamble. As for Aristotle, like other men he was fallible and subject to error. But, even so, he was an eminent philosopher whose eminence was recognized by his unique title as the Philosopher. Yet he earned this eminence not because he had spoken, but because what he said contained so much truth within it. As St. Thomas saw him, Aristotle served truth well as a philosopher, so that St. Thomas was often able to speak "according to truth and Aristotle."

These views were present in St. Thomas' mind towards the year 1257 when he was commenting on Boethius' theological tract *On the Trinity*. In this commentary, St. Thomas raised many questions, of which two in particular concern us. Were revelation and faith necessary to men? Should faith use philosophical arguments? Since the SCG deals directly with the first of these questions (I, 5), we shall note here only an objection that St. Thomas poses and answers. The objection is a question well known to the ancients. Why should man seek things greater than himself? To this St. Thomas replies in a way that includes a realistic assessment of the accomplishments of the philosophers:

"Whoever is tending to beatitude must know the things in which he is to seek beatitude and how to do it. This cannot take place more easily than through faith, since the inquiry of the reason cannot arrive at such a knowledge except by already knowing many things that it is not easy to know. Nor, likewise, could the reason come to know them with less danger, since human inquiry easily succumbs to error because of the weakness of our intellect. This is also shown from the philosophers themselves who, searching for the end of human life following the way of the reason, and not finding the manner of reaching that end, fell into many and most shameful errors. Moreover, they disagreed among themselves so much that scarcely two or three of them had in all of these questions one doctrine in common, whereas, as against this, we see that through faith even the greatest number of people are united in one common teaching."[3]

St. Thomas Aquinas has ample evidence for this conclusion throughout the first half of Book Three of the *SCG*. But the errors of the philosophers, while indicating the appropriateness of the divine revelation, do not lead St. Thomas to sacrifice reason to its fallibility or philosophy to the errors of men. In fact, the following rather lengthy citation is an interesting witness to St. Thomas' belief in the unity of truth and in the service of philosophy to revelation. The question at issue, as has been indicated, is whether faith should use philosophical arguments. The answer is as follows.

"The gifts of grace are added to nature in such a manner that they do not remove it but perfect it. So it is with the light of faith that is infused in us gratuitously: it does not destroy the light of natural knowledge with which we are by nature endowed. Now, although the natural light of the human mind does not suffice for the manifestation of the things that are made manifest by faith, yet it is impossible that what is divinely taught to us by faith be contrary to the things with which we are endowed by nature. For one or the other would then have to be false, and, since both come to us from God, God would be to

3. *In B. de Trinitate*, q. III, a. 1, ad 3 (in *S. Thomae Aquinatis Opuscula Omnia*, ed. P. Mandonnet [5 vols., Paris: P. Lethielleux, 1927], vol. III, p. 64).

us an author of falsehood, which is impossible. Rather, the situation is this. Since within the imperfect there is a certain imitation of what is perfect, though an incomplete one, in what is known through natural knowledge there is a certain likeness of what is taught to us by faith.

"Now just as Sacred Teaching is founded on the light of faith, so philosophy is founded on the natural light of reason. It is therefore impossible that what belongs to philosophy be contrary to what belongs to faith; it rather falls short of it. It contains, however, certain likenesses of what belongs to faith, and certain preambles to it, as nature is a preamble to grace. And if in what the philosophers have said we come upon something that is contrary to faith, this does not belong to philosophy but is rather an abuse of philosophy arising from a defect in reason. It is therefore possible for the principles of philosophy to refute such an error by showing either that it is absolutely impossible or that it is not necessary. For just as what belongs to faith cannot be proved demonstratively, so certain notions contrary to these cannot be shown demonstratively to be wrong but can be shown not to be necessary.

"Thus, therefore, in Sacred Teaching we can use philosophy in a threefold way.

"*First*, we can use it to demonstrate the preambles of faith, which are necessary in the science of faith as being the things that are proved of God by natural arguments, e.g., that God exists, that God is one, or similar propositions concerning God or creatures that faith proposes as having been proved in philosophy.

"*Second*, we can use philosophy to make known through certain likenesses what belongs to faith, as Augustine in his book *On the Trinity* uses many likenesses drawn from the teachings of the philosophers to explain the Trinity.

"*Third*, we can use philosophy to oppose what is said

against faith, either by showing that these things are false or by showing that they are not necessary.

"However, those who use philosophy in Sacred Scripture can err in a twofold way. In one way, by using the things that are contrary to faith, as did Origen, which are not a part of philosophy but are rather an error or an abuse of philosophy. In another way, so as to enclose what belongs to faith under the limits of philosophy, as if one should wish to believe nothing except what can be acquired through philosophy, when, on the contrary, philosophy should be reduced to the limits of faith, according to the words of the Apostle: 'bringing into captivity every understanding unto the obedience of Christ'" (II Corinth. x, 5).[4]

III. THE PLAN OF THE
Summa Contra Gentiles

The question of the occasion of the SCG is a historical problem that cannot be settled definitively. But the allied question of the internal doctrinal purpose of the work is one that can be submitted to a systematic examination. Indirectly, too, the structure and purpose of the SCG can throw some light on the original destination of the work. To the present writer it seems, on internal grounds, that the SCG did not have a Christian audience in view but rather, through the teaching of Christian missionaries, an intellectual Arab audience. No doubt, even if we accept the testimony of Peter Marsilio and agree on the Penafort inspiration of the SCG, we can still recognize that St. Thomas wrote this work with a full awareness of the development of Arabian Aristotelianism in the Faculty of Arts at the University of Paris.

4. Op. cit., q. II, a. 3; ed. cit., pp. 50–52.

But, however this may be, the internal purpose of the SCG can be determined by examining its structure, organization and development. Here, too, the historians of St. Thomas Aquinas are not in agreement. The controversy precipitated in 1924 by Guy de Broglie, S.J., suggests the necessity of seeing in some detail the unity and order of the SCG according to St. Thomas himself. Those who have had the occasion to read the pages devoted by the Leonine Editors in 1948 to the plan of the SCG will recognize, furthermore, how difficult it can seem to some interpreters of St. Thomas to consider the SCG a unified doctrinal work with a unified purpose.

The SCG, as it is generally known, is a work in four books. The matter that St. Thomas considers in these books he distributes as follows. In Book One he studies God, His existence and perfections, especially His perfect actuality, the autonomy of His knowledge, the independence of His will, the perfection of His life, and the generosity of His love. In Book Two, St. Thomas studies creation, especially God's freedom in creation, the nature of man, and particularly the unity of soul and body within man. In Book Three, St. Thomas studies the order of creation and especially of man to God, the divine providence over all things and especially man. In Book Four, St. Thomas studies the Trinity, the Incarnation and the end of the universe. Moreover, at the beginning of each book St. Thomas sets down a number of rubrics whose purpose is to make clear to the reader the plan of the whole work and the unity and continuity of the four books among themselves.[5] Taken together, these rubrics give a clear conception of the plan and purpose of the SCG as seen by its author. A study of this plan offers the surest introduction to the work and to St. Thomas' purpose in writing it.

5. These rubrics are, in order, located in the following chapters: SCG, I, ch. 1–9; II, ch. 1–5; III, ch. 1 (see also ch. 64 and 111); IV, ch. 1.

A

The *SCG* is a work of wisdom and, in writing it, St. Thomas set himself the task of being a wise man. The absolutely wise man is he who considers the whole universe in its end and beginning. This is the intelligent being that is the source and the author of the universe. Because the good of the universe is the good aimed at by the intellectual being that is its author, that good must be truth. Truth, therefore, as the aim and purpose of the whole universe, is the principal object of the wise man. This truth is God. Divine Wisdom testifies that He has assumed flesh and come into the world in order to make divine truth known to men. And Aristotle himself said that first philosophy is the science of truth, that is, of that truth which is the origin of all truth and all things. In brief, then, the office of the wise man is to meditate on divine truth and to communicate his meditation to others. The wise man will also oppose the falsehoods that are contrary to this truth. St. Thomas' own purpose is to be a wise man, that is to say, a student of divine truth. He lists four reasons for this purpose. The pursuit of wisdom is the source of true beatitude; it makes man approach to a likeness to God; it is the road to the kingdom of immortality; it is full of joy without any bitterness. St. Thomas, therefore, dedicates his life as a student of the truth professed by the Catholic faith. He makes his own the words of St. Hilary that we have already cited: "I am aware that I owe this to God as the chief duty of my life, that my every word and sense may speak of Him."[6]

What is the method available to the wise man for the manifestation of divine truth? To answer this question we must consider that in the things that we profess about God there is a twofold truth. Some truths about God exceed the grasp of reason, as does the doctrine of the Trinity, but

6. *SCG,* I, ch. 2 (below, p. 62).

some can be reached by reason, for example, the existence and unity of God. The truths accessible to the reason were also proved by the philosophers guided by the light of natural reason. That there are truths about God that exceed the reason can be seen if we consider that our knowledge begins in the world of sensible things and reaches to whatever sensible things enable us to reach. God transcends the world of sense as well as our knowledge of it. Aristotle and Scripture are agreed on this point. To St. Thomas this means that we should not immediately reject as false whatever is said about God even though we cannot investigate it by means of reason. In the presence of a transcending God, reason must be open to many truths that surpass its power.

Given that divine truth is twofold, namely, that which can and that which cannot be investigated by reason, St. Thomas thinks it fitting that both should be proposed to men by a divine revelation for their belief. Consider, first, the truths about God that are accessible to reason. If these truths had not been revealed, three harmful consequences would follow. Few men would come to know God, they would need a long time to reach this knowledge, and they would be subject to many errors and uncertainties in the process of reaching it. Hence the conclusion: "Beneficially, therefore, did the divine mercy provide that it should instruct us to hold by faith even those truths that the human reason is able to investigate. In this way, all men would easily be able to have a share in the knowledge of God, and this without uncertainty and error."[7]

It was also necessary that men believe even what they could not grasp by means of the reason. Men had to learn to direct their desire towards a divine good that transcends human experience in the present life. To call men to some-

---

7. SCG, I, ch. 4, ¶6 (below, p. 68).—For the dependence of St. Thomas on Maimonides in the reasons for revelation, see the study of P. Synave (in *Mélanges Mandonnet* [2 vols., Paris: Librairie J. Vrin, 1930], vol. II, pp. 327–370).

thing that is higher than the reason can reach is a way of preparing them for their destiny beyond time. This is especially true of the Christian religion, which teaches men spiritual goods to be found in eternity. The philosophers themselves were going in this direction, pointing out to men the nobility and the joys of a life devoted to the contemplation of truth. Then, too, the revelation of transcendent truths about God would strengthen our conception of Him as a transcendent being. Needless to say, the acceptance of these same truths would help us to avoid presumption. Finally, such truths, however difficult, offer us the greatest satisfaction. For, as Aristotle says, "although what we know of the higher substances is very little, yet that little is loved and desired more than all the knowledge that we have about less noble substances."[8]

We may thus note three essential points in the life of a believing intellect as St. Thomas sees it. Man has serious reasons for believing in the Christian Revelation, even though what is proposed to him for belief is above his reason. There are visible signs such as miracles and the remarkable spread of the Christian faith. Wasn't it miraculous, St. Thomas asks, that Christianity, promising what it did, should yet have grown at all? In short, there is evidence for saying that the Christian faith rests on divine truth. But, furthermore, the Christian faith transcends, but it does not contradict, the truths that reason can know. God is the same author and teacher both for faith and for reason. Faith cannot be opposed to the principles and the truths of which men have a natural knowledge nor can there be any proper argument against faith proceeding from the natural principles of reason and of knowledge. This means that arguments "against the doctrines of faith are conclusions incorrectly derived from the first and self-evident principles imbedded in nature."[9] Such arguments are not demonstrations and they can always be answered.

8. SCG, I, ch. 5, ¶5 (below, pp. 70–71).
9. SCG, I, ch. 7, ¶7 (below, p. 75).

In short, the harmony of faith and reason within the unity of truth is complete. This leads St. Thomas to the third point. Man has in this life no vision of divine truth; he knows God only by the likeness that he finds in His effects. So long as man does not pretend to comprehend divine truth, to seek after it will be to him a cause of the greatest joy.[10]

The life of man the believer, as here described by St. Thomas, should be noted. If the world of divine truths infinitely transcends man's reason, this means that man should not have the presumption to comprehend divine truth. And yet, within the world of divine truth, man's reason is wholly free and wholly at home. The truths that he can know and demonstrate have a divine origin, and nothing in the world of faith will ever oppose or contradict them. The reason of the Christian believer, therefore, lives freely in a world of luminous mystery and truth.

Having justified the revelation to men of the twofold divine truth; having, furthermore, characterized the life of a believing intellect, St. Thomas turns to the question of the procedure to be followed in the exposition of divine truth that will occupy the SCG.

It should be clear, at this point, that the twofold divine truth whose exposition St. Thomas is about to undertake is proposed to men for belief. It should likewise be clear that the wise man who is undertaking this exposition of divine truth is himself a believer and that, as a believer, he is here seeking to discover the method of exposition proper to divine truth in its twofold character. As to the divine truth that is accessible to the reason but yet proposed to men by revelation, St. Thomas will proceed by way of demonstrative arguments with a view to convincing his adversaries. With reference to those truths about God that surpass the capacity of the reason, St. Thomas will not pro-

10. SCG, I, ch. 6–8 (below, pp. 71–76).

ceed by demonstration nor will he aim to convince his adversaries; rather than at a conviction born of demonstration,
he will aim at remaining faithful to the authority of Sacred
Scripture. He will also use certain "likely arguments" in
order to make divine truth known; but, be it noted, "this
should be done for the training and consolation of the
faithful, and not with any idea of refuting those who are
adversaries." Otherwise, the opponents of Christianity
would be strengthened in their error, "since they would
imagine that our acceptance of the truth of faith was based
on such weak arguments."[11]

St. Thomas is now in possession of his procedure. He
will "first seek to make known that truth which faith professes and reason investigates." This he will do "by bringing
forward both demonstrative and probable arguments, some
of which were drawn from the books of the philosophers
and of the saints, through which truth is strengthened and
its adversary overcome."[12] The exposition of the truths that
faith professes and reason investigates occupies St. Thomas
during the first three books of the SCG. With the opening
of Book Four, he takes up the second part of the exposition
of the truth revealed by God, namely, the truth that surpasses the reason.

According to this general plan, we may characterize the
SCG as a work devoted to the exposition and defense of
divine truth. This exposition has two main parts, namely,
the consideration of that truth that faith professes and
reason investigates, and the consideration of the truth that
faith professes and reason is not competent to investigate.
Furthermore, the procedure of the reason in the first order
of truth is by demonstration, aiming at conviction, although
probable arguments may be added to demonstrations. The
procedure of the reason in the second order of truth is by
an appeal to the authority of Scripture, aiming, through

11. SCG, I, ch. 9, ¶2 (below, p. 77).
12. SCG, I, ch. 9, ¶3 (below, p. 78).

that authority, to answer the arguments of unbelievers. In its plan and procedure, therefore, the SCG is the work of a Christian believer expounding what he believes about God by means of demonstration where the truths in question allow it and by means of an appeal to Scripture where the truths in question surpass the reason.

It is now possible to turn to a somewhat more detailed breakdown of the two main parts of the SCG.

With respect to the first kind of truth, St. Thomas intends to proceed thus. His general purpose, as is now clear, is to follow "the way of the reason and to inquire into what the human reason can investigate about God." This aim has three parts. The first is to consider "that which belongs to God Himself." This St. Thomas does in Book One of the SCG. The second part "concerns the coming forth of creatures from God." St. Thomas devotes Book Two to this consideration. The third part "concerns the ordering of creatures to God as to their end."[13] The development from Book One to Book Three, according to St. Thomas' own indications, will reinforce and further clarify the conception that we have so far formed of the aim and plan of the SCG. This may be seen by examining the opening chapters of Books Two and Three.

B

The continuation of Book Two of the SCG with Book One is clear. Book One deals with our knowledge of what belongs to God Himself—His existence and nature, and especially His life and blessedness. Book One considered the activity and operation of God as it is in God. Book Two now argues that we do not know the nature of a thing perfectly unless we know its operation; for how a thing acts shows forth the measure and quality of its power, which in turn reveals the nature. Now, according to Aris-

13. SCG, I, ch. 9, ¶4 (below, p. 78).

totle,[14] operation is twofold, namely, one that remains in
the agent and is his perfection (for example, understanding, willing, and sensing) and one that goes out to an
external thing, being the perfection of the thing produced
(for example, heating, cutting, and building). Both of
these operations belong to God. God understands, wills,
rejoices, and loves; but He also produces things in being,
and He conserves and rules them. Of these two kinds of
operation, the first is God's perfection, the second is the
perfection of what He makes. Furthermore, since the agent
of an operation is naturally prior to what he makes and is its
cause, the first operation is the source of the second and
precedes it as a cause precedes its effect. Finally, the first
type of operation is called operation or action, while the
second type, being the perfection of the thing made and
not of the agent, is called making. Thus, just as Book One
of the SCG was devoted to the first divine operation, so
Book Two is devoted to the second. "Hence, to complete
the consideration of divine truth, we must deal with the
second operation, namely, the operation through which
things are produced and governed by God."[15]

There is more. A meditation on the things that God has
made is necessary for the instruction of man's faith. There
are four reasons for this fact. Since God has made things
by His wisdom, by considering what God has made we can
gather the divine wisdom as it is scattered by a kind of
communication in God's works. In fact, this consideration
will help us to admire and to know the divine wisdom.
Then, too, the admiration of the power of God leads to a
growth of reverence in man's heart. God has made great
and wondrous things, but He is greater than what He has

14. The main Aristotelian texts on the distinction between im-
    manent and transitive action are the following: Metaphysics
    IX, 6 (1048b 28-36); IX, 8 (1050a 21-b 1); XI, 9 (1065b
    14-1066a 7); De Anima, I, 3 (407a 32-33); III, 7 (431a
    4-8); Nicomachean Ethics, VII, 14 (1154b 26).
15. SCG, II, ch. 1, ¶6.

made. Admiration, therefore, leads to fear and reverence. Third, the admiring consideration of things will kindle a desire of the divine goodness. Whatever goodness and perfection we see scattered in creation, all this is found wholly united in God as in the fountain of all goodness. If the goodness and beauty of creatures attract the soul of man, the sea of goodness in God Himself, zealously pursued through the rivulets of goodness found in things, will inflame and completely draw the souls of men to itself. Finally, the consideration of creatures gives to man a certain likeness of the divine perfection. Now precisely, "since the Christian faith instructs man principally about God, and gives him a knowledge of creatures through the light of the divine revelation, there comes to be in man a certain likeness of the divine wisdom." Hence the conclusion: "It is thus clear that the consideration of creatures belongs to the Christian faith."[16]

The consideration of creatures is also necessary to set aside errors. For errors about creatures lead men away from the truth of faith by being opposed to the true knowledge of God. This can happen in many ways. When men think that air or the sun or the stars are God, they hold nothing in esteem beyond visible creatures. When men do not know the nature of creatures, they sometimes give to them the name of God. Sometimes, too, they also detract from God's power by saying that there are two first principles, or that God acts through necessity, or that some creatures are not under His providence, or that His providence cannot act otherwise than as it ordinarily does. When man does not know the nature of creatures, he does not know his place in the universe and he will sometimes subject himself to creatures (as did those who thought things were ruled by the stars) instead of subjecting himself to God. It is therefore false to say that what we think about creatures is unimportant so long as we think correctly about

16. *SCG*, II, ch. 2, ¶6.

God. For an error concerning creatures leads to a false opinion about God; at the same time it directs the minds of men away from God by subjecting them to other beings.[17]

This conclusion leads St. Thomas to explain in what way the "teaching of the Christian faith" (*doctrina fidei Christianae*) is concerned with creatures. It is concerned with them "in so far as there comes to be in them a certain likeness of God, and in so far as an error about creatures leads to an error about God." "Human philosophy" (*philosophia humana*), on the other hand, considers creatures according to what they are in themselves. That is why the "philosopher" (*philosophus*) and the "believer" (*fidelis*) consider different things in creatures. The philosopher considers what befits a creature according to its nature. The believer considers what belongs to a creature in so far as it stands in relation to God. Thus, it is not an imperfection in the teaching of faith if it omits many of the characteristics of things—if, for example, it omits any reference to the configuration of the heavens or the nature of motion.

Even when the philosopher and the believer consider the same things in creatures they do so through different principles. The philosopher bases himself on the immediate causes of things, whereas the believer begins with the first cause, God. That is why the consideration of the believer should be called the highest wisdom, since it deals with the highest cause. That is why, too, human philosophy serves it as the principal wisdom. And for this reason the divine wisdom of the believer makes use of the principles of human philosophy, in the same way as the first philosophy of the philosophers "uses the teachings of all the sciences in order to make known its own objective."

There is a last and decisive difference between philosophy and the teaching of faith. In philosophy, the consideration of creatures comes first, that of God comes last. "In the teaching of faith, however, which considers creatures

17. SCG, II, ch. 3, ¶6.

only within their order to God, the consideration of God comes first, after which comes the consideration of creatures." This order of the teaching of faith is St. Thomas' order: "Hence, *following this order*, after what has been said about God Himself in the First Book it remains for us to continue with the things that are from God."[18] St. Thomas could hardly say more clearly that the SCG is a work of Christian teaching rather than a work of "human philosophy."

C

After considering the perfection of the divine nature in Book One of the *SCG*, and in Book Two the perfection of His power as creator and lord of all things, in Book Three St. Thomas sets out to study God as the end and ruler of created things.

Up to this point St. Thomas has proved (as he says) that there exists a first being, God, possessing within Himself the full perfection of being. Out of the abundance of His perfection, God generously gives being to all existing things. He is therefore not only the First Being, but also the source of being for all things. Moreover, God has given being to other things, not by any necessity of His nature, but according to the choice of His will. God is therefore the lord and master of His works; for we have mastery over the things that are subject to our will. Even more, God's mastery over His creatures is perfect since, as the cause of all being, God needs neither the aid of an outside agent nor the underlying presence of matter for the production of creatures.

18. *SCG*, II, ch. 4. For the order of Book Two, see ch. 5, where the main divisions are indicated (namely, the production of things, their distinction, and their nature). On the study of the nature of things, St. Thomas limits his consideration to what "pertains to the truth of faith" (ch. 5, repeated in ch. 46, ¶1). Book Two omits a study of material creatures as such.

What is produced by the will of an agent, St. Thomas continues, is directed to some end by that agent. For the proper object of will is what we call the good or the end, so that whatever proceeds from a will must be directed to an end. Each thing, furthermore, attains its end through its own action, which must be directed to the end by the one who gave things their principles of action. God, then, being in every way perfect, and through His power freely giving being to all things, is the ruler of all things, Himself subject to no one's rule. Nothing escapes God's rule, just as there is nothing that did not receive being from Him. Perfect as a being and as a cause, God is therefore perfect as a ruler.

The effect of God's rule may be seen in different things according to their nature. Intellectual creatures bear God's likeness and they manifest His image. Such beings are not only directed by God, they also direct themselves through their own actions to their appropriate end. And if in the direction of themselves they are subject to the divine rule, they are admitted by it to gain the last end; but if in their direction of themselves they proceed otherwise, they are turned away. Creatures without an intellect are merely directed by another; they do not direct themselves. They too do not escape from the power of the first ruler.

We are now ready for Book Three of the SCG. "Since, then, in the First Book we have dealt with the perfection of the divine nature and in the Second Book with the perfection of its power, according as God is the maker and lord of all things, it remains for us in this Third Book to treat of the perfect authority or dignity of God according as He is the end and ruler of all things."[19]

---

19. SCG, III, ch. 1, ¶11, where the plan of Book Three is likewise indicated. St. Thomas proposes to deal with God as the end of all things, with His government in general, and with His special government over intellectual creatures.

D

We have been prepared for Book Four in general by what St. Thomas has already said. After studying the truth about God "that faith professes and reason investigates," with Book Four we proceed to that divine truth which is beyond the comprehension of reason. How does St. Thomas make the transition to Book Four? He does so by meeting clearly and directly the central difficulty contained in man's destiny.

"The human intellect, to which it is connatural to derive its knowledge from sensible things, is not able through itself to reach the vision of the divine substance in itself, which is above all sensible things and indeed immeasurably above all other things. Yet because man's perfect good is that he somehow know God, lest such a noble creature might seem to be created to no purpose, as being unable to reach its own end, there is given to man a certain way through which he can rise to the knowledge of God: so that, since the perfections of things descend in a certain order from the highest summit of things, God, man may progress in the knowledge of God by beginning with lower things and gradually ascending."[20]

But this is only the beginning of the story. St. Thomas first considers the perfections descending from God, which are the ladder of man's ascent to God. These perfections are governed by two principles, of which one refers to the first origin of things. In order that perfection might be found in things, the divine wisdom produced them in a certain order. As a result, the universe of creatures is filled with both the highest and the lowest beings. In other words, things were created in a hierarchy. The other principle refers to a hierarchy in cause and effect. Causes are more noble than their effects. The first divine effects fall short of God the first cause, but the effects of these effects in

20. SCG, IV, ch. 1, ¶2.

turn fall short of them. This continues until we reach the lowest realities. Now there is perfect unity in God, and it is a fact that the more one a thing is the more powerful and eminent it is. This means that, as we descend from the first principle, the more we find diversity and variety in things. The procession of things from God is united in its source, and is multiplied according to the lowest things in which it terminates. "In this way, according to the diversity of things, there appears the diversity of the ways, as though these ways began in one principle and terminated in various ends." These are the many ways in things that the human intellect can ascend in its search of God. The trouble begins at this point, and the following paragraph of St. Thomas needs careful reading.

"Through these ways our intellect can rise to the knowledge of God. But because of the weakness of the intellect we are not able to know perfectly even the ways themselves. For the sense, from which our knowledge begins, is occupied with external accidents, which are the proper sensibles, e.g., color, odor, and the like. As a result, through such external accidents the intellect can scarcely reach the perfect knowledge of a lower nature, even in the case of those natures whose accidents it comprehends perfectly through the sense. Much less will the intellect arrive at comprehending the natures of those things of which we grasp few accidents by sense; and it will do so even less in the case of those things whose accidents cannot be grasped by the senses, though they may be perceived through certain deficient effects. But even though the natures of things themselves were known to us, we can have only a little knowledge of their order, according as the divine providence disposes them in relation to one another and directs them to the end, since we do not come to know the plan of the divine providence: *cum ad cognoscendam rationem divinae providentiae non pertingamus.* If, then, the ways themselves are known imperfectly by us, how shall we be able to arrive at a perfect knowledge of the source of these ways? And because that source transcends the abovementioned ways beyond proportion, even if we knew the ways themselves perfectly, we would yet not have within our grasp a perfect knowledge of the source."[21]

This impasse was broken by God. Man could reach only a weak knowledge of God by pursuing the ways upward in creation with his intellect, and he could see little. "Out of a superabundant goodness, therefore, so that man might have a firmer knowledge of Him, God revealed certain things about Himself that transcend the human intellect." There is a certain order in this revelation, suited to man's needs. In the beginning, the revelation is such that man cannot understand it but only hears and believes it: his intellect, which in the present life is united to the senses, cannot be raised to seeing what lies above sense. When the intellect is freed from this union with the senses, it will be raised to see what has been revealed.

Man has therefore a threefold knowledge of God. The first is according as man, by the natural light of reason, mounts through creatures to a knowledge of God. The second is according as the divine truth, which transcends his intellect, descends within him as a revelation, not indeed made clear so as to be seen, but expressed in speech so as to be believed. The third is according as the mind of man will be raised to the perfect vision of what has been revealed.

Within this setting we can now see the transition to Book Four in the SCG, and we can see it from the vantage point of Book Four itself. "In what has preceded, we have dealt with divine things according as the natural reason can arrive at the knowledge of divine things through creatures. This way is imperfect, nevertheless, and in keeping with the reason's native capacity. That is why we can say with Job (26:14): 'These things are said in part of His ways.' We must now deal with those divine things that have been divinely revealed to us to be believed, since they

21. SCG, IV, ch. 1, ¶4.

transcend the human intellect." Furthermore, in turning
to the things that have been revealed by God, we shall take
the things we find in Scripture as our principles, and we
shall try, as best we can, to understand and to defend
against unbelievers what is taught in Scripture in a hidden
way. We shall not have the presumption to understand
perfectly, for we shall prove these hidden truths by the
authority of Scripture, not by natural reason. Nevertheless,
we are called upon to show that the truths hidden in
Scripture are not opposed to natural reason and can be
defended against the attack of unbelievers. This mode of
procedure, St. Thomas adds, was established in the beginning of the SCG.[22]

E

Such, in simple outline, is the general plan of the SCG
as set down by St. Thomas himself. Beginning with the
notion that the wise man par excellence studies divine
truth, St. Thomas undertakes the work of making known
the divine truth professed by the Catholic faith.

The SCG is a manifestation of divine truth. It is con-
ducted by a believer as a meditation on God. Embracing
all truth about God under revelation, this meditation de-
fends the right of the revealed truth taught by faith to the
title of principal wisdom and to the ministerial use of the
principles of human philosophy. There are explicit formulas
linking all four books to faith and there are allusions and
marks of organization that proceed from considerations
concerning the needs of faith. Most important of all, St.
Thomas acknowledges that the order of the SCG is delib-
erately that of "the teaching of faith," and not that of
"human philosophy."

In a sense, to determine the transition from Book Three
to Book Four in the SCG is also to determine the plan
of the whole work. That transition is not a question of

22. SCG, IV, ch. 1, ¶¶5-7, 11-12. See SCG, I, ch. 9.

going from reason to faith, or from philosophy to theology. St. Thomas rather goes from "what faith affirms and reason investigates" to "what faith affirms and reason cannot investigate." The transition, therefore, takes place entirely within faith, but it proceeds from the level of reason's connatural competence to a supra-rational level within faith. The development of the whole *SCG* is thus within faith.

With this conclusion we rejoin an old interpretation of the *SCG* propounded some two hundred years ago by the Dominican Bernard de Rubeis (1687–1775) in his *Critical and Apologetical Dissertations* on the life, writings, and teachings of St. Thomas Aquinas. Printed in Venice in 1750, the *Dissertations* can today be found in the first volume of the Leonine edition of the writings of St. Thomas. In the twelfth *Dissertation*, de Rubeis quotes most of the text of Peter Marsilio on the occasion of the *SCG* that we have seen. Then he goes on to discuss the title of the work and argues that, given the intention of St. Thomas, the title should be *On the Truth of the Catholic Faith*. At this point he raises a difficulty that is to our purpose, as is his solution.

"The divine truths that Aquinas illumines painstakingly and at length, and that are open to our natural light, create for us a difficulty at this point. I am referring to the existence and unity of God, the other several divine attributes, and His power and providence. It does not seem that they should have been called *truths of the Catholic faith*, nor, likewise, should the title of the work have been *On the Truth of the Catholic Faith*.

"This difficulty Thomas himself anticipates, and he removes every doubt concerning the genuineness of the title that we have advanced. For he distinguishes in chapter 3 [I, ch. 3] a twofold mode for divine truth: one, which surpasses the whole ability of the human reason, the other, to which the natural reason can attain. Truths of the first kind are made known through the free revelation of God; we believe them, but we cannot know them. Truths of the second kind can fall under human science. Nevertheless, although they are open to the inquiry of reason, St. Thomas shows by many arguments that it was fitting for them to be proposed for belief by supernatural revelation. Hence it is that the integral body of the Catholic faith is constituted of both kinds of truth; and Sacred Scripture, which embraces the divine revelation, without doubt sets forth these two kinds of truth. The work composed by Thomas, therefore, could and should have been called, with the greatest appropriateness, On the Truth of the Catholic Faith: in it the abovementioned truths are expounded and defended."[23]

This conclusion is as sound today as it was two hundred years ago when de Rubeis wrote it.

23. B. de Rubeis, Dissertationes Criticae et Apologeticae, XII, ch. 2, no. 2 (S. Thomae Aquinatis . . . Opera, vol. I, 1882, pp. CLXXXI–CLXXXII).

Summa Contra Gentiles, Book One: God.

I. THE CHRISTIAN GOD

Considered in itself, Book One of the SCG is a treatise on the existence and nature of God. This is, in fact, the first movement in man's consideration of divine things. The consideration begins with the existence of God because, as St. Thomas has said, unless that existence is established, "all consideration of divine things is necessarily suppressed."[24]

Book One of the SCG is devoted by St. Thomas to the study of God in His substance and in His life and operation. These two divisions are further subdivided according to the following general headings:

A. Book One, Part I (ch. 10–43)
  1. the existence of God (ch. 10–13)
  2. our knowledge of God
    a. the way of remotion (ch. 14–28)
    b. the divine names and analogy (ch. 29–36)
  3. the divine attributes (ch. 37–43)

B. Book One, Part II (ch. 44–102)
  1. the intelligence and knowledge of God (ch. 44–71)
  2. the will, love, and blessedness of God (ch. 72–102)

The development of this plan depends on two considerations that dominate not only the doctrine of the SCG but also the immediate objective that it has in view. The first of these considerations concerns the divine perfection, and especially the total independence of the divine will, on which in turn hinges the idea of a free creation and a free

24. SCG, I, ch. 9, ¶5 (below, p. 78).

divine government over the universe. The second consideration depends on St. Thomas' audience. In the presence
of the philosophers, and especially Aristotle, St. Thomas
is anxious to show not only the errors that they committed
but also the truths that they reached and even the core
of truth contained in their very errors. Not that St.
Thomas is conciliatory towards the failings of the philosophers. In point of fact, there is a serious polemical section
in Book One of the SCG in which St. Thomas shows
against Avicenna and especially Averroes that God has a
perfect knowledge of creatures and that He creates them
with complete freedom and generosity.[25] But over and above
correcting the errors of the philosophers, we find St.
Thomas insisting on how much truth the philosophers
know, how far they have gone in the direction of the truth
professed by Christianity, and how much the Christian
Revelation has clarified their problems, removed their errors,
and completed their search as philosophers. The St.
Thomas who believes that grace perfects nature, also believes that faith perfects reason, and he is sincerely at
pains to show that the philosophy of an Aristotle has grown
and deepened by living within the light of revelation.

The doctrinal development of Book One begins with
the existence of God. This St. Thomas proves after showing that it needs to be proved and that it can be proved.
The proof itself is noteworthy for its almost academic
completeness in the methodological interpretation of Aristotle. St. Thomas says that he will set down the truths
by which "both the philosophers and Catholic teachers
have proved that God exists." But, except for a brief paragraph devoted to St. John Damascene and a passing reference to Averroes, his whole exposition comes from Aristotle.[26] St. Thomas notices that, according to Aristotle,

25. SCG, I, ch. 63–71, 79–88 (below, pp. 209ff., 253ff.). See
also SCG, II, ch. 23–30, 39–45.
26. SCG, I, ch. 13 (below, pp. 85–96). Note that ¶s2–34 deal
with Aristotle, while ¶35 deals with St. John Damascene and
Averroes.

the proof for the existence of God involves the supposition of the eternity of motion. How can a Catholic teacher make this supposition? St. Thomas' answer to the question should be noted. To prove that God exists on the supposition of the eternity of motion is the strongest way of doing so, since on this supposition the existence of God is not so evident. St. Thomas' point is clear. It is not that the world is eternal; rather, it is that, even if the world were eternal, it would still lead to a separate and unmoved source of its motion, namely, God.[27]

The argumentation of Aristotle has enabled St. Thomas to conclude that there is a first unmoved mover, God. Now God is Himself completely free from motion. This freedom further enables St. Thomas to arrive at a knowledge of what God is by means of determining what He is not. Thus, as absolutely unmoved, God is eternal, without potency and therefore without matter, and also without composition.[28] God is not a body, as the philosophers themselves proved.[29] Furthermore, since God is not composite, He is His own essence.[30] Being His own essence, He is His own being: God's essence is being.[31] This is the sublime truth taught to Moses by the Lord Himself. *He Who Is* sent Moses to the children of Israel (Exod. 3:13–14). St. Thomas comments: "By this our Lord showed that His own proper name is *He Who Is*. Now names have been devised to signify the natures or essences of things. It remains, then, that the divine being is God's essence or nature."[32]

In the presence of Greek and Arabian notions on God, what is uppermost in St. Thomas' mind is to defend the

27. *SCG*, I, ch. 13, ¶s29–30 (below, pp. 94–95).
28. *SCG*, I, ch. 14–18 (below, pp. 96–104).
29. *SCG*, I, ch. 20 (below, pp. 106ff.). Note the attitude toward the philosophers on the perpetuity of motion in ¶32.
30. *SCG*, I, ch. 21 (below, pp. 116–117).
31. *SCG*, I, ch. 22 (below, pp. 118–121).
32. *SCG*, I, ch. 22, ¶10 (below, p. 121).

eminence of the divine knowledge and the total liberty of the divine will. The philosophers had never known the idea of creation, and if they had an obscure understanding of the divine unity they were rather unaware of the divine liberty and even more so of the divine liberality. Where the Greeks had taught the Arabs the doctrine of an eternal and necessary world, the Christian Revelation was making known to men a world whose origin, existence, and final destination depended purely and simply on the will of God. Now the will of God is intelligent, and it works with a plan and a purpose. Moreover, there is an order in its work. But there is no necessity compelling the divine will to work as it does, for in the very perfection of its nature, it has supreme independence of action. The world that hangs upon such a divine will is radically contingent: neither need it be, nor need it be what it is. But given the free decision of God to create the world, and this for reasons that lie infinitely beyond every possible universe, then this world must be what it is. Any world that God would create would be an orderly world, and in its order it would reveal God. But no world, absolutely speaking, would be a necessary world, whatever its intelligibility. The divine perfection needs no world: it is infinitely full in itself. Why God has created, therefore, is a divine secret that infinitely transcends the limits of the world in which we are living.

The Christian Revelation transformed Greek and Arabian philosophy by locating the world between a divine liberty that the philosophers appreciated very imperfectly and a divine finality that they could not appreciate at all. The divine liberty is rooted in the divine perfection, and in creating God had one motive, namely, the generous communication of that perfection. But we must go farther than this. If God has created a universe composed of both spiritual and material creatures, the latter exist for the sake of the former. The beatitude of spiritual creatures is the central and unifying purpose of creation. From this point of view, the physical universe in which we are living is, for St. Thomas Aquinas, anthropocentric in a way that remained unknown to the Greeks and Arabs. The physical world exists for man, man exists for beatitude, and beatitude is offered to man as a free gift from God. The Incarnation was not an afterthought added by God to creation. Intended as the way of man's salvation, it is also the way of the perfection of his nature in its search for beatitude. God crossed the distance from the infinite to the finite in order to lead mankind to an infinite beatitude.[33] Philosophy could not have any greater completion and triumph than this. By the same token, the Incarnation is the culminating moment in the argument of St. Thomas with the Greeks and the Arabs: God became man and gave to men true beatitude—Himself.

This conclusion unites the whole apologetic effort of the SCG. It also gives to Book One its proper location. The God Who is being, Who knows and loves with perfect autonomy, Who creates with generosity, Who watches over the fall of every sparrow just as He waits for man's response to His love, is the God of love Who came on earth to unite man to Himself. This God the Greeks and the Arabs came to know very imperfectly even in the truths that were accessible to their reason. But this very fact was, after all, one of the reasons for the existence of revelation. If St. Thomas' reason is better than that of Aristotle or Averroes, that is not because he is a better philosopher. Or rather, he is better as a philosopher and in philosophy because he is a believer and because his reason is being taught by God. The Christian reason, in believing, becomes more rational in its life as a reason. Such is the deep Christian conviction that St. Thomas wishes to communicate to the followers of "human philosophy." Having embarked upon the right road, the philosophy of the ancients was disfigured by its errors and frustrated by its

33. On beatitude and the Incarnation, see SCG, IV, ch. 54.

ignorance. On both counts the Christian Revelation was a source of light. Beatitude is the destiny of man and the end of creation. Man cannot reach it by himself because the goal is infinitely high. Therein lies the mystery of his destiny—and the dark night of the philosophers. Therein lies also the point of the liberating message to whose exposition the SCG is dedicated by St. Thomas.

II.　THE PRESENT TRANSLATION

After publishing *What Plato Said* in 1933, Paul Shorey had intended to write a sequel, *What Plato Meant*. There is a lesson here for translators; at least, there is a lesson for the present translator in relation to St. Thomas.

In translating Book One of the SCG, I have thought it my business to set down what St. Thomas said, not what he meant. This is harder to do than is sometimes imagined. Additions to St. Thomas' texts, even when they seem legitimate, are nevertheless additions; they are interpretations and commentaries, more or less slight, but yet clarifications that the original text does not have. For my part, I have tried to do as little interpreting as possible in the present translation. Only rarely have I ventured to add words to the original text in order to preserve its sense. As much as possible, I have likewise refrained from recasting the form of his sentences because this would have given to his thought an order and a development that the original Latin does not contain.

It may be useful to the reader to know how I have translated St. Thomas' technical vocabulary. Here are some examples. *Esse* is translated as *being*, and a few times as *act of being*. *Ens* becomes *that which is*, or *a being*. On the analogy of *esse*, *intelligere* is translated as *understanding*. *Principium* is *principle*, *source* or *origin*; hence, *principaliter* is *originally*, that is, *in origin*. *Doctrina* is translated as *teaching* and, less often, as *doctrine*. Hence, *sacra doctrina* is *sacred teaching*.

On the whole, the present translation is literal in the sense of preserving, as much as possible, what St. Thomas said. For the student of St. Thomas, at least, such a translation has seemed the proper one to achieve.

As for the footnotes to the text, they are limited mainly to the sources of St. Thomas. In citing these sources, I have followed current practice, including some of its inconsistencies. Thus, though I refer to the *Metaphysics*, I have preferred to cite Aristotle's treatise on the soul as the *De Anima* rather than as *On the Soul*. This mixing of Latin and English seems impossible to avoid at present, and I have followed it not only in the notes to the text, but also in citing titles within the text itself.

The text used in preparing the present translation is the Manual Leonine text of the *SCG* published in 1934. The paragraph numbers in the translation follow the paragraphing of the Latin original.

There is one person to whom I am particularly indebted in preparing the present translation. It is a great pleasure for me to acknowledge the generous help that my friend Professor Etienne Gilson has given me. We read the translation and the text of St. Thomas together in Toronto during the fall and winter of 1954. My translation owes much to Professor Gilson's counsel, and I thank him sincerely for his many insights, comments, and criticisms. If the translation is not better than it is, the responsibility is my own.

ANTON C. PEGIS

Riverdale, New York
5 April, 1955

Bibliography.

The present bibliography is limited strictly to those books that were used in the preparation of the translation of *SCG*, Book I. The bibliography on St. Thomas for the years up to 1920 is covered by P. Mandonnet-J. Destrez, *Bibliographie Thomiste* (Kain, Le Saulchoir, 1921); for 1920 to 1940 there is Vernon J. Bourke, *Thomistic Bibliography* (St. Louis, St. Louis University Press, 1945). For the years after 1940, the indispensable guide is the *Bulletin Thomiste* published by the Dominicans of the Saulchoir since 1924. The most recent historical assessment of St. Thomas and his work in the thirteenth century can be found in Etienne Gilson, *History of Christian Philosophy in the Middle Ages* (New York, Random House, 1955), pp. 361–383, 707–717.

I. ST. THOMAS AQUINAS

S. *Thomae Aquinatis Doctoris Angelici Opera Omnia, iussu impensaque Leonis XIII P. M. edita*, 16 vols., Romae, Ex Typographia Polyglotta, 1882–1948.

S. *Thomae Aquinatis Scriptum Super Sententiis*, 4 vols. (incomplete), ed. P. Mandonnet (vols. 1–2) and M. F. Moos (vols 3–4), Paris, P. Lethielleux, 1929–1947.

S. *Thomae de Aquino Ordinis Praedicatorum Summa Theologiae*, 5 vols., Ottawa, Impensis Studii Generalis O. Pr., 1941–1945.

S. *Thomae de Aquino Doctoris Angelici Summa Contra Gentiles*, Romae, Apud Sedem Commissionis Leoninae, 1934.

Basic Writings of St. Thomas Aquinas, 2 vols., edited by Anton C. Pegis, New York, Random House, 1945.

II. THE SUMMA CONTRA GENTILES

1. The date of the SCG.

A. Motte, "Note sur la date du Contra Gentiles," *Revue Thomiste*, 44 (1938), 806–809.

H. Dondaine, "Le Contra Errores Graecorum de s. Thomas d'Aquin et le livre IV Contra Gentiles," *Revue des sciences philosophiques et théologiques*, 41 (1941), 155–162.

2. The occasion and aim of the work

M.-M. Gorce, "La lutte 'contra Gentiles' à Paris," *Mélanges Mandonnet*, Paris, J. Vrin, 1930, Vol. I, pp. 223–243. The pages on the SCG have been reprinted in the same author's *L'Essor de la pensée au moyen âge*, Paris, Letouzey et Ané, 1933, pp. 242–247.

D. Salman, "Sur la lutte 'contra Gentiles' de s. Thomas," *Divus Thomas* (Piacenza), 40 (1937), 488–509. By the same author: "Note sur la première influence d'Averroès," *Revue néo-scolastique de philosophie*, 40 (1937), 203–212; "Albert le Grand et l'Averroisme latin," *Revue des sciences philosophiques et théologiques*, 24 (1935), 38–64.

H. Féret, review in *Bulletin Thomiste*, 3 (1930–1933), 105–112, nos. 86–87.

M.-M. Gorce, in *Bulletin Thomiste*, 3 (1930–1933), 183–186, no. 126.

M.-D. Chenu, *Introduction à l'étude de saint Thomas d'Aquin*, Paris, J. Vrin, 1950, pp. 247–254.

3. The plan of the work

G. de Broglie, "De la place du surnaturel dans la philosophie de saint Thomas," *Recherches de science religieuse*, 14 (1924), 193–246, 481–496.

G. de Broglie, "La place de la vision béatifique dans la philosophie de saint Thomas," *Revue de philosophe,* 24 (1924), 441–443.

M. Blanche, *ibid.,* 443–449. (Reply to de Broglie)

R. Mulard, "Desir naturel de connaître et vision béatifique," *Revue des sciences philosophiques et théologiques,* 14 (1925), 5–19. (Reply to de Broglie)

———, in *Bulletin Thomiste,* 1–3 (1924–1926), 192–195, nos. 195–196. (Review of de Broglie and Blanche)

G. de Broglie, "Sur la place du surnaturel dans la philosophie de saint Thomas," *Recherches de science religieuse,* 15 (1925), 5–53; pp. 40–50 treat of *SCG.* (Reply to Blanche)

M. Bouyges, "Le plan du *Contra Gentiles* de saint Thomas," *Archives de philosophie,* III, 2 (1925), 176–197.

N. Balthazar-A. Simonet, "Le plan de la somme contre les gentils de saint Thomas," *Revue néo-scolastique de philosophie,* 32 (1930), 183–210.

H.-M. Laurent, "Autour de la Summa contra Gentiles," *Angelicum,* 8 (1931), 237–245.

"De Principiis et Compositione Comparatis Summae Theoologiae et Summae Contra Gentiles," *S. Thomae Aquinatis . . . Opera Omnia iussu edita Leonis XIII P. M. Tomus Decimus Sextus: Indices* (Romae, Ex Typographia Polyglotta, 1948, 285–293).

III.   THE SOURCES

1. Aristotle

Aristotelis Opera, 2 vols., Berlin Academy Edition based on I. Bekker, Berlin, G. Reimer, 1831.—The Oxford editions of the Greek text of Aristotle prepared by W. D. Ross are extremely useful: *Metaphysics* (2 vols., 1924; reprinted 1948), *Physics* (1936), *Prior and Posterior Analytics* (1949). The *De anima* was edited, among others, by R. D. Hicks, Cambridge, University Press, 1907.

The Works of Aristotle, English translation, edited by W. D. Ross, 11 vols., Oxford, Clarendon Press, 1928–1931.

The Basic Works of Aristotle, edited, and with an introduction, by R. McKeon, New York, Random House, 1941.

2. Averroes

Aristotelis de Physico Auditu libri octo cum Averrois . . . Commentario, Venetiis, apud Iuntas, 1562.

Metaphysicorum libri XIII cum Averrois . . . Commentariis, et Epitome, Venetiis, apud Iuntas, 1574.

Averrois Cordubensis Commentarium Magnum in Aristotelis de Anima Libros, edited by F. Stuart Crawford, Cambridge, Mass., The Mediaeval Academy of America, 1953.

3. Avicenna

Avicennae perhypatetici philosophi ac medicorum facile primi opera in luce redacta, Venetiis, 1508.

4. Maimonides

Rabi Mossei Aegyptii Dux seu Director dubitantium aut perplexorum, in tres libros divisus, & summa accuratione R. p. Augustini Justiniani . . . recognitus, Paris, 1520.

5. Latin writers (St. Hilary, St. Augustine, Boethius, St. Gregory) are quoted from J. P. Migne, *Patrologia Latina*, 221 vols., Paris, 1844–1864 (with later printings).

6. The Pseudo-Dionysius and St. John Damascene are quoted from J. P. Migne, *Patrologia Graeca*, 162 vols., Paris, 1857–1866 (with later printings).

Three abbreviations are used in the notes:
PL: *Patrologia Latina*
PG: *Patrologia Graeca*
SCG: *Summa Contra Gentiles*

Saint Thomas Aquinas

ON THE TRUTH OF THE CATHOLIC FAITH

BOOK ONE: GOD

Chapter 1.

THE OFFICE OF THE WISE MAN

*"My mouth shall meditate truth, and my
lips shall hate impiety"* (Prov. 8:7).

[1] The usage of the multitude, which according to the
Philosopher is to be followed in giving names to things,[1]
has commonly held that they are to be called wise who
order things rightly and govern them well. Hence, among
other things that men have conceived about the wise man,
the Philosopher includes the notion that "it belongs to the
wise man to order."[2] Now, the rule of government and
order for all things directed to an end must be taken from
the end. For, since the end of each thing is its good, a thing
is then best disposed when it is fittingly ordered to its end.
And so we see among the arts that one functions as the
governor and the ruler of another because it controls its
end. Thus, the art of medicine rules and orders the art of
the chemist because health, with which medicine is concerned, is the end of all the medications prepared by the
art of the chemist. A similar situation obtains in the art of
ship navigation in relation to shipbuilding, and in the mili-
tary art with respect to the equestrian art and the equip-
ment of war. The arts that rule other arts are called
architectonic, as being the ruling arts. That is why the
artisans devoted to these arts, who are called master artisans,
appropriate to themselves the name of wise men. But, since
these artisans are concerned, in each case, with the ends of
certain particular things, they do not reach to the universal
end of all things. They are therefore said to be wise with
respect to this or that thing; in which sense it is said that

1. Aristotle, *Topics*, II, 1 (102a 30).
2. Aristotle, *Metaphysics*, I, 2 (982a 18).

"as a wise architect, I have laid the foundation" (I Cor. 3:10). The name of the absolutely wise man, however, is reserved for him whose consideration is directed to the end of the universe, which is also the origin of the universe. That is why, according to the Philosopher, it belongs to the wise man to consider the highest causes.[3]

[2] Now, the end of each thing is that which is intended by its first author or mover. But the first author and mover of the universe is an intellect, as will be later shown.[4] The ultimate end of the universe must, therefore, be the good of an intellect. This good is truth. Truth must consequently be the ultimate end of the whole universe, and the consideration of the wise man aims principally at truth. So it is that, according to His own statement, divine Wisdom testifies that He has assumed flesh and come into the world in order to make the truth known: "For this was I born, and for this came I into the world, that I should give testimony to the truth" (John 18:37). The Philosopher himself establishes that first philosophy is the science of truth, not of any truth, but of that truth which is the origin of all truth, namely, which belongs to the first principle whereby all things are. The truth belonging to such a principle is, clearly, the source of all truth; for things have the same disposition in truth as in being.[5]

[3] It belongs to one and the same science, however, both to pursue one of two contraries and to oppose the other. Medicine, for example, seeks to effect health and to eliminate illness. Hence, just as it belongs to the wise man to meditate especially on the truth belonging to the first principle and to teach it to others, so it belongs to him to refute the opposing falsehood.

[4] Appropriately, therefore, is the twofold office of the wise man shown from the mouth of Wisdom in our open-

3. Aristotle, *Metaphysics*, I, 1 (981b 28).
4. See below, ch. 44; also *SCG*, II, ch. 24
5. Aristotle, *Metaphysics*, Ia, 1 (993b 30).

ing words: to meditate and speak forth of the divine truth, which is truth in person (Wisdom touches on this in the words *my mouth shall meditate truth*), and to refute the opposing error (which Wisdom touches on in the words *and my lips shall hate impiety*). By *impiety* is here meant falsehood against the divine truth. This falsehood is contrary to religion, which is likewise named *piety*. Hence, the falsehood contrary to it is called *impiety*.[6]

Chapter 2.

THE AUTHOR'S INTENTION IN
THE PRESENT WORK

[1] Among all human pursuits, the pursuit of wisdom is more perfect, more noble, more useful, and more full of joy.

It is more perfect because, in so far as a man gives himself to the pursuit of wisdom, so far does he even now have some share in true beatitude. And so a wise man has said: "Blessed is the man that shall continue in wisdom" (Ecclus. 14:22).

It is more noble because through this pursuit man especially approaches to a likeness to God Who "made all things in wisdom" (Ps. 103:24). And since likeness is the cause of love, the pursuit of wisdom especially joins man to God in friendship. That is why it is said of wisdom that "she is an infinite treasure to men! which they that use become the friends of God" (Wis. 7:14).

It is more useful because through wisdom we arrive at the kingdom of immortality. For "the desire of wisdom bringeth to the everlasting kingdom" (Wis. 6:21).

6. In the present chapter, I have changed *wickedness* in the Douay text to *impiety*, since this is demanded by the sense.

It is more full of joy because "her conversation hath no bitterness, nor her company any tediousness, but joy and gladness" (Wis. 7:16).

[2]   And so, in the name of the divine Mercy, I have the confidence to embark upon the work of a wise man, even though this may surpass my powers, and I have set myself the task of making known, as far as my limited powers will allow, the truth that the Catholic faith professes, and of setting aside the errors that are opposed to it. To use the words of Hilary: "I am aware that I owe this to God as the chief duty of my life, that my every word and sense may speak of Him."[1]

[3]   To proceed against individual errors, however, is a difficult business, and this for two reasons. In the first place, it is difficult because the sacrilegious remarks of individual men who have erred are not so well known to us so that we may use what they say as the basis of proceeding to a refutation of their errors. This is, indeed, the method that the ancient Doctors of the Church used in the refutation of the errors of the Gentiles. For they could know the positions taken by the Gentiles since they themselves had been Gentiles, or at least had lived among the Gentiles and had been instructed in their teaching. In the second place, it is difficult because some of them, such as the Mohammedans and the pagans, do not agree with us in accepting the authority of any Scripture, by which they may be convinced of their error. Thus, against the Jews we are able to argue by means of the Old Testament, while against heretics we are able to argue by means of the New Testament. But the Mohammedans and the pagans accept neither the one nor the other. We must, therefore, have recourse to the natural reason, to which all men are forced to give their assent. However, it is true, in divine matters the natural reason has its failings.

[4]   Now, while we are investigating some given truth, we shall also show what errors are set aside by it; and we shall

1. St. Hilary, De Trinitate, I, 37 (PL, 10, 48).

likewise show how the truth that we come to know by demonstration is in accord with the Christian religion.

Chapter 3.

ON THE WAY IN WHICH DIVINE TRUTH IS TO BE MADE KNOWN

[1]   The way of making truth known is not always the same, and, as the Philosopher has very well said, "it belongs to an educated man to seek such certitude in each thing as the nature of that thing allows."[1] The remark is also introduced by Boethius.[2] But, since such is the case, we must first show what way is open to us in order that we may make known the truth which is our object.

[2]   There is a twofold mode of truth in what we profess about God. Some truths about God exceed all the ability of the human reason. Such is the truth that God is triune. But there are some truths which the natural reason also is able to reach. Such are that God exists, that He is one, and the like. In fact, such truths about God have been proved demonstratively by the philosophers, guided by the light of the natural reason.

[3]   That there are certain truths about God that totally surpass man's ability appears with the greatest evidence. Since, indeed, the principle of all knowledge that the reason perceives about some thing is the understanding of the very substance of that being (for according to Aristotle "what a thing is" is the principle of demonstration),[3] it is necessary that the way in which we understand the substance of a thing determines the way in which we know what belongs to it. Hence, if the human intellect compre-

1. Aristotle, *Nicomachean Ethics*, I, 3 (1094b 24).
2. Boethius, *De Trinitate*, II (PL, 64, col. 1250).
3. Aristotle, *Posterior Analytics*, II, 3 (90b 31).

hends the substance of some thing, for example, that of a stone or of a triangle, no intelligible characteristic belonging to that thing surpasses the grasp of the human reason. But this does not happen to us in the case of God. For the human intellect is not able to reach a comprehension of the divine substance through its natural power. For, according to its manner of knowing in the present life, the intellect depends on the sense for the origin of knowledge; and so those things that do not fall under the senses cannot be grasped by the human intellect except in so far as the knowledge of them is gathered from sensible things. Now, sensible things cannot lead the human intellect to the point of seeing in them the nature of the divine substance; for sensible things are effects that fall short of the power of their cause. Yet, beginning with sensible things, our intellect is led to the point of knowing about God that He exists, and other such characteristics that must be attributed to the First Principle. There are, consequently, some intelligible truths about God that are open to the human reason; but there are others that absolutely surpass its power.

[4]   We may easily see the same point from the gradation of intellects. Consider the case of two persons of whom one has a more penetrating grasp of a thing by his intellect than does the other. He who has the superior intellect understands many things that the other cannot grasp at all. Such is the case with a very simple person who cannot at all grasp the subtle speculations of philosophy. But the intellect of an angel surpasses the human intellect much more than the intellect of the greatest philosopher surpasses the intellect of the most uncultivated simple person; for the distance between the best philosopher and a simple person is contained within the limits of the human species, which the angelic intellect surpasses. For the angel knows God on the basis of a more noble effect than does man; and this by as much as the substance of an angel, through which the angel in his natural knowledge is led to the knowledge of

God, is nobler than sensible things and even than the soul itself, through which the human intellect mounts to the knowledge of God. The divine intellect surpasses the angelic intellect much more than the angelic surpasses the human. For the divine intellect is in its capacity equal to its substance, and therefore it understands fully what it is, including all its intelligible attributes. But by his natural knowledge the angel does not know what God is, since the substance itself of the angel, through which he is led to the knowledge of God, is an effect that is not equal to the power of its cause. Hence, the angel is not able, by means of his natural knowledge, to grasp all the things that God understands in Himself; nor is the human reason sufficient to grasp all the things that the angel understands through his own natural power. Just as, therefore, it would be the height of folly for a simple person to assert that what a philosopher proposes is false on the ground that he himself cannot understand it, so (and even more so) it is the acme of stupidity for a man to suspect as false what is divinely revealed through the ministry of the angels simply because it cannot be investigated by reason.

[5] The same thing, moreover, appears quite clearly from the defect that we experience every day in our knowledge of things. We do not know a great many of the properties of sensible things, and in most cases we are not able to discover fully the natures of those properties that we apprehend by the sense. Much more is it the case, therefore, that the human reason is not equal to the task of investigating all the intelligible characteristics of that most excellent substance.

[6] The remark of Aristotle likewise agrees with this conclusion. He says that "our intellect is related to the prime beings, which are most evident in their nature, as the eye of an owl is related to the sun."[4]

[7] Sacred Scripture also gives testimony to this truth. We read in Job: "Peradventure thou wilt comprehend the

4. Aristotle, *Metaphysics*, Ia, 1 (993b 9).

steps of God, and wilt find out the Almighty perfectly?"
(11:7). And again: "Behold, God is great, exceeding our
knowledge" (Job 36:26). And St. Paul: "We know in part"
(I Cor. 13:9).

[8]   We should not, therefore, immediately reject as false,
following the opinion of the Manicheans and many unbelievers, everything that is said about God even though it
cannot be investigated by reason.

Chapter 4.

THAT THE TRUTH ABOUT GOD TO WHICH THE
NATURAL REASON REACHES IS FITTINGLY
PROPOSED TO MEN FOR BELIEF

[1]   Since, therefore, there exists a twofold truth concerning the divine being, one to which the inquiry of the reason
can reach, the other which surpasses the whole ability of the
human reason, it is fitting that both of these truths be proposed to man divinely for belief. This point must first be
shown concerning the truth that is open to the inquiry of
the reason; otherwise, it might perhaps seem to someone
that, since such a truth can be known by the reason, it was
uselessly given to men through a supernatural inspiration
as an object of belief.

[2]   Yet, if this truth were left solely as a matter of inquiry
for the human reason, three awkward consequences would
follow.

[3]   The first is that few men would possess the knowledge
of God. For there are three reasons why most men are cut
off from the fruit of diligent inquiry which is the discovery
of truth. Some do not have the physical disposition for such
work. As a result, there are many who are naturally not
fitted to pursue knowledge; and so, however much they

tried, they would be unable to reach the highest level of human knowledge which consists in knowing God. Others are cut off from pursuing this truth by the necessities imposed upon them by their daily lives. For some men must devote themselves to taking care of temporal matters. Such men would not be able to give so much time to the leisure of contemplative inquiry as to reach the highest peak at which human investigation can arrive, namely, the knowledge of God. Finally, there are some who are cut off by indolence. In order to know the things that the reason can investigate concerning God, a knowledge of many things must already be possessed. For almost all of philosophy is directed towards the knowledge of God, and that is why metaphysics, which deals with divine things, is the last part of philosophy to be learned. This means that we are able to arrive at the inquiry concerning the aforementioned truth only on the basis of a great deal of labor spent in study. Now, those who wish to undergo such a labor for the mere love of knowledge are few, even though God has inserted into the minds of men a natural appetite for knowledge.

[4] The second awkward effect is that those who would come to discover the abovementioned truth would barely reach it after a great deal of time. The reasons are several. There is the profundity of this truth, which the human intellect is made capable of grasping by natural inquiry only after a long training. Then, there are many things that must be presupposed, as we have said. There is also the fact that, in youth, when the soul is swayed by the various movements of the passions, it is not in a suitable state for the knowledge of such lofty truth. On the contrary, "one becomes wise and knowing in repose," as it is said in the *Physics*.[1] The result is this. If the only way open to us for the knowledge of God were solely that of the reason, the human race would remain in the blackest shadows of ignorance. For then the knowledge of God, which especially renders men perfect and good, would come to be

1. Aristotle, *Physics*, VII, 3 (247b 9).

possessed only by a few, and these few would require a great deal of time in order to reach it.

[5]   The third awkward effect is this. The investigation of the human reason for the most part has falsity present within it, and this is due partly to the weakness of our intellect in judgment, and partly to the admixture of images. The result is that many, remaining ignorant of the power of demonstration, would hold in doubt those things that have been most truly demonstrated. This would be particularly the case since they see that, among those who are reputed to be wise men, each one teaches his own brand of doctrine. Furthermore, with the many truths that are demonstrated, there sometimes is mingled something that is false, which is not demonstrated but rather asserted on the basis of some probable or sophistical argument, which yet has the credit of being a demonstration. That is why it was necessary that the unshakeable certitude and pure truth concerning divine things should be presented to men by way of faith.[2]

[6]   Beneficially, therefore, did the divine Mercy provide that it should instruct us to hold by faith even those truths that the human reason is able to investigate. In this way, all men would easily be able to have a share in the knowledge of God, and this without uncertainty and error.

[7]   Hence it is written: "Henceforward you walk not as also the Gentiles walk in the vanity of their mind, having their understanding darkened" (Eph. 4:17–18). And again: "All thy children shall be taught of the Lord" (Isa. 54:13).

2. Although St. Thomas does not name Maimonides or his *Guide for the Perplexed* (*Dux neutrorum*), there are evident points of contact between the Catholic and the Jewish theologian. On the reasons for revelation given here, on our knowledge of God, on creation and the eternity of the world, and on Aristotelianism in general, St. Thomas has Maimonides in mind both to agree and to disagree with him. By way of background for *SCG*, I, the reader can usefully consult the references to Maimonides in E. Gilson, *History of Christian Philosophy in the Middle Ages* (New York, 1955), pp. 649–651.

Chapter 5.

THAT THE TRUTHS THE HUMAN REASON IS NOT ABLE TO INVESTIGATE ARE FITTINGLY PROPOSED TO MEN FOR BELIEF

[1] Now, perhaps some will think that men should not be asked to believe what the reason is not adequate to investigate, since the divine Wisdom provides in the case of each thing according to the mode of its nature. We must therefore prove that it is necessary for man to receive from God as objects of belief even those truths that are above the human reason.

[2] No one tends with desire and zeal towards something that is not already known to him. But, as we shall examine later on in this work, men are ordained by the divine Providence towards a higher good than human fragility can experience in the present life.[1] That is why it was necessary for the human mind to be called to something higher than the human reason here and now can reach, so that it would thus learn to desire something and with zeal tend towards something that surpasses the whole state of the present life. This belongs especially to the Christian religion, which in a unique way promises spiritual and eternal goods. And so there are many things proposed to men in it that transcend human sense. The Old Law, on the other hand, whose promises were of a temporal character, contained very few proposals that transcended the inquiry of the human reason. Following this same direction, the philosophers themselves, in order that they might lead men from the pleasure of sensible things to virtue, were concerned to show that there were in existence other goods of a higher nature than these things of sense, and that those who gave

1. *SCG*, III, ch. 48.

themselves to the active or contemplative virtues would find much sweeter enjoyment in the taste of these higher goods.

[3]   It is also necessary that such truth be proposed to men for belief so that they may have a truer knowledge of God. For then only do we know God truly when we believe Him to be above everything that it is possible for man to think about Him; for, as we have shown,[2] the divine substance surpasses the natural knowledge of which man is capable. Hence, by the fact that some things about God are proposed to man that surpass his reason, there is strengthened in man the view that God is something above what he can think.

[4]   Another benefit that comes from the revelation to men of truths that exceed the reason is the curbing of presumption, which is the mother of error. For there are some who have such a presumptuous opinion of their own ability that they deem themselves able to measure the nature of everything; I mean to say that, in their estimation, everything is true that seems to them so, and everything is false that does not. So that the human mind, therefore, might be freed from this presumption and come to a humble inquiry after truth, it was necessary that some things should be proposed to man by God that would completely surpass his intellect.

[5]   A still further benefit may also be seen in what Aristotle says in the Ethics.[3] There was a certain Simonides who exhorted people to put aside the knowledge of divine things and to apply their talents to human occupations. He said that "he who is a man should know human things, and he who is mortal, things that are mortal." Against Simonides Aristotle says that "man should draw himself towards what is immortal and divine as much as he can." And so he says in the De animalibus that, although what we know of the higher substances is very little, yet that little is loved and

2. See above, ch. 3.
3. Aristotle, Nicomachean Ethics, X, 7 (1177b 31).

desired more than all the knowledge that we have about less noble substances.[4] He also says in the *De caelo et mundo* that when questions about the heavenly bodies can be given even a modest and merely plausible solution, he who hears this experiences intense joy.[5] From all these considerations it is clear that even the most imperfect knowledge about the most noble realities brings the greatest perfection to the soul. Therefore, although the human reason cannot grasp fully the truths that are above it, yet, if it somehow holds these truths at least by faith, it acquires great perfection for itself.

[6]   Therefore it is written: "For many things are shown to thee above the understanding of men" (Ecclus. 3:25). Again: "So the things that are of God no man knoweth but the Spirit of God. But to us God hath revealed them by His Spirit" (I Cor. 2:11, 10).

Chapter 6.

THAT TO GIVE ASSENT TO THE TRUTHS OF FAITH IS NOT FOOLISHNESS EVEN THOUGH THEY ARE ABOVE REASON

[1]   Those who place their faith in this truth, however, "for which the human reason offers no experimental evidence,"[1] do not believe foolishly, as though "following artificial fables" (II Peter 1:16). For these "secrets of divine Wisdom" (Job 11:6) the divine Wisdom itself, which knows all things to the full, has deigned to reveal to men. It reveals its own presence, as well as the truth of its teaching and inspiration, by fitting arguments; and in order to confirm those truths that exceed natural knowledge, it

4. Aristotle, *De partibus animalium*, I, 5 (644b 32).

5. Aristotle, *De caelo et mundo*, II, 12 (291b 26).

1. St. Gregory, *Homiliae in evangelia*, II, hom. 26, i (*PL*, 76, col. 1197).

gives visible manifestation to works that surpass the ability of all nature. Thus, there are the wonderful cures of illnesses, there is the raising of the dead, and the wonderful immutation in the heavenly bodies; and what is more wonderful, there is the inspiration given to human minds, so that simple and untutored persons, filled with the gift of the Holy Spirit, come to possess instantaneously the highest wisdom and the readiest eloquence. When these arguments were examined, through the efficacy of the abovementioned proof, and not the violent assault of arms or the promise of pleasures, and (what is most wonderful of all) in the midst of the tyranny of the persecutors, an innumerable throng of people, both simple and most learned, flocked to the Christian faith. In this faith there are truths preached that surpass every human intellect; the pleasures of the flesh are curbed; it is taught that the things of the world should be spurned. Now, for the minds of mortal men to assent to these things is the greatest of miracles, just as it is a manifest work of divine inspiration that, spurning visible things, men should seek only what is invisible. Now, that this has happened neither without preparation nor by chance, but as a result of the disposition of God, is clear from the fact that through many pronouncements of the ancient prophets God had foretold that He would do this. The books of these prophets are held in veneration among us Christians, since they give witness to our faith.

[2] The manner of this confirmation is touched on by St. Paul: "Which," that is, human salvation, "having begun to be declared by the Lord, was confirmed unto us by them that hear Him: God also bearing them witness of signs, and wonders, and divers miracles, and distributions of the Holy Ghost" (Heb. 2:3–4).

[3] This wonderful conversion of the world to the Christian faith is the clearest witness of the signs given in the past; so that it is not necessary that they should be further repeated, since they appear most clearly in their effect. For

it would be truly more wonderful than all signs if the world had been led by simple and humble men to believe such lofty truths, to accomplish such difficult actions, and to have such high hopes. Yet it is also a fact that, even in our own time, God does not cease to work miracles through His saints for the confirmation of the faith.

[4] On the other hand, those who founded sects committed to erroneous doctrines proceeded in a way that is opposite to this. The point is clear in the case of Mohammed. He seduced the people by promises of carnal pleasure to which the concupiscence of the flesh goads us. His teaching also contained precepts that were in conformity with his promises, and he gave free rein to carnal pleasure. In all this, as is not unexpected, he was obeyed by carnal men. As for proofs of the truth of his doctrine, he brought forward only such as could be grasped by the natural ability of anyone with a very modest wisdom. Indeed, the truths that he taught he mingled with many fables and with doctrines of the greatest falsity. He did not bring forth any signs produced in a supernatural way, which alone fittingly gives witness to divine inspiration; for a visible action that can be only divine reveals an invisibly inspired teacher of truth. On the contrary, Mohammed said that he was sent in the power of his arms—which are signs not lacking even to robbers and tyrants. What is more, no wise men, men trained in things divine and human, believed in him from the beginning. Those who believed in him were brutal men and desert wanderers, utterly ignorant of all divine teaching, through whose numbers Mohammed forced others to become his followers by the violence of his arms. Nor do divine pronouncements on the part of preceding prophets offer him any witness. On the contrary, he perverts almost all the testimonies of the Old and New Testaments by making them into fabrications of his own, as can be seen by anyone who examines his law. It was, therefore, a shrewd decision on his part to forbid his followers to read the Old and New Testaments, lest these books convict him of

falsity. It is thus clear that those who place any faith in his words believe foolishly.

Chapter 7.

THAT THE TRUTH OF REASON IS NOT OPPOSED TO THE TRUTH OF THE CHRISTIAN FAITH

[1] Now, although the truth of the Christian faith which we have discussed surpasses the capacity of the reason, nevertheless that truth that the human reason is naturally endowed to know cannot be opposed to the truth of the Christian faith. For that with which the human reason is naturally endowed is clearly most true; so much so, that it is impossible for us to think of such truths as false. Nor is it permissible to believe as false that which we hold by faith, since this is confirmed in a way that is so clearly divine. Since, therefore, only the false is opposed to the true, as is clearly evident from an examination of their definitions, it is impossible that the truth of faith should be opposed to those principles that the human reason knows naturally.

[2] Furthermore, that which is introduced into the soul of the student by the teacher is contained in the knowledge of the teacher—unless his teaching is fictitious, which it is improper to say of God. Now, the knowledge of the principles that are known to us naturally has been implanted in us by God; for God is the Author of our nature. These principles, therefore, are also contained by the divine Wisdom. Hence, whatever is opposed to them is opposed to the divine Wisdom, and, therefore, cannot come from God. That which we hold by faith as divinely revealed, therefore, cannot be contrary to our natural knowledge.

[3] Again. In the presence of contrary arguments our intellect is chained, so that it cannot proceed to the knowl-

edge of the truth. If, therefore, contrary knowledges were implanted in us by God, our intellect would be hindered from knowing truth by this very fact. Now, such an effect cannot come from God.

[4] And again. What is natural cannot change as long as nature does not. Now, it is impossible that contrary opinions should exist in the same knowing subject at the same time. No opinion or belief, therefore, is implanted in man by God which is contrary to man's natural knowledge.

[5] Therefore, the Apostle says: "The word is nigh thee, even in thy mouth and in thy heart. This is the word of faith, which we preach" (Rom. 10:8). But because it overcomes reason, there are some who think that it is opposed to it: which is impossible.

[6] The authority of St. Augustine also agrees with this. He writes as follows: "That which truth will reveal cannot in any way be opposed to the sacred books of the Old and the New Testament."[1]

[7] From this we evidently gather the following conclusion: whatever arguments are brought forward against the doctrines of faith are conclusions incorrectly derived from the first and self-evident principles imbedded in nature. Such conclusions do not have the force of demonstration; they are arguments that are either probable or sophistical. And so, there exists the possibility to answer them.

Chapter 8.

HOW THE HUMAN REASON IS RELATED TO THE TRUTH OF FAITH

[1] There is also a further consideration. Sensible things, from which the human reason takes the origin of its knowl-

1. St. Augustine, *De genesi ad litteram*, II, c. 18 (*PL*, 34, col. 280).

edge, retain within themselves some sort of trace of a likeness to God. This is so imperfect, however, that it is
absolutely inadequate to manifest the substance of God.
For effects bear within themselves, in their own way, the
likeness of their causes, since an agent produces its like;
yet an effect does not always reach to the full likeness of
its cause. Now, the human reason is related to the knowledge of the truth of faith (a truth which can be most evident only to those who see the divine substance) in such a
way that it can gather certain likenesses of it, which are yet
not sufficient so that the truth of faith may be comprehended as being understood demonstratively or through
itself. Yet it is useful for the human reason to exercise
itself in such arguments, however weak they may be, provided only that there be present no presumption to comprehend or to demonstrate. For to be able to see something
of the loftiest realities, however thin and weak the sight
may be, is, as our previous remarks indicate, a cause of the
greatest joy.

[2]   The testimony of Hilary agrees with this. Speaking of
this same truth, he writes as follows in his De Trinitate:
"Enter these truths by believing, press forward, persevere.
And though I may know that you will not arrive at an end,
yet I will congratulate you in your progress. For, though he
who pursues the infinite with reverence will never finally
reach the end, yet he will always progress by pressing on-
ward. But do not intrude yourself into the divine secret,
do not, presuming to comprehend the sum total of intelligence, plunge yourself into the mystery of the unending
nativity; rather, understand that these things are incompre-
hensible."[1]

1. St. Hilary, De Trinitate, II, 10, ii (PL, 10, coll. 58–59).

Chapter 9.

THE ORDER AND MANNER OF PROCEDURE IN THE PRESENT WORK

[1] It is clearly apparent, from what has been said, that the intention of the wise man ought to be directed toward the twofold truth of divine things, and toward the destruction of the errors that are contrary to this truth. One kind of divine truth the investigation of the reason is competent to reach, whereas the other surpasses every effort of the reason. I am speaking of a "twofold truth of divine things," not on the part of God Himself, Who is truth one and simple, but from the point of view of our knowledge, which is variously related to the knowledge of divine things.

[2] Now, to make the first kind of divine truth known, we must proceed through demonstrative arguments, by which our adversary may become convinced. However, since such arguments are not available for the second kind of divine truth, our intention should not be to convince our adversary by arguments: it should be to answer his arguments against the truth; for, as we have shown,[1] the natural reason cannot be contrary to the truth of faith. The sole way to overcome an adversary of divine truth is from the authority of Scripture—an authority divinely confirmed by miracles. For that which is above the human reason we believe only because God has revealed it. Nevertheless, there are certain likely arguments that should be brought forth in order to make divine truth known. This should be done for the training and consolation of the faithful, and not with any idea of refuting those who are adversaries. For the very inadequacy of the arguments would rather strengthen them in their error, since they would imagine

1. See above, ch. 7.

that our acceptance of the truth of faith was based on such weak arguments.

[3]   This, then, is the manner of procedure we intend to follow. We shall first seek to make known that truth which faith professes and reason investigates.[2] This we shall do by bringing forward both demonstrative and probable arguments, some of which were drawn from the books of the philosophers and of the saints, through which truth is strengthened and its adversary overcome. Then, in order to follow a development from the more manifest to the less manifest, we shall proceed to make known that truth which surpasses reason, answering the objections of its adversaries and setting forth the truth of faith by probable arguments and by authorities, to the best of our ability.[3]

[4]   We are aiming, then, to set out following the way of the reason and to inquire into what the human reason can investigate about God. In this aim the first consideration that confronts us is of that which belongs to God in Himself.[4] The second consideration concerns the coming forth of creatures from God.[5] The third concerns the ordering of creatures to God as to their end.[6]

[5]   Now, among the inquiries that we must undertake concerning God in Himself, we must set down in the beginning that whereby His Existence is demonstrated, as the necessary foundation of the whole work. For, if we do not demonstrate that God exists, all consideration of divine things is necessarily suppressed.

2. This effort occupies St. Thomas through Books I–III of the present work.
3. The transition of Books I–III to Book IV may be clearly seen from the last two paragraphs of the first chapter of Book IV.
4. This is the subject of Book I.
5. This is the subject of Book II.
6. This is the subject of Book III.

Chapter 10.

THE OPINION OF THOSE WHO SAY THAT THE EXISTENCE OF GOD, BEING SELF-EVIDENT, CANNOT BE DEMONSTRATED

[1] There are some persons to whom the inquiry seeking to demonstrate that God exists may perhaps appear superfluous. These are the persons who assert that the existence of God is self-evident, in such wise that its contrary cannot be entertained in the mind. It thus appears that the existence of God cannot be demonstrated, as may be seen from the following arguments.

[2] Those propositions are said to be self-evident that are known immediately upon the knowledge of their terms. Thus, as soon as you know the nature of a *whole* and the nature of a *part*, you know immediately that every whole is greater than its part. The proposition *God exists* is of this sort. For by the name *God* we understand something than which a greater cannot be thought. This notion is formed in the intellect by one who hears and understands the name *God*. As a result, God must exist already at least in the intellect. But He cannot exist solely in the intellect, since that which exists both in the intellect and in reality is greater than that which exists in the intellect alone. Now, as the very definition of the name points out, nothing can be greater than God. Consequently, the proposition that God exists is self-evident, as being evident from the very meaning of the name *God*.

[3] Again, it is possible to think that something exists whose non-existence cannot be thought. Clearly, such a being is greater than the being whose non-existence can be thought. Consequently, if God Himself could be thought not to be, then something greater than God could be

thought. This, however, is contrary to the definition of the name God. Hence, the proposition that God exists is self-evident.

[4]   Furthermore, those propositions ought to be the most evident in which the same thing is predicated of itself, for example, *man is man*, or whose predicates are included in the definition of their subjects, for example, *man is an animal*. Now, in God, as will be shown in a later chapter,[1] it is pre-eminently the case that His being is His essence, so that to the question *what is He?* and to the question *is He?* the answer is one and the same. Thus, in the proposition *God exists*, the predicate is consequently either identical with the subject or at least included in the definition of the subject. Hence, that God exists is self-evident.

[5]   What is naturally known is known through itself, for we do not come to such propositions through an effort of inquiry. But the proposition that God exists is naturally known since, as will be shown later on,[2] the desire of man naturally tends towards God as towards the ultimate end. The proposition that God exists is, therefore, self-evident.

[6]   There is also the consideration that that through which all the rest are known ought itself to be self-evident. Now, God is of this sort. For just as the light of the sun is the principle of all visible perception, so the divine light is the principle of all intelligible knowledge; since the divine light is that in which intelligible illumination is found first and in its highest degree. That God exists, therefore, must be self-evident.

[7]   These, then, and others like them are the arguments by which some think that the proposition *God exists* is so self-evident that its contrary cannot be entertained by the mind.

1. See below, ch. 22.
2. *SCG*, III, ch. 25.

Chapter 11.

A REFUTATION OF THE ABOVEMENTIONED OPINION AND A SOLUTION OF THE ARGUMENTS

[1] In part, the above opinion arises from the custom by which from their earliest days people are brought up to hear and to call upon the name of God. Custom, and especially custom in a child, comes to have the force of nature. As a result, what the mind is steeped in from childhood it clings to very firmly, as something known naturally and self-evidently.

[2] In part, however, the above opinion comes about because of a failure to distinguish between that which is self-evident in an absolute sense and that which is self-evident in relation to us. For assuredly that God exists is, absolutely speaking, self-evident, since what God is is His own being. Yet, because we are not able to conceive in our minds that which God is, that God exists remains unknown in relation to us. So, too, that every whole is greater than its part is, absolutely speaking, self-evident; but it would perforce be unknown to one who could not conceive the nature of a whole. Hence it comes about, as it is said in *Metaphysics* II, that "our intellect is related to the most knowable things in reality as the eye of an owl is related to the sun."[1]

[3] And, contrary to the point made by the first argument, it does not follow immediately that, as soon as we know the meaning of the name God, the existence of God is known. It does not follow first because it is not known to all, even including those who admit that God exists, that God is that than which a greater cannot be thought. After all, many ancients said that this world itself was God. Furthermore, no such inference can be drawn from the

1. Aristotle, *Metaphysics*, Iα, 1 (993b 9).

interpretations of the name God to be found in Dama-scene.[2] What is more, granted that everyone should under-stand by the name God something than which a greater cannot be thought, it will still not be necessary that there exist in reality something than which a greater cannot be thought. For a thing and the definition of a name are posited in the same way. Now, from the fact that that which is indicated by the name God is conceived by the mind, it does not follow that God exists save only in the intellect. Hence, that than which a greater cannot be thought will likewise not have to exist save only in the intellect. From this it does not follow that there exists in reality something than which a greater cannot be thought. No difficulty, consequently, befalls anyone who posits that God does not exist. For that something greater can be thought than anything given in reality or in the intellect is a difficulty only to him who admits that there is some-thing than which a greater cannot be thought in reality.

[4] Nor, again, is it necessary, as the second argument advanced, that something greater than God can be thought if God can be thought not to be. For that He can be thought not to be does not arise either from the imperfec-tion or the uncertainty of His own being, since this is in itself most manifest. It arises, rather, from the weakness of our intellect, which cannot behold God Himself except through His effects and which is thus led to know His existence through reasoning.

[5] This enables us to solve the third argument as well. For just as it is evident to us that a whole is greater than a part of itself, so to those seeing the divine essence in itself it is supremely self-evident that God exists because His essence is His being. But, because we are not able to see His essence, we arrive at the knowledge of His being, not through God Himself, but through His effects.

2. St. John Damascene, De fide orthodoxa, I, 9 (PG, 94, coll. 836B–837B).

[6]   The answer to the *fourth* argument is likewise clear. For man naturally knows God in the same way as he naturally desires God. Now, man naturally desires God in so far as he naturally desires beatitude, which is a certain likeness of the divine goodness. On this basis, it is not necessary that God considered in Himself be naturally known to man, but only a likeness of God. It remains, therefore, that man is to reach the knowledge of God through reasoning by way of the likenesses of God found in His effects.

[7]   So, too, with the *fifth* argument, an easy solution is available. For God is indeed that by which all things are known, not in the sense that they are not known un-less He is known (as obtains among self-evident princi-ples), but because all our knowledge is caused in us through His influence.

Chapter 12.

THE OPINION OF THOSE WHO SAY THAT THE EXISTENCE OF GOD CANNOT BE DEMON-STRATED BUT IS HELD BY FAITH ALONE

[1]   There are others who hold a certain opinion, contrary to the position mentioned above, through which the efforts of those seeking to prove the existence of God would like-wise be rendered futile. For they say that we cannot arrive at the existence of God through the reason; it is received by way of faith and revelation alone.

[2]   What led some persons to hold this view was the weakness of the arguments which had been brought forth by others to prove that God exists.

[3]   Nevertheless, the present error might erroneously find support in its behalf in the words of some philosophers who show that in God essence and being are identical, that

is, that that which answers to the question *what is it?* is identical with that which answers to the question *is it?* Now, following the way of the reason we cannot arrive at a knowledge of what God is. Hence, it seems likewise impossible to demonstrate by the reason that God exists.

[4]   Furthermore, according to the logic of the Philosopher, as a principle to demonstrate whether a thing is we must take the signification of the name of that thing;[1] and, again according to the Philosopher, the meaning signified by a name is its definition.[2] If this be so, if we set aside a knowledge of the divine essence or quiddity, no means will be available whereby to demonstrate that God exists.

[5]   Again, if, as is shown in the *Posterior Analytics*,[3] the knowledge of the principles of demonstration takes its origin from sense, whatever transcends all sense and sensibles seems to be indemonstrable. That God exists appears to be a proposition of this sort and is therefore indemonstrable.

[6]   The falsity of this opinion is shown to us, first, from the art of demonstration which teaches us to arrive at causes from their effects. Then, it is shown to us from the order of the sciences. For, as it is said in the *Metaphysics*,[4] if there is no knowable substance higher than sensible substance, there will be no science higher than physics. It is shown, thirdly, from the pursuit of the philosophers, who have striven to demonstrate that God exists. Finally, it is shown to us by the truth in the words of the Apostle Paul: "For the invisible things of God . . . are clearly seen, being understood by the things that are made" (Rom. 1:20).

[7]   Nor, contrary to the *first* argument, is there any problem in the fact that in God essence and being are identical.

1. Aristotle, *Posterior Analytics*, II, 9 (93b 23).
2. Aristotle, *Metaphysics*, IV, 7 (1012a 23–24).
3. Aristotle, *Posterior Analytics*, I, 18 (81a 38).
4. Aristotle, *Metaphysics*, IV, 3 (1005a 18).

For this is understood of the being by which God subsists in Himself. But we do not know of what sort this being is, just as we do not know the divine essence. The reference is not to the being that signifies the composition of intellect. For thus the existence of God does fall under demonstration; this happens when our mind is led from demonstrative arguments to form such a proposition of God whereby it expresses that He exists.

[8] Now, in arguments proving the existence of God, it is not necessary to assume the divine essence or quiddity as the middle term of the demonstration. This was the second view proposed above. In place of the quiddity, an effect is taken as the middle term, as in demonstrations *quia*.[5] It is from such effects that the meaning of the name God is taken. For all divine names are imposed either by removing the effects of God from Him or by relating God in some way to His effects.

[9] It is thereby likewise evident that, although God transcends all sensible things and the sense itself, His effects, on which the demonstration proving His existence is based, are nevertheless sensible things. And thus, the origin of our knowledge in the sense applies also to those things that transcend the sense.

Chapter 13.

ARGUMENTS IN PROOF OF THE EXISTENCE OF GOD

[1] We have now shown that the effort to demonstrate the existence of God is not a vain one. We shall therefore proceed to set forth the arguments by which both philosophers and Catholic teachers have proved that God exists.

5. That is, demonstrations proving that something is so—for example, *that* God exists.

[2]   We shall first set forth the arguments by which Aristotle proceeds to prove that God exists. The aim of Aristotle is to do this in two ways, beginning with motion.

[3]   Of these ways the first is as follows.[1] Everything that is moved is moved by another. That some things are in motion—for example, the sun—is evident from sense. Therefore, it is moved by something else that moves it. This mover is itself either moved or not moved. If it is not, we have reached our conclusion—namely, that we must posit some unmoved mover. This we call God. If it is moved, it is moved by another mover. We must, consequently, either proceed to infinity, or we must arrive at some unmoved mover. Now, it is not possible to proceed to infinity. Hence, we must posit some prime unmoved mover.

[4]   In this proof, there are two propositions that need to be proved, namely, that *everything that is moved is moved by another*, and that *in movers and things moved one cannot proceed to infinity*.

[5]   The first of these propositions Aristotle proves in three ways. The first way is as follows. If something moves itself, it must have within itself the principle of its own motion; otherwise, it is clearly moved by another. Furthermore, it must be primarily moved. This means that it must be moved by reason of itself, and not by reason of a part of itself, as happens when an animal is moved by the motion of its foot. For, in this sense, a whole would not be moved by itself, but a part, and one part would be moved by another. It is also necessary that a self-moving being be divisible and have parts, since, as it is proved in the *Physics*,[2] whatever is moved is divisible.

[6]   On the basis of these suppositions Aristotle argues as follows. That which is held to be moved by itself is primarily moved. For if, while one part was at rest, another part in it were moved, then the whole itself would not be pri-

1. Aristotle, *Physics*, VII, 1 (241b 24).
2. Aristotle, *Physics*, VI, 4 (234b 10).

marily moved; it would be that part in it which is moved while another part is at rest. But nothing that is at rest because something else is at rest is moved by itself; for that being whose rest follows upon the rest of another must have its motion follow upon the motion of another. It is thus not moved by itself. Therefore, that which was posited as being moved by itself is not moved by itself. Consequently, everything that is moved must be moved by another.

[7] Nor is it an objection to this argument if one might say that, when something is held, to move itself, a part of it cannot be at rest; or, again, if one might say that a part is not subject to rest or motion except accidentally, which is the unfounded argument of Avicenna.[3] For, indeed, the force of Aristotle's argument lies in this: *if something moves itself primarily and through itself, rather than through its parts, that it is moved cannot depend on another*. But the moving of the divisible itself, like its being, depends on its parts; it cannot therefore move itself primarily and through itself. Hence, for the truth of the inferred conclusion it is not necessary to assume as an absolute truth that a part of a being moving itself is at rest. What must rather be true is this conditional proposition: *if the part were at rest, the whole would be at rest*. Now, this proposition would be true even though its antecedent be impossible. In the same way, the following conditional proposition is true: *if man is an ass, he is irrational*.

[8] In the second way, Aristotle proves the proposition by induction.[4] Whatever is moved by accident is not moved by itself, since it is moved upon the motion of another. So, too, as is evident, what is moved by violence is not moved by itself. Nor are those beings moved by themselves that are moved by their nature as being moved from within; such is the case with animals, which evidently are moved by the soul. Nor, again, is this true of those beings, such

3. Avicenna, *Sufficientia*, II, 1 (fol. 24ra).
4. Aristotle, *Physics*, VIII, 4 (254b 8).

as heavy and light bodies, which are moved through nature. For such beings are moved by the generating cause and the cause removing impediments. Now, whatever is moved is moved through itself or by accident. If it is moved through itself, then it is moved either violently or by nature; if by nature, then either through itself, as the animal, or not through itself, as heavy and light bodies. Therefore, everything that is moved is moved by another.

[9]   In the *third* way, Aristotle proves the proposition as follows.[5] The same thing cannot be at once in act and in potency with respect to the same thing. But everything that is moved is, as such, in potency. For motion is *the act of something that is in potency inasmuch as it is in potency.*[6] That which moves, however, is as such in act, for nothing acts except according as it is in act. Therefore, with respect to the same motion, nothing is both mover and moved. Thus, nothing moves itself.

[10]   It is to be noted, however, that Plato, who held that every mover is moved,[7] understood the name *motion* in a wider sense than did Aristotle. For Aristotle understood motion strictly, according as it is the act of what exists in potency inasmuch as it is such. So understood, motion belongs only to divisible bodies, as it is proved in the *Physics.*[8] According to Plato, however, that which moves itself is not a body. Plato understood by motion any given operation, so that *to understand* and *to judge* are a kind of motion. Aristotle likewise touches upon this manner of speaking in the *De anima.*[9] Plato accordingly said that the first mover moves himself because he knows himself and wills or loves himself. In a way, this is not opposed to the reasons of Aristotle. There is no difference between reaching a first being that moves himself, as understood by Plato,

5. Aristotle, *Physics*, VIII, 5 (257a 39).
6. Aristotle, *Physics*, III, 1 (201a 10).
7. Plato, *Phaedrus*, p. 247C.
8. Aristotle, *Physics*, VI, 4 (234b 10).
9. Aristotle, *De anima*, III, 7 (431a 6).

and reaching a first being that is absolutely unmoved, as understood by Aristotle.

[11] The second proposition, namely, *that there is no procession to infinity among movers and things moved,* Aristotle proves in three ways.

[12] The first is as follows.[10] If among movers and things moved we proceed to infinity, all these infinite beings must be bodies. For whatever is moved is divisible and a body, as is proved in the *Physics*.[11] But every body that moves some thing moved is itself moved while moving it. Therefore, all these infinites are moved together while one of them is moved. But one of them, being finite, is moved in a finite time. Therefore, all those infinites are moved in a finite time. This, however, is impossible. It is, therefore, impossible that among movers and things moved one can proceed to infinity.

[13] Furthermore, that it is impossible for the above-mentioned infinites to be moved in a finite time Aristotle proves as follows. The mover and the thing moved must exist simultaneously. This Aristotle proves by induction in the various species of motion. But bodies cannot be simultaneous except through continuity or contiguity. Now, since, as has been proved, all the aforementioned movers and things moved are bodies, they must constitute by continuity or contiguity a sort of single mobile. In this way, one infinite is moved in a finite time. This is impossible, as is proved in the *Physics*.[12]

[14] The second argument proving the same conclusion is the following.[13] In an ordered series of movers and things moved (this is a series in which one is moved by another according to an order), it is necessarily the fact that, when the first mover is removed or ceases to move, no other

10. Aristotle, *Physics*, VII, 1 (241b 24).
11. Aristotle, *Physics*, VI, 4 (234b 10).
12. Aristotle, *Physics*, VII, 1 (241b 12); VI, 7 (237b 23ff.).
13. Aristotle, *Physics*, VIII, 5 (256a 12).

mover will move or be moved. For the first mover is the cause of motion for all the others. But, if there are movers and things moved following an order to infinity, there will be no first mover, but all would be as intermediate movers. Therefore, none of the others will be able to be moved, and thus nothing in the world will be moved.

[15]   The third proof comes to the same conclusion, except that, by beginning with the superior, it has a reversed order. It is as follows. That which moves as an instrumental cause cannot move unless there be a principal moving cause. But, if we proceed to infinity among movers and things moved, all movers will be as instrumental causes, because they will be moved movers and there will be nothing as a principal mover. Therefore, nothing will be moved.

[16]   Such, then, is the proof of both propositions assumed by Aristotle in the first demonstrative way by which he proved that a first unmoved mover exists.

[17]   The second way is this. If every mover is moved, this proposition is true either by itself or by accident. If by accident, then it is not necessary, since what is true by accident is not necessary. It is something possible, therefore, that no mover is moved. But, if a mover is not moved, it does not move: as the adversary says. It is therefore possible that nothing is moved. For, if nothing moves, nothing is moved. This, however, Aristotle considers to be impossible—namely, that at any time there be no motion.[14] Therefore, the first proposition was not possible, since from a false possible, a false impossible does not follow. Hence, this proposition, *every mover is moved by another*, was not true by accident.

[18]   Again, if two things are accidentally joined in some being, and one of them is found without the other, it is probable that the other can be found without it. For example, if *white* and *musical* are found in Socrates, and in Plato we find *musical* but not *white*, it is probable that in

14. Aristotle, *Physics*, VIII, 5 (256b 4–13).

some other being we can find the *white* without the *musical*. Therefore, if mover and thing moved are accidentally joined in some being, and the thing moved be found without the mover in some being, it is probable that the mover is found without that which is moved. Nor can the example of two things, of which one depends on the other, be brought as an objection against this. For the union we are speaking of is not essential, but accidental.

[19] But, if the proposition that every mover is moved is true by itself, something impossible or awkward likewise follows. For the mover must be moved either by the same kind of motion as that by which he moves, or by another. If the same, a cause of alteration must itself be altered, and further, a healing cause must itself be healed, and a teacher must himself be taught and this with respect to the same knowledge. Now, this is impossible. A teacher must have science, whereas he who is a learner of necessity does not have it. So that, if the proposition were true, the same thing would be possessed and not possessed by the same being—which is impossible. If, however, the mover is moved by another species of motion, so that (namely) the altering cause is moved according to place, and the cause moving according to place is increased, and so forth, since the genera and species of motion are finite in number, it will follow that we cannot proceed to infinity. There will thus be a first mover, which is not moved by another. Will someone say that there will be a recurrence, so that when all the genera and species of motion have been completed the series will be repeated and return to the first motion? This would involve saying, for example, that a mover according to place would be altered, the altering cause would be increased, and the increasing cause would be moved according to place. Yet this whole view would arrive at the same conclusion as before: whatever moves according to a certain species of motion is itself moved according to the same species of motion, though mediately and not immediately.

[20]   It remains, therefore, that we must posit some first mover that is not moved by any exterior moving cause.

[21]   Granted this conclusion—namely, that there is a first mover that is not moved by an exterior moving cause —it yet does not follow that this mover is absolutely unmoved. That is why Aristotle goes on to say that the condition of the first mover may be twofold.[15] The first mover can be absolutely unmoved. If so, we have the conclusion we are seeking: there is a first unmoved mover. On the other hand, the first mover can be self-moved. This may be argued, because that which is through itself is prior to what is through another. Hence, among things moved as well, it seems reasonable that the first moved is moved through itself and not by another.

[22]   But, on this basis, the same conclusion again follows.[16] For it cannot be said that, when a mover moves himself, the whole is moved by the whole. Otherwise, the same difficulties would follow as before: one person would both teach and be taught, and the same would be true among other motions. It would also follow that a being would be both in potency and in act; for a mover is, as such, in act, whereas the thing moved is in potency. Consequently, one part of the self-moved mover is solely moving, and the other part solely moved. We thus reach the same conclusion as before: there exists an unmoved mover.

[23]   Nor can it be held that both parts of the self-moved mover are moved, so that one is moved by the other, or that one moves both itself and the other, or that the whole moves a part, or that a part moves the whole. All this would involve the return of the aforementioned difficulties: something would both move and be moved according to the same species of motion; something would be at once in potency and in act; and, furthermore, the whole would not be primarily moving itself, it would move through the

15. Aristotle, *Physics*, VIII, 5 (256a 13).
16. Aristotle, *Physics*, VIII, 5 (257b 2).

motion of a part. The conclusion thus stands: one part of a self-moved mover must be unmoved and moving the other part.

[24] But there is another point to consider. Among self-moved beings known to us, namely, animals, although the moving part, which is to say the soul, is unmoved through itself, it is yet moved by accident. That is why Aristotle further shows that the moving part of the first self-moving being is not moved either through itself or by accident.[17] For, since self-moving beings known to us, namely, animals, are corruptible, the moving part in them is moved by accident. But corruptible self-moving beings must be reduced to some first self-moving being that is everlasting. Therefore, some self-moving being must have a mover that is moved neither through itself nor by accident.

[25] It is further evident that, according to the position of Aristotle, some self-moved being must be everlasting. For if, as Aristotle supposes, motion is everlasting, the generation of self-moving beings (this means beings that are generable and corruptible) must be endless. But the cause of this endlessness cannot be one of the self-moving beings, since it does not always exist. Nor can the cause be all the self-moving beings together, both because they would be infinite and because they would not be simultaneous. There must therefore be some endlessly self-moving being, causing the endlessness of generation among these sublunary self-movers. Thus, the mover of the self-moving being is not moved, either through itself or by accident.

[26] Again, we see that among beings that move themselves some initiate a new motion as a result of some motion. This new motion is other than the motion by which an animal moves itself, for example, digested food or altered air. By such a motion the self-moving mover is moved by accident. From this we may infer that no self-moved being is

17. Aristotle, *Physics*, VIII, 6 (258b 15).

moved everlastingly whose mover is moved either by itself
or by accident. But the first self-mover is everlastingly in
motion; otherwise, motion could not be everlasting, since
every other motion is caused by the motion of the self-
moving first mover. The first self-moving being, therefore, is
moved by a mover who is himself moved neither through
himself nor by accident.

[27]   Nor is it against this argument that the movers of
the lower spheres produce an everlasting motion and yet are
said to be moved by accident. For they are said to be moved
by accident, not on their own account, but on account of
their movable subjects, which follow the motion of the
higher sphere.

[28]   Now, God is not part of any self-moving mover. In
his *Metaphysics*, therefore, Aristotle goes on from the
mover who is a part of the self-moved mover to seek another mover—God—who is absolutely separate.[18] For,
since everything moving itself is moved through appetite,
the mover who is part of the self-moving being moves because of the appetite of some appetible object. This object
is higher, in the order of motion, than the mover desiring
it; for the one desiring is in a manner a moved mover,
whereas an appetible object is an absolutely unmoved
mover. There must, therefore, be an absolutely unmoved
separate first mover. This is God.

[29]   Two considerations seem to invalidate these arguments. The first consideration is that, as arguments, they
presuppose the eternity of motion, which Catholics consider to be false.

[30]   To this consideration the reply is as follows. The
most efficacious way to prove that God exists is on the
supposition that the world is eternal. Granted this supposition, that God exists is less manifest. For, if the world
and motion have a first beginning, some cause must clearly
be posited to account for this origin of the world and of

18. Aristotle, *Metaphysics*, XII, 7 (1072a 23).

motion. That which comes to be anew must take its origin from some innovating cause; since nothing brings itself from potency to act, or from non-being to being.

[31]   The second consideration is that the demonstrations given above presuppose that the first moved being, namely, a heavenly body, is self-moved. This means that it is animated, which many do not admit.

[32]   The reply to this consideration is that, if the prime mover is not held to be self-moved, then it must be moved immediately by something absolutely unmoved. Hence, even Aristotle himself proposed this conclusion as a disjunction: it is necessary either to arrive immediately at an unmoved separate first mover, or to arrive at a self-moved mover from whom, in turn, an unmoved separate first mover is reached.[19]

[33]   In *Metaphysics* II Aristotle also uses another argument to show that there is no infinite regress in efficient causes and that we must reach one first cause—God.[20] This way is as follows. In all ordered efficient causes, the first is the cause of the intermediate cause, whether one or many, and this is the cause of the last cause. But, when you suppress a cause, you suppress its effect. Therefore, if you suppress the first cause, the intermediate cause cannot be a cause. Now, if there were an infinite regress among efficient causes, no cause would be first. Therefore, all the other causes, which are intermediate, will be suppressed. But this is manifestly false. We must, therefore, posit that there exists a first efficient cause. This is God.

[34]   Another argument may also be gathered from the words of Aristotle. In *Metaphysics* II he shows that what is most true is also most a being.[21] But in *Metaphysics* IV he shows the existence of something supremely true from the observed fact that of two false things one is more false

19. Aristotle, *Physics*, VIII, 5 (258a 1; b 4).
20. Aristotle, *Metaphysics*, Ia, 2 (994a 1).
21. Aristotle, *Metaphysics*, Ia, 1 (993b 30).

than the other, which means that one is more true than the other.[22] This comparison is based on the nearness to that which is absolutely and supremely true. From these Aristotelian texts we may further infer that there is something that is supremely being. This we call God.

[35] Damascene proposes another argument for the same conclusion taken from the government of the world.[23] Averroes likewise hints at it.[24] The argument runs thus. Contrary and discordant things cannot, always or for the most part, be parts of one order except under someone's government, which enables all and each to tend to a definite end. But in the world we find that things of diverse natures come together under one order, and this not rarely or by chance, but always or for the most part. There must therefore be some being by whose providence the world is governed. This we call God.

Chapter 14.

THAT TO KNOW GOD WE MUST USE THE WAY OF REMOTION

[1] We have shown that there exists a first being, whom we call God. We must, accordingly, now investigate the properties of this being.

[2] Now, in considering the divine substance, we should especially make use of the method of remotion. For, by its immensity, the divine substance surpasses every form that our intellect reaches. Thus we are unable to apprehend it by knowing what it is. Yet we are able to have some knowledge of it by knowing what it is not. Furthermore, we ap-

---

22. Aristotle, *Metaphysics*, IV, 4 (1008b 37).
23. St. John Damascene, *De fide orthodoxa*, I, 3 (PG, 94, col. 796CD).
24. Averroes, *In II Physicorum*, t.c. 75 (fol. 75v–76r).

proach nearer to a knowledge of God according as through our intellect we are able to remove more and more things from Him. For we know each thing more perfectly the more fully we see its differences from other things; for each thing has within itself its own being, distinct from all other things. So, too, in the case of the things whose definitions we know. We locate them in a genus, through which we know in a general way what they are. Then we add differences to each thing, by which it may be distinguished from other things. In this way, a complete knowledge of a substance is built up.

[3] However, in the consideration of the divine substance we cannot take a *what* as a genus; nor can we derive the distinction of God from things by differences affirmed of God. For this reason, we must derive the distinction of God from other beings by means of negative differences. And just as among affirmative differences one contracts the other, so one negative difference is contracted by another that makes it to differ from many beings. For example, if we say that God is not an accident, we thereby distinguish Him from all accidents. Then, if we add that He is not a body, we shall further distinguish Him from certain substances. And thus, proceeding in order, by such negations God will be distinguished from all that He is not. Finally, there will then be a proper consideration of God's substance when He will be known as distinct from all things. Yet, this knowledge will not be perfect, since it will not tell us what God is in Himself.

[4] As a principle of procedure in knowing God by way of remotion, therefore, let us adopt the proposition which, from what we have said, is now manifest, namely, that God is absolutely unmoved. The authority of Sacred Scripture also confirms this. For it is written: "I am the Lord and I change not" (Mal. 3:6); . . . "with whom there is no change" (James 1:17). Again: "God is not man . . . that He should be changed (Num. 23:19).

Chapter 15.

THAT GOD IS ETERNAL

[1]   From what we have said it is further apparent that God is eternal.

[2]   Everything that begins to be or ceases to be does so through motion or change. Since, however, we have shown that God is absolutely immutable, He is eternal, lacking all beginning or end.

[3]   Again. Those beings alone are measured by time that are moved. For time, as is made clear in *Physics* IV, is "the number of motion."[1] But God, as has been proved, is absolutely without motion, and is consequently not measured by time. There is, therefore, no *before* and *after* in Him; He does not have being after non-being, nor non-being after being, nor can any succession be found in His being. For none of these characteristics can be understood without time. God, therefore, is without beginning and end, having His whole being at once. In this consists the nature of eternity.

[4]   What is more, if it were true that there was a time when He existed after not existing, then He must have been brought by someone from non-being to being. Not by Himself, since what does not exist cannot act. If by another, then this other is prior to God. But we have shown that God is the first cause. Hence, He did not begin to be, nor consequently will He cease to be, for that which has been everlastingly has the power to be everlastingly. God is, therefore, eternal.

[5]   We find in the world, furthermore, certain beings, those namely that are subject to generation and corruption,

1. Aristotle, *Physics*, IV, 11 (219b 1).—The cross-references in ¶s 1–4 of the text are to ch. 13, above.

which can be and not-be. But what can be has a cause because, since it is equally related to two contraries, namely, being and non-being, it must be owing to some cause that being accrues to it. Now, as we have proved by the reasoning of Aristotle, one cannot proceed to infinity among causes.[2] We must therefore posit something that is a necessary being. Every necessary being, however, either has the cause of its necessity in an outside source or, if it does not, it is necessary through itself. But one cannot proceed to infinity among necessary beings the cause of whose necessity lies in an outside source. We must therefore posit a first necessary being, which is necessary through itself. This is God, since, as we have shown,[3] He is the first cause. God, therefore, is eternal, since whatever is necessary through itself is eternal.

[6] From the everlastingness of time, likewise, Aristotle shows the everlastingness of motion,[4] from which he further shows the everlastingness of the moving substance.[5] Now, the first moving substance is God. God is therefore everlasting. If we deny the everlastingness of time and motion, we are still able to prove the everlastingness of the moving substance. For, if motion had a beginning, it must have done so through some moving cause. If this moving cause began, it did so through the action of some cause. Hence, either one will proceed to infinity, or he will arrive at a moving cause that had no beginning.

[7] To this truth divine authority offers witness. The Psalmist says: "But Thou, O Lord, endurest forever"; and he goes on to say: "But Thou art always the selfsame: and Thy years shall not fail" (Ps. 101:13, 28).

2. See above, ch. 13, ¶11ff.
3. See above, ch. 13, ¶28.
4. Aristotle, *Physics*, VIII, 1 (251b 12).
5. Aristotle, *Physics*, VIII, 6 (258b 13).

Chapter 16.

THAT THERE IS NO PASSIVE POTENCY IN GOD

[1]   If God is eternal, of necessity there is no potency in Him.

[2]   The being whose substance has an admixture of potency is liable not to be by as much as it has potency; for that which can be, can not-be. But, God, being everlasting, in His substance cannot not-be. In God, therefore, there is no potency to being.

[3]   Though a being that is sometime in potency and sometime in act is in time in potency before being in act, absolutely speaking act is prior to potency. For potency does not raise itself to act; it must be raised to act by something that is in act. Hence, whatever is in some way in potency has something prior to it. But, as is evident from what was said above,[1] God is the first being and the first cause. Hence, He has no admixture of potency in Himself.

[4]   Moreover, that which is a necessary being through itself is in no way a possible being, since that which is through itself a necessary being has no cause, whereas, as we have shown above,[2] whatever is a possible being has a cause. But God is through Himself a necessary being. He is, therefore, in no way a possible being, and so no potency is found in His substance.

[5]   Again, each thing acts in so far as it is in act. Therefore, what is not wholly act acts, not with the whole of itself, but with part of itself. But what does not act with the whole of itself is not the first agent, since it does not act through its essence but through participation in some-

1. See above, ch. 13, ¶34.
2. See above, ch. 15, ¶5.

thing. The first agent, therefore, namely, God, has no admixture of potency but is pure act.

[6]   Further, just as each thing naturally acts in so far as it is in act, so it is naturally receptive in so far as it is in potency; for motion is the act of that which exists in potency.[3] But God is absolutely impassible and immutable, as is clear from what we have said.[4] He has, therefore, no part of potency—that is, passive potency.

[7]   Then, too, we see something in the world that emerges from potency to act. Now, it does not educe itself from potency to act, since that which is in potency, being still in potency, can therefore not act. Some prior being is therefore needed by which it may be brought forth from potency to act. This cannot go on to infinity. We must, therefore, arrive at some being that is only in act and in no wise in potency. This being we call God.

Chapter 17.

THAT THERE IS NO MATTER IN GOD

[1]   From this it is likewise evident that God is not matter.

[2]   Whatever matter is, it is in potency.

[3]   Matter, furthermore, is not a principle of acting. That is why, according to Aristotle, the efficient cause and matter do not coincide.[1] But, as we have said, it belongs to God to be the first efficient cause of things.[2] Therefore, He is not matter.

[4]   Moreover, for those who reduced all things to matter as to the first cause it follows that natural things exist by

3. Aristotle, *Physics*, III, 1 (201a 10).
4. See above, ch. 13, ¶s 24 and 28.
1. Aristotle, *Physics*, II, 7 (198a 25).
2. See above, ch. 13, ¶33.

chance. Aristotle argues against these thinkers in *Physics* II.[3] Hence, if God, Who is the first cause, is the material cause of things, it follows that all things exist by chance.

[5]   Again, matter does not become the cause of something actual except by being altered and changed. But if, as we have proved, God is absolutely immobile, He cannot in any way be the cause of things according to the mode of matter.

[6]   Now, the Catholic faith professes this truth, namely, it asserts that God has created all things, not out of His own substance, but out of nothing.

[7]   On this point, however, the madness of David of Dinant stands confounded. He dared to assert that God is the same as prime matter on the ground that, if He were not, He would have to differ from it by some differences, and thus they would not be simple. For in the being that differs from another by a difference, the difference itself produces a composition. David's position was the result of ignorance. He did not know how to distinguish between *difference* and *diversity*. The *different*, as is determined in *Metaphysics* x,[4] is said relationally, for every different is different by something. Something is called *diverse*, however, absolutely, from the fact that it is not the same. Difference, therefore, must be sought among those things that agree in something, for we must point to something in them according to which they differ: for example, two species agree in genus and must therefore be distinguished by differences. But in things that agree in nothing we need not seek the whereby they differ; they are diverse by themselves. In the same way, opposite differences are distinguished from one another. For they do not share in the genus as a part of their essence, and therefore, since they are by themselves diverse, there is no need to seek that by which they differ.

3. Aristotle, *Physics*, II, 8 (198b 10).
4. Aristotle, *Metaphysics*, X, 3 (1054a 30).—On David of Dinant, see G. Théry, *David de Dinant* (Paris, 1925), and E. Gilson, *History of Christian Philosophy in the Middle Ages* (New York, 1955), pp. 241–243, 654 (note 9).

In this way, too, God and prime matter are distinguished: one is pure act, the other is pure potency, and they agree in nothing.

Chapter 18.

THAT THERE IS NO COMPOSITION IN GOD

[1] From what we have set down we can conclude that there is no composition in God.

[2] In every composite there must be act and potency. For several things cannot become absolutely one unless among them something is act and something potency. Now, beings in act are not united except by being, so to speak, bound or joined together, which means that they are not absolutely one. Their parts, likewise, are brought together as being in potency with respect to the union, since they are united in act after being potentially unitable. But in God there is no potency. Therefore, there is no composition in Him.

[3] Every composite, moreover, is subsequent to its components. The first being, therefore, which is God, has no components.

[4] Every composite, furthermore, is potentially dissoluble. This arises from the nature of composition, although in some composites there is another element that resists dissolution. Now, what is dissoluble can not-be. This does not befit God, since He is through Himself the necessary being. There is, therefore, no composition in God.

[5] Every composition, likewise, needs some composer. For, if there is composition, it is made up of a plurality, and a plurality cannot be fitted into a unity except by some composer. If, then, God were composite, He would have a composer. He could not compose Himself, since nothing is

its own cause, because it would be prior to itself, which is impossible. Now, the composer is the efficient cause of the composite. Thus, God would have an efficient cause. Thus, too, He would not be the first cause—which was proved above.[1]

[6]   Again, in every genus the simpler a being, the more noble it is: e.g., in the genus of the hot, fire, which has no admixture of cold. That, therefore, which is at the peak of nobility among all beings must be at the peak of simplicity. But the being that is at the peak of nobility among all beings we call God, since He is the first cause. For a cause is nobler than an effect. God can, therefore, have no composition.

[7]   Furthermore, in every composite the good belongs, not to this or that part, but to the whole—and I say good according to the goodness that is proper to the whole and its perfection. For parts are imperfect in comparison with the whole, as the parts of man are not a man, the parts of the number six do not have the perfection of six, and similarly the parts of a line do not reach the perfection of the measure found in the whole line. If, then, God is composite, His proper perfection and goodness is found in the whole, not in any part of the whole. Thus, there will not be in God purely that good which is proper to Him. God, then, is not the first and highest good.

[8]   Again, prior to all multitude we must find unity. But there is multitude in every composite. Therefore, that which is before all things, namely, God, must be free of all composition.

1. See above, ch. 13, ¶11ff.

Chapter 19.

THAT IN GOD THERE IS NOTHING VIOLENT OR UNNATURAL

[1] From this Aristotle concludes that in God there can be nothing violent or unnatural.

[2] Everything in which there is found something violent and outside nature has something added to itself, for what belongs to the substance of a thing can be neither violent nor outside nature. Now, nothing simple has anything added to itself, since this would render it composite. Since, then, God is simple, as we have shown, nothing in Him can be violent or outside nature.[1]

[3] Furthermore, the necessity of coaction is a necessity from another. But in God there is no necessity from another; He is necessary through Himself and the cause of necessity for other things. Therefore, nothing in God is due to coaction.

[4] Again, wherever there is something violent, there can be something beyond what befits a thing through itself; for the violent is opposed to what is according to nature. But in God there cannot be anything beyond what befits Him according to Himself; for God, as we have shown, is of Himself the necessary being.[2] There can, therefore, be nothing violent in God.

[5] Then, too, everything in which there can be something violent or unnatural is by nature able to be moved by another. For the violent is "that whose source is from the outside, the receiver being completely passive."[3] Now, as

1. Aristotle, *Metaphysics*, IV, 5 (1015b 14).
2. See above, ch. 15.
3. Aristotle, *Nicomachean Ethics*, III, 1 (1110a 1).

we have shown, God is absolutely immobile.[4] There can, therefore, be nothing violent or unnatural in Him.

Chapter 20.

THAT GOD IS NOT A BODY

[1]   From the preceding remarks it is also shown that God is not a body.

[2]   Every body, being a continuum, is composite and has parts. But, as we have shown, God is not composite, and is, therefore, not a body.

[3]   Again, everything possessed of quantity is in a certain manner in potency. For a continuum is potentially divisible to infinity, while numbers can be increased to infinity. But every body has quantity and is therefore in potency. But God is not in potency, being pure act, as has been shown.[1] Therefore, God is not a body.

[4]   Furthermore, if God is a body, He must be some natural body, since, as the Philosopher proves, a mathematical body is not something self-existing, since dimensions are accidents.[2] But God is not a natural body, being immobile, as we have shown,[3] whereas every natural body is movable. God is, therefore, not a body.

[5]   Again, every body is finite, as is proved in De caelo I of a circular body and a rectilinear body.[4] Now, we can transcend any given finite body by means of the intellect and the imagination. If, then, God is a body, our intellect and imagination can think of something greater than God.

4. See above ch. 13, ¶s 24 and 28, and ch. 16.
1. See above, ch. 18.—On God as pure act, see above, ch. 16.
2. Aristotle, Metaphysics, III, 5 (1002a 26).
3. See above, ch. 13, ¶28.
4. Aristotle, De caelo et mundo, I, 5 (271b 27ff.).

God is thus not greater than our intellect—which is awkward. God is, therefore, not a body.

[6] Intellectual knowledge, moreover, is more certain than sensitive knowledge. In nature we find an object for the sense and therefore for the intellect as well. But the order and distinction of powers is according to the order of objects. Therefore, above all sensible things there is something intelligible among things. Now, every body having actual existence is sensible. Therefore, we can find something nobler above all bodies. Hence, if God is a body, He will not be the first and greatest being.

[7] A living thing, likewise, is nobler than any non-living body, and the life of a living body is nobler than it, since it is this life that gives to the living body its nobility above other bodies. Therefore, that than which nothing is nobler is not a body. This is God. God is, therefore, not a body.

[8] Then, too, there are the arguments of the philosophers to the same effect, based on the eternity of motion. They are as follows. In every everlasting motion, the first mover cannot be moved either through Himself or by accident, as is clear from the above.[5] Now, the body of the heavens is moved in a circle with an everlasting motion. Therefore, its first mover is not moved either through Himself or by accident. Now, no body moves locally unless it be moved, since the mover and the moved must be together. The moving body must thus be moved in order to be together with the moved body. But no power in a body moves unless it itself be moved by accident, since, when a body is moved, its power is by accident moved. The first mover of the heavens, therefore, is neither a body nor a power in a body. Now, that to which the motion of the heavens is ultimately reduced as to its first unmoved mover is God. God is, therefore, not a body.

[9] Again, no infinite power is a power in a magnitude. But the power of the prime mover is an infinite power.

5. See above, ch. 13, ¶24.

Therefore, it is not in any magnitude. Therefore, God, Who is the prime mover, is neither a body nor a power in a body.

[10]   The first proposition is proved thus. If the power of some magnitude is infinite, it will be the power either of a finite magnitude or an infinite one. But there is no infinite magnitude, as is proved in *Physics* III and *De caelo* I.[6] But a finite magnitude cannot have an infinite power. Therefore, an infinite power cannot reside in any magnitude. That an infinite power cannot reside in a finite magnitude is proved thus. A greater power produces an equal effect in a shorter time than a lesser power does in a longer time. This is true whether that effect be according to alteration, local motion, or any other motion whatever. But an infinite power is greater than every finite power. Therefore, by moving more swiftly, it should produce its effect in a shorter time than any finite power. Nor can it be in something lesser that still is in time. Therefore, this will be in an indivisible point of time. And thus to move, to be moved, and motion will take place in an instant—of which the contrary has been proved in *Physics* VI.[7] That an infinite power in a finite magnitude cannot move in time is likewise proved as follows. Let there be an infinite power A. Let us assume a part of that power to be AB. This part will, therefore, move in a greater time. Yet there must be some proportion of this time to the time in which the whole power moves, since both times are finite. Let these two times be related to one another in the proportion of one to ten, since for the present argument this proportion will do as well as any other. Now, if we add to the aforementioned finite power, we must diminish its time according to the proportion of the addition to the power; for a greater power moves in a lesser time. If the decuple be added, that power will move in a time that will be a tenth part of the time in which the first assumed part of the infinite power, namely,

6. Aristotle, *Physics*, III, 5 (204a 10); *De caelo et mundo*, I, 5 (271b 24).
7. Aristotle, *Physics*, VI, 3 (233b 33).

AB, moved. And yet this power, which is its decuple, is a finite power, since it has a determinate proportion to the finite power. Therefore, the finite and the infinite power will move in the same time—which is impossible. Therefore, the infinite power of a finite magnitude cannot move in time.

[11] That the power of the first mover is infinite is proved thus. No finite power can move in an infinite time. But the power of the first mover moves in an infinite time because the first motion is endless. Therefore, the power of the prime mover is infinite. The first proposition is proved thus. If the finite power of some body moves in an infinite time, a part of that body, having a part of the power, will move in a shorter time; for the greater the power of a mover, the more it will be able to keep up its motion in a longer time. Thus, the aforementioned part will move in a finite time, and a greater part will be able to move in a longer time. Thus, as we add to the power of the mover, we shall always add to the time according to the same proportion. But after a certain addition has been made, the addition will reach the quantity of the whole or even exceed it. So, too, an addition of time will reach the quantity of time in which it moves the whole. But the time in which it moved the whole was said to be infinite. Therefore, a finite time will measure an infinite time—which is impossible.

[12] But against this reasoning there are several objections.

[13] One objection is this. It can be assumed that the body that moves the first moved is not divisible, as is the case with a heavenly body. But the preceding proof is based on the division of the first body.

[14] The reply to this objection is as follows. There can be a true conditional proposition whose antecedent is impossible. If there is something that destroys the truth of this conditional proposition, it is then impossible. For example, if someone destroys the truth of the conditional proposi-

tion, *If man flies, he has wings,* it would be impossible. It is in this manner that the above proof is to be understood. For the following conditional proposition is true: *If a heavenly body is divided, a part of it will have less power than the whole.* Now, the truth of this conditional proposition is taken away if it be posited that the first mover is a body; and the reason is the impossibilities that follow from it. Therefore, to posit this is impossible. A similar reply can be given if objection is made concerning the increase of finite powers. We cannot assume powers in nature according to all proportions of time to any given time. Nevertheless, the proposition required in the above proof is a true conditional proposition.

[15]   The second objection is this. Although a body is divided, it is possible to find in a given body a power that is not divided when the body is divided. For example, the rational soul is not divided if the body is divided.

[16]   The reply is as follows. The above argument does not prove that God is not joined to a body as the rational soul is joined to the human body; it proves that He is not a power in a body in the manner of a material power, which is divided upon the division of the body. So, too, it is said of the human intellect that it is not a body or a power in a body. However, that God is not joined to a body as the soul is, this is another issue.[8]

[17]   The third objection is this. If some given body has a finite power, as the above argument shows, and if through a finite power nothing can endure through an infinite time, it will follow that no body can endure through an infinite time. Thus, a heavenly body will of necessity be corrupted.

[18]   To this objection some reply that, as far as its own power is concerned, a heavenly body can fail, but it acquires an eternal duration from another being of an infinite power. Plato[9] seems to speak for this solution when he introduces

8. See below, ch. 27 and SCG, II, ch. 56.
9. Plato, Timaeus, p. 41AB.

God addressing the heavenly bodies as follows: "By your natures you are dissoluble, but through my will you are indissoluble; for my will is greater than your bond."

[19]   The Commentator attacks this position in *Metaphysics* XI. According to him, it is impossible that what can of itself not-be should acquire a perpetuity of being from another. This would mean that something corruptible becomes incorruptible, which according to him is impossible. Hence, Averroes answers the objection as follows. All the potency that is in a heavenly body is finite, but there is no reason why a heavenly body should have every potency. For, according to Aristotle in *Metaphysics* VIII, there is in a heavenly body potency with respect to place, but not with respect to being.[10] Hence, a heavenly body need not have a potency to non-being.

[20]   This reply of the Commentator, however, is not sufficient. Even if we should grant that in a heavenly body there is no sort of a passive potency to being, which is the potency of matter, yet there is in it a potency of an active kind, which is the power of being. For Aristotle expressly says in *De caelo* I that the heavens have the power to be forever.[11]

[21]   Hence, it is better to reply as follows. Since potency is said relatively to act, we must judge of potency according to the mode of the act. Now, according to its nature, motion has quantity and extension, and hence its infinite duration requires that the potency moving it be infinite. But being does not have any quantitative extension, especially in the case of a thing, such as the heavens, whose being is without change. Hence, the power of being need not be infinite in a finite body, even though it will endure to infinity. For it is one and the same whether through that power something will endure for an instant or for an infinite time, since its changeless being is not touched by time except by accident.

10. Averroes, *In XII Metaphysicorum*, t. c. 41 (fol. 324va); Aristotle, *Metaphysics*, VIII, 4 (1044b 8).

11. Aristotle, *De caelo et mundo*, I, 3 (270a 19ff.).

[22] The *fourth* objection is this. In those beings that in moving are not themselves altered, it does not seem necessary that what moves in an infinite time should have an infinite power. For such a motion consumes nothing of their power, so that after they have moved for a time they are able to move for no less a time than before. Thus, the power of the sun is finite, and because its active power is not lessened by acting, it is able, according to its nature, to act on the sublunary world during an infinite time.

[23] To this the reply is, as we have proved, that a body does not move unless it be moved. If, then, it should happen that a certain body is not moved, that body will consequently not move. But in everything that is moved there is a potency towards opposites, since the termini of motion are opposites. Therefore, of itself, every body that is moved can also not-be-moved. But what can not-be-moved is not of itself able to be moved through endless time, and hence neither to move through endless time.

[24] The above demonstration, consequently, holds of the finite power of a finite body, which power of itself cannot move in an infinite time. But a body that of itself can be moved and not-moved, move and not-move, can acquire perpetuity of motion from another. This must be incorporeal. The first mover must, therefore, be incorporeal. Thus, according to its nature, nothing prevents a finite body, which acquires from another a perpetuity in being moved, from likewise having a perpetuity in moving. For the first heavenly body itself, according to its nature, can revolve the lower heavenly bodies with a perpetual motion, according as sphere moves sphere. Nor, according to the Commentator, is it impossible (as it was impossible in the case of perpetuity of being) that what of itself can be moved and not-moved should acquire perpetuity of motion from another. For motion is a certain flow out of the mover to the thing moved, and hence something moved can acquire from another a perpetuity of motion that it does not have of itself. *To be*, on the other hand, is something fixed

and at rest in being, and, therefore, that which of itself is in potency to non-being cannot, as Averroes himself says,[12] following the course of nature acquire from another a perpetuity of being.

[25] The fifth objection is that, following the above reasoning, there does not seem to be a greater reason why an infinite power is not in a magnitude rather than outside a magnitude. For in either case it will follow that it moves in null time.

[26] To this the reply is that, in magnitude, time, and motion, finite and infinite are found according to one and the same notion, as is proved in *Physics* III and VI.[13] Therefore, the infinite in one of them removes a finite proportion in the others. But in beings without magnitude there is no finite or infinite except equivocally. Hence, the aforementioned method of demonstration is not applicable among such potencies.

[27] There is, however, another and better answer. The heavens have two movers, a proximate one with a finite power, which is responsible for the fact that they have a finite velocity, and a remote mover with an infinite power, which is responsible for the fact that their motion can be of an infinite duration. And thus it is evident that an infinite power that is not in a magnitude can move a body in time, but not immediately. But a power that is in a magnitude must move immediately, since no body moves except by being moved. Hence, if it did move, it would follow that it would move in null time.

[28] An even better reply is this.[14] A power that is not in a magnitude is an intellect, and moves by will. For we have proved that the intellect is not a corporeal power. There-

12. Averroes, *In XII Metaphysicorum*, t.c. 41 (fol. 324va).
13. Aristotle, *Physics*, III, 4 (202b 30); VI, 2 (232a 17); VI, 7 (237b 23).
14. I have transposed the sentences in this paragraph in order to preserve the continuity of the argument.

fore, it moves according to the needs of the movable body and not the proportion of its power; whereas a power that is in a magnitude can move only through the necessity of nature. Thus, of necessity, it moves according to the proportion of its quantity. Hence, if it moves, it moves in an instant.

[29]   Thus, with the removal of the preceding objections, we see that the argumentation of Aristotle stands.

[30]   No motion, furthermore, which is from a corporeal mover can be continuous and regular, because in local motion a corporeal mover moves by pulling and pushing. Now, what is pulled or pushed is not uniformly disposed towards its mover from the beginning to the end of the motion, since at times it will be nearer and at other times farther away. Thus, no body can move with a continuous and regular motion. But the first motion is continuous and regular, as is proved in *Physics* VIII.[15] Therefore, the mover of the first motion is not a body.

[31]   Again, no motion to an end that passes from potency to act can be endless, since when it reaches act the motion comes to rest. If, then, the first motion is endless, it must aim at an end that is always and in all ways in act. But such an end is not a body or a power in a body, since all such things are movable either through themselves or by accident. Therefore, the end of the first motion is neither a body nor a power in a body. But the end of the first motion is the first mover, which moves as something desired.[16] This, however, is God. God, therefore, is neither a body nor a power in a body.

[32]   However, although according to our faith it is false that the motion of the heavens is perpetual, as will be made evident later on,[17] yet it is true that it will not fail either through a failure of power in the mover or through the

15. Aristotle, *Physics*, VIII, 7 (260a 24).
16. Aristotle, *Metaphysics*, XII, 7 (1072b 3).
17. See *SCG*, IV, ch. 97.

corruption of the substance in the moved; for there is no evidence that the passing of time has slowed down the motion of the heavens. Hence, the above demonstrations do not lose their force.

[33] With this demonstrated truth divine authority stands in agreement. For it is said in John (4:24): "God is a spirit, and they that adore Him must adore Him in spirit and in truth." It is likewise said: "To the King of ages, immortal, invisible, the only God" (I Tim. 1:17). Again: "The invisible things of God . . . are clearly seen, being understood by the things that are made" (Rom. 1:20); for what is seen, not by sight, but by the intellect, is incorporeal.

[34] Thereby is destroyed the error of the early natural philosophers, who posited only material causes, such as fire or water or the like, and who thus said that the first principles of things were bodies and called them gods. Among them there were some who further posited *friendship* and *strife* as moving causes. (They, too, were refuted through the above arguments.) For since, according to them, strife and friendship are in bodies, it will follow that the first moving principles are bodily powers. They also held that God is composed of the four elements and friendship, which would give us to understand that for them God was a heavenly body. Among the early thinkers,[18] Anaxagoras alone approached the truth by positing that an intellect moved all things.

[35] By this truth, too, are refuted the Gentiles, who, taking their beginning in the errors of the philosophers we have listed, posited that the elements of the world and the powers in them are gods; for example, the sun, the moon, the earth, water, and the like.

[36] By the same arguments, moreover, are set aside the wild fantasies of the simple Jews, Tertullian, the Vodiani or Anthropomorphite heretics, who endowed God with a

18. On this paragraph, see Aristotle, *Metaphysics*, I, 8 (988b 23ff.).—On Anaxagoras, *Metaphysics*, I, 3 (984b 15).

bodily figure; and also of the Manicheans, who thought that God was a certain infinite substance of light, stretched out through an infinite space.

[37]   The occasion of all these errors was that, in thinking of divine things, men were made the victims of their imagination, through which it is not possible to receive anything except the likeness of a body. This is why, in meditating on what is incorporeal, we must stop following the imagination.

Chapter 21.

THAT GOD IS HIS ESSENCE

[1]   From what has been laid down we can infer that God is His essence, quiddity, or nature.

[2]   There must be some composition in every being that is not its essence or quiddity. Since, indeed, each thing possesses its own essence, if there were nothing in a thing outside its essence all that the thing is would be its essence; which would mean that the thing is its essence. But, if some thing were not its essence, there should be something in it outside its essence. Thus, there must be composition in it. Hence it is that the essence in composite things is signified as a part, for example, *humanity* in man. Now, it has been shown that there is no composition in God.[1] God is, therefore, His essence.

[3]   Moreover, only that which does not enter the definition of a thing seems to be outside its essence or quiddity; for the definition signifies what a thing is. But it is only the accidents of a thing that do not fall in the definition; and therefore only the accidents in any thing are outside its essence. But, as will be shown, in God there are no acci-

1. See above, ch. 18.

dents.[2] There is, therefore, nothing in God outside His essence; and hence He is His essence.

[4] Furthermore, forms that are not predicated of subsisting things, whether these be considered universally or each is taken singly, are forms that do not subsist through themselves as singulars individuated in themselves. We do not say that Socrates, or man, or animal is whiteness, because whiteness does not subsist as a singular through itself but is individuated through its subsisting subjects. In the same way, also, natural forms do not subsist as singulars through themselves but are individuated in their proper matters. That is why we do not say that this fire, or fire, is its own form. The very essences or quiddities of genera and species are individuated through the designated matter of this or that individual, even though the quiddity of the genus or the species should include common form and matter. That is why we do not say that Socrates or man is humanity. But the divine essence exists through itself as a singular existent and individuated through itself; for, as we have shown, it is not in any matter.[3] The divine essence is predicated of God, therefore, so that we may say: *God is His essence.*

[5] Again, the essence of a thing is either the thing itself or is related to the thing in some way as its cause; for a thing derives its species through its essence. But nothing can in any way be the cause of God, since, as we have shown, He is the first being.[4] God is, therefore, His essence.

[6] Then, too, what is not its essence is related to its essence, according to some part of itself, as potency to act. That is why the essence is signified in the manner of a form, for example, *humanity.* But, as was shown above, there is no potentiality in God.[5] He must, therefore, be His essence.

2. See below, ch. 23.
3. See above, ch. 17.
4. See above, ch. 13, ¶34.
5. See above, ch. 16.

Chapter 22.

THAT IN GOD BEING AND ESSENCE ARE THE SAME

[1]   From what was proved above, however, we can further prove that His essence or quiddity is not something other than His being.

[2]   For it was shown above[1] that there is some being that must be through itself, and this is God. If, then, this being that must be belongs to an essence that is not that which it is, either it is incompatible with that essence or repugnant to it, as to exist through itself is repugnant to the quiddity of whiteness, or it is compatible with it or appropriate to it, as to be in another is to whiteness. If the first alternative be the case, the being that is through itself necessary will not befit that quiddity, just as it does not befit whiteness to exist through itself. If the second alternative be the case, either such being must depend on the essence, or both must depend on another cause, or the essence must depend on the being. The first two alternatives are contrary to the nature of that which is through itself a necessary being; for if it depends on another, it is no longer a necessary being. From the third alternative it follows that that quiddity is added accidentally to the thing that is through itself a necessary being; for what follows upon a thing's being is accidental to it and hence not its quiddity. God, therefore, does not have an essence that is not His being.

[3]   But against this conclusion it can be objected that that being does not absolutely depend on that essence, so as not to be unless the essence existed; it depends, rather, on the essence with reference to the union by which it is

1. See above, ch. 13.

joined to it. Thus, that being is through itself necessary, but its union with the essence is not.

[4] However, this reply does not escape the aforementioned difficulties. For, if that being can be understood without that essence, it will follow that the essence is related to that being in an accidental way. But that being is that which is through itself a necessary being. Therefore, that essence is related in an accidental way to that which is through itself a necessary being. It is, therefore, not its essence. But that which is through itself a necessary being is God. That essence, then, is not the essence of God, but some essence below God. On the other hand, if that being cannot be understood without that essence, it depends absolutely on that on which its union to that essence depends. We then reach the same impasse as before.

[5] Another argument. Each thing is through its own being. Hence, that which is not its own being is not through itself a necessary being. But God is through Himself a necessary being. He is, therefore, His own being.

[6] Again, if God's being is not His essence, and cannot be part of that essence, since, as we have shown, the divine essence is simple,[2] such a being must be something outside the divine essence. But whatever belongs to a thing and is yet not of its essence belongs to it through some cause; for, if things that are not through themselves one are joined, they must be joined through some cause. Being, therefore, belongs to that quiddity through some cause. This is either through something that is part of the essence of that thing, or the essence itself, or through something else. If we adopt the first alternative, and it is a fact that the essence is through that being, it follows that something is the cause of its own being. This is impossible, because, in their notions, the existence of the cause is prior to that of the effect. If, then, something were its own cause of being, it would be understood to be before it had being—which is impos-

2. See above, ch. 18.

sible, unless we understand that something is the cause of its own being in an accidental order, which is being in an accidental way. This is not impossible. It is possible that there be an accidental being that is caused by the principles of its subject before the substantial being of its subject is understood as given. Here, however, we are speaking of substantial being, not accidental being. On the other hand, if the being belongs to the essence through some other cause, then this follows: given that what acquires its being from another cause is something caused, and is not the first cause, whereas God, as was demonstrated above, is the first cause and has no cause, the quiddity that acquires its being from another is not the quiddity of God. God's being must, therefore, be His quiddity.

[7]   *Being*, furthermore, is the name of an act, for a thing is not said to be because it is in potency but because it is in act. Everything, however, that has an act diverse from it is related to that act as potency to act; for potency and act are said relatively to one another. If, then, the divine essence is something other than its being, the essence and the being are thereby related as potency and act. But we have shown that in God there is no potency, but that He is pure act.[3] God's essence, therefore, is not something other than His being.

[8]   Moreover, if something can exist only when several elements come together, it is composite. But no thing in which the essence is other than the being can exist unless several elements come together, namely, the essence and the being. Hence, every thing in which the essence is other than the being is composite. But, as we have shown, God is not composite.[4] Therefore, God's being is His essence.

[9]   Every thing, furthermore, exists because it has being. A thing whose essence is not its being, consequently, is not through its essence but by participation in something,

3. See above, ch. 16.
4. See above, ch. 18.

namely, being itself. But that which is through participation in something cannot be the first being, because prior to it is the being in which it participates in order to be. But God is the first being, with nothing prior to Him. His essence is, therefore, His being.

[10] This sublime truth Moses was taught by our Lord. When Moses asked our Lord: "If the children of Israel say to me: what is His name? What shall I say to them?" The Lord replied: "I AM WHO AM . . . Thou shalt say to the children of Israel: HE WHO IS hath sent me to you" (Exod. 3:13, 14). By this our Lord showed that His own proper name is HE WHO IS. Now, names have been devised to signify the natures or essences of things. It remains, then, that the divine being is God's essence or nature.

[11] Catholic teachers have likewise professed this truth. For Hilary writes in his book *De Trinitate*: "Being is not an accident in God but subsisting truth, the abiding cause and the natural property His nature." Boethius also says in his own work *De Trinitate*: "The divine substance is being itself, and from it comes being."[5]

Chapter 23.

THAT NO ACCIDENT IS FOUND IN GOD

[1] It follows necessarily from this truth that nothing can come to God beyond His essence, nor can there be anything in Him in an accidental way.

[2] For being cannot participate in anything that is not of its essence, although that which is can participate in something. The reason is that nothing is more formal or more simple than being, which thus participates in nothing. But the divine substance is being itself, and therefore

5. St. Hilary, *De Trinitate*, VII, 11 (PL, 10, col. 208B); Boethius, *De Trinitate*, II (PL, 64, col. 1250B).

has nothing that is not of its substance. Hence, no accident can reside in it.

[3]   Furthermore, what is present in a thing accidentally has a cause of its presence, since it is outside the essence of the thing in which it is found. If, then, something is found in God accidentally, this must be through some cause. Now, the cause of the accident is either the divine essence itself or something else. If something else, it must act on the divine essence, since nothing will cause the introduction of some form, substantial or accidental, in some receiving subject except by acting on it in some way. For to act is nothing other than to make something actual, which takes place through a form. Thus, God will suffer and receive the action of some cause—which is contrary to what we already established.[1] On the other hand, let us suppose that the divine substance is the cause of the accident inhering in it. Now it is impossible that it be, as receiving it, the cause of the accident, for then one and the same thing would make itself to be actual in the same respect. Therefore, if there is an accident in God, it will be according to different respects that He receives and causes that accident, just as bodily things receive their accidents through the nature of their matter and cause them through their form. Thus, God will be composite. But, we have proved the contrary of this proposition above.[2]

[4]   Every subject of an accident, moreover, is related to it as potency to act, since the accident is a certain form making the subject to be actual according to an accidental being. But, as we have shown above, there is no potentiality in God.[3] There can, therefore, be no accident in Him.

[5]   Then, too, when a being has an accident inhering in it, it is in some way mutable according to its nature, since

1. See above, ch. 13.
2. See above, ch. 18.
3. See above, ch. 16.

an accident can inhere or not-inhere. If, then, God has something belonging to Him in an accidental way, He will consequently be mutable. But the contrary of this was demonstrated above.[4]

[6] Again, that which has an accident inhering in it is not whatever it has in itself, since an accident is not part of the essence of the subject. But God is what He has in Himself. There is, therefore, no accident in God. The minor proposition is proved thus. Everything is found in a more noble way in the cause than in an effect. But God is the cause of all things. Hence, whatever is in Him is there in the most noble way. Now, what a thing itself is, this belongs to it in a most perfect way. For this is something more perfectly one than when something is joined to something else substantially as form to matter; just as substantial union is more perfect than when something inheres in something else as an accident. God, then, is whatever He has.

[7] It is also a fact that a substance does not depend on an accident, although an accident depends on a substance. But what does not depend on something can sometimes be found without it. Some substance, then, can be found without an accident. This seems especially to fit the substance that is most simple, such as the divine substance is. The divine substance, therefore, has no accidents whatever.

[8] In dealing with this problem, Catholics likewise give assent to this opinion. Whence Augustine says in his *De Trinitate* that "there is no accident in God."[5]

[9] The proof of this truth serves as a refutation of the error of some Saracen theologians "who posit certain intentions superadded to the divine essence."[6]

4. See above, ch. 13.
5. St. Augustine, *De Trinitate*, V, 4 (PL, 42, col. 913).
6. Averroes, *In XII Metaphysicorum*, t.c. 39 (fol. 322vab).

Chapter 24.

THAT THE DIVINE BEING CANNOT BE DETER-
MINED BY THE ADDITION OF SOME
SUBSTANTIAL DIFFERENCE

[1]   We can likewise show from what we have said that nothing can be added to the divine being to determine it with an essential determination, as a genus is determined by its differences.

[2]   Nothing can be in act unless everything that determines its substantial act of being exists. Thus, there cannot be an actual animal unless it be a rational or an irrational animal. Hence, the Platonists themselves, in positing the Ideas, did not posit self-existing Ideas of genera, which are determined to the being of their species through essential differences; rather, they posited self-existing Ideas solely of species, which for their determination need no essential differences. If, then, the divine being is determined essentially through something else superadded to it, it will be in act only if what is superadded is present. But the divine being, as we have shown, is the divine substance itself.[1] Therefore the divine substance cannot be in act without the presence of something added; from which it can be concluded that it is not through itself a necessary being. But, we have proved the contrary of this proposition above.[2]

[3]   Moreover, what needs an addition in order to be is in potency in relation to this addition. But, as we have shown, the divine substance is not in any way in potency;[3] rather, the divine substance is its being. The divine being,

1. See above, ch. 22.
2. See above, ch. 13.
3. See above, ch. 16.

therefore, cannot be determined in its substance through something superadded to it.

[4] Again, that through which a thing derives being in act and is intrinsic to it is either the whole essence of that thing or a part of the essence. But that which determines something in an essential way makes that thing to be in act and is intrinsic to the determined thing; otherwise, the thing could not be determined substantially by it. It must therefore be either the essence itself or a part of the essence. But, if something is added to the divine being, this cannot be the whole essence of God, since it has already been shown that God's being is not other than His essence.[4] It must, then, be a part of the essence, which means that God will be composed of essential parts. But, we have proved the contrary of this above.[5]

[5] Furthermore, what is added to a thing to give it a certain essential determination does not constitute its nature but only its being in act. For *rational* added to *animal* gains for animal being in act, but it does not constitute the nature of animal as animal, since the difference does not enter the definition of the genus. But, if something is added in God by which He is determined in His essence, that addition must constitute for the being to which it is added the nature of its own quiddity or essence, since what is thus added gains for a thing its being in act. But in God this "being in act" is the divine essence itself, as we have shown above.[6] It remains, then, that to the divine being nothing can be added that determines it in an essential way, as the difference determines the genus.

4. See above, ch. 22.
5. See above, ch. 18.
6. See above, ch. 22.

Chapter 25.

THAT GOD IS NOT IN SOME GENUS

[1]   From this we infer necessarily that God is not in some genus.

[2]   Every thing in a genus has something within it by which the nature of the genus is determined to its species; for nothing is in a genus that is not in some species of that genus. But, as we have shown, this determination cannot take place in God.[1] God cannot, then, be in some genus.

[3]   If, moreover, God is in a genus, either He is in the genus of accident or in that of substance. He is not in the genus of accident, since the first being and the first cause cannot be an accident. Neither can God be in the genus of substance, since the substance that is a genus is not being itself; otherwise, every substance would be its being and would thus not be caused by another—which is impossible, as is evident from what we have said. Therefore, God is not in some genus.

[4]   Again, whatever is in a genus differs in being from the other things in that genus; otherwise, the genus would not be predicated of many things. But all the things that are in the same genus must agree in the quiddity of the genus, since the genus is predicated of all things in it in terms of what they are. In other words, the being of each thing found in a genus is outside the quiddity of the genus. This is impossible in God. God, therefore, is not in a genus.

[5]   Then, too, each thing is placed in a genus through the nature of its quiddity, for the genus is a predicate expressing what a thing is. But the quiddity of God is His very being. Accordingly, God is not located in a genus, be-

1. See above, ch. 24.

cause then *being*, which signifies the act of being, would be a genus. Therefore, God is not in a genus.

[6] Now, that *being* cannot be a genus is proved by the Philosopher in the following way.[2] If being were a genus we should have to find a difference through which to contract it to a species. But no difference shares in the genus in such a way that the genus is included in the notion of the difference, for thus the genus would be included twice in the definition of the species. Rather, the difference is outside what is understood in the nature of the genus. But there can be nothing that is outside that which is understood by being, if being is included in the concept of the things of which it is predicated. Thus, being cannot be contracted by any difference. Being is, therefore, not a genus. From this we conclude necessarily that God is not in a genus.

[7] From this it is likewise evident that God cannot be defined, for every definition is constituted from the genus and the differences.

[8] It is also clear that no demonstration is possible about God, except through an effect; for the principle of demonstration is the definition of that of which the demonstration is made.

[9] Now it can seem to someone that, although the name *substance* cannot properly apply to God because God does not *substand* accidents, yet the thing signified by the name is appropriate and thus God is in the genus of substance. For a substance is a being through itself. Now, this is appropriate to God, since we have proved that He is not an accident.

[10] To this contention we must reply, in accord with what we have said, that *being through itself* is not included in the definition of substance. For, if something is called

2. Aristotle, *Metaphysics*, III, 3 (998b 21).

being, it cannot be a genus, since we have already proved that being does not have the nature of a genus. Neither can what is *through itself* be a genus, since the expression seems to indicate nothing more than a negation. Something is said to be a being through itself because it is not in another. This is a pure negation, which likewise cannot constitute the nature of a genus; for a genus would then say, not what a thing is, but what it is not. The nature of substance, therefore, must be understood as follows. A substance is *a thing to which it belongs to be not in a subject*. The name *thing* takes its origin from the *quiddity*, just as the name *being* comes from *to be*. In this way, the definition of substance is understood as *that which has a quiddity to which it belongs to be not in another*. Now, this is not appropriate to God, for He has no quiddity save His being. In no way, then, is God in the genus of substance. Thus, He is in no genus, since we have shown that He is not in the genus of accident.

Chapter 26.

THAT GOD IS NOT THE FORMAL BEING
OF ALL THINGS

[1]   We are now able to refute the error of certain persons who said that God is nothing other than the formal being of each thing.[1]

[2]   This being is divided into the being of substance and the being of accident. Now, we have proved that the divine being is neither the being of substance nor that of accident.[2] God, therefore, cannot be that being by which each thing formally is.

1. See E. Gilson, *History of Christian Philosophy in the Middle Ages*, pp. 240–241, 654 (note 8).
2. See above, ch. 25.

[3] Furthermore, things are not distinguished from one another in having being, for in this they agree. If, then, things differ from one another, either their being must be specified through certain added differences, so that diverse things have a diverse being according to their species, or things must differ in that the being itself is appropriate to natures that are diverse in species. The first of these alternatives is impossible, since, as we have said, no addition can be made to a being in the manner in which a difference is added to a genus.[3] It remains, then, that things differ because they have diverse natures, to which being accrues in a diverse way. Now, the divine being does not accrue to a nature that is *other* than it; it is the nature itself, as we have said.[4] If, therefore, the divine being were the formal being of all things, all things would have to be absolutely one.

[4] Then, too, a principle is naturally prior to that whose principle it is. Now, in certain things being has something that is as its principle. For the form is said to be a principle of being, and so is the agent, that makes things to be in act. If, therefore, the divine being is the being of each thing, it will follow that God, Who is His own being, has some cause. Thus, He is not through Himself a necessary being. But, we have proved the contrary of this conclusion above.[5]

[5] Moreover, that which is common to many is not outside the many except by the reason alone. Thus, *animal* is not something outside Socrates and Plato and the other animals except in the intellect that apprehends the form of animal stripped of all its individuating and specifying characteristics. For man is that which truly is animal; otherwise, it would follow that in Socrates and Plato there are several animals, namely, *common animal* itself, *common man*, and *Plato* himself. Much less, then, is common being

3. *Ibid.*
4. See above, ch. 22.
5. See above, ch. 15, ¶5.

itself something outside all existing things, save only for being in the intellect. Hence, if God is common being, the only thing that will exist is that which exists solely in the intellect. But we showed above that God is something not only in the intellect but also in reality.[6] Therefore, God is not the common being of all things.

[6]   Again, strictly speaking, generation is the way to being and corruption the way to non-being. For form is not the terminus of generation, and privation is not the terminus of corruption, except because a form causes being and privation non-being. If a form did not cause being, a thing which received such a form would not be said to be generated. Hence, if God is the formal being of all things, He will consequently be the terminus of generation. This is false, since, as we have shown above, God is eternal.[7]

[7]   It will also follow that the being of each thing has existed from eternity. Generation or corruption is therefore impossible. If it does exist, pre-existing being must accrue to something anew. It will therefore accrue either to something pre-existing or to something in no way pre-existing. In the first instance, since according to the above position the being of all existing things is one, it will follow that a thing that is said to be generated acquires, not a new being, but a new mode of being. The result is alteration, not generation. But, if the generated thing in no way pre-existed, it will follow that it is produced from nothing—which is contrary to the nature of generation. This position, therefore, entirely ruins generation and corruption and, as a consequence, is evidently impossible.

[8]   Sacred Teaching as well casts aside this error in confessing that God is "high and elevated," according to Isaias (6:1), and that He is "over all," according to Romans (9:5). For, if He is the being of all things, He is part of all things, but not over them.

6. See above, ch. 11.
7. See above, ch. 15.

[9]   So, too, those who committed this error are condemned by the same judgment as are the idolators who "gave the incommunicable name," that is, of God, "to wood and stones," as it is written (Wis. 14:21). If, indeed, God is the being of all things, there will be no more reason to say truly that a *stone is a being* than to say that a *stone is God.*

[10]   Four factors seem to have contributed to the rise of this error. The first is the warped interpretation of certain authoritative texts. There is in Dionysius this remark: "The being of all things is the super-essential divinity."[8] From this remark they wished to infer that God is the formal being of all things, without considering that this interpretation could not square with the words themselves. For, if the divinity is the formal being of all things, it will not be over all but among all, indeed a part of all. Now, since Dionysius said that the divinity was above all things, he showed that according to its nature it was distinct from all things and raised above all things. And when he said that the divinity is the being of all things, he showed that there was in all things a certain likeness of the divine being, coming from God. Elsewhere Dionysius has rather openly set aside this warped interpretation. He has said: "God neither touches nor is in any way mingled with other things, as a point touches a line or the figure of a seal touches wax."[9]

[11]   The second cause leading them to this error is a failure of reason. For, since that which is common is specified or individuated through addition, they thought that the divine being, which receives no addition, was not some proper being but the common being of all things. They ignored the fact that what is common or universal cannot exist without addition, but is considered without addition.

8. Pseudo-Dionysius, *De caelesti hierarchia,* IV, 1 (PG, 3, col. 177D).

9. Pseudo-Dionysius, *De divinis nominibus,* II, 5 (PG, 3, col. 664).

For animal cannot be without the difference rational or the difference irrational, although it is considered without these differences. What is more, although a universal may be considered without addition, it is not without the receptibility of addition; for, if no difference could be added to animal, it would not be a genus. The same is true of all other names. But the divine being is without addition not only in thought but also in reality; and not only without addition but also without the receptibility of addition. From the fact, then, that it neither receives nor can receive addition we can rather conclude that God is not common being but proper being; for His being is distinguished from all the rest by the fact that nothing can be added to it. Hence the Commentator says in the Book of Causes that, out of the purity of its goodness, the first cause is distinguished from the rest and in a manner individuated.[10]

[12] The third factor that led them into this error concerns the divine simplicity. God is at the peak of simplicity. They therefore thought that the last point of resolution in our way of seeing things is God, as being absolutely simple. For it is not possible to proceed to infinity in composition among the things we know. Their reason also failed because they did not observe that what is most simple in our understanding of things is not so much a complete thing as a part of a thing. But, simplicity is predicated of God as of some perfect subsisting thing.

[13] A fourth factor that could have led them to their error is the mode of expression we use when we say that God is in all things. By this we do not mean that God is in things as a part of a thing, but as the cause of a thing that

10. If this Commentator is Averroes, then we are led to suppose that, in writing SCG, I, St. Thomas still believed in the Aristotelian authorship of the Liber de Causis. On the general question of the history of this famous work in the middle ages, see H. D. Saffrey, O.P., Sancti Thomae de Aquino Super Librum de Causis Expositio (Fribourg: Société Philosophique, 1954), pp. xv–xxv.

is never lacking to its effect. For we do not say that a form is in matter as a sailor is in a ship.

Chapter 27.

THAT GOD IS NOT THE FORM OF ANY BODY

[1] Having shown that God is not the being of all things, we can likewise show that He is not the form of any thing.

[2] As we have shown, the divine being cannot belong to any quiddity that is not being itself.[1] Now, only God is the divine being itself. It is impossible, therefore, for God to be the form of some other being.

[3] Furthermore, the form of a body is not the being itself, but a principle of being. But God is being itself. He is, therefore, not the form of a body.

[4] Again, the union of form and matter results in a composite, which is a whole with respect to the matter and the form. But the parts are in potency in relation to the whole. In God, however, there is no potentiality. Therefore, God cannot be a form united to some thing.

[5] Moreover, that which has being through itself is nobler than that which has being in another. But every form of a body has being in another. Since, then, God, as the first cause of being, is the noblest being, He cannot be the form of any being.

[6] The same conclusion can also be reached in the following way from the eternity of motion. If God is the form of some movable body, since He is the first mover, the composite will be self-moving. But something self-moving can be moved and not-moved. Both possibilities are found in it. But such a being does not of itself have an indefecti-

1. See above, ch. 22.

bility of motion. Above the self-moving being, therefore, we must posit another first mover, which gives to the self-moving being the endlessness of its motion. Thus, God, Who is the first mover, is not the form of a self-moving body.

[7]   This argumentation is suitable for those who posit the eternity of motion. Those who do not posit it can reach the same conclusion from the regularity of the motion of the heavens. For just as a self-mover can be at rest and in motion, so it can be moved more swiftly and less so. The necessity in the uniformity of the motion of the heavens, therefore, depends on some higher and absolutely immobile principle, which is not a part of a self-moving body as the form of that body.

[8]   The authority of Scripture is in agreement with this truth. For it is said in a Psalm (8:2): "Thy magnificence is elevated above the heavens"; and in Job (11:8, 9): "He is higher than heaven, and what wilt thou do? . . . the measure of Him is longer than the earth and deeper [Douay, broader] than the sea."

[9]   Thus, then, is removed the error of the Gentiles, who said that God is the soul of the heavens, or even the soul of the whole world. Thereby they defended the error of idolatry, by saying that the whole world was God not by reason of the body but by reason of the soul; just as man is said to be wise not by reason of the body but by reason of the soul. On the basis of this error the Gentiles thought it to follow that, not unfittingly, divine worship should be shown to the world and its parts. The Commentator also says that this point was the place where the Zabii stumbled and fell from wisdom—because, namely, they posited that God is the form of the heavens.[2]

2. Averroes, In XII Metaphysicorum, t.c. 41 (fol. 325ra).

Chapter 28.

ON THE DIVINE PERFECTION

[1] Although the things that exist and live are more perfect than the things that merely exist, nevertheless, God, Who is not other than His being, is a universally perfect being. And I call *universally perfect* that to which the excellence of no genus is lacking.

[2] Every excellence in any given thing belongs to it according to its being. For man would have no excellence as a result of his wisdom unless through it he were wise. So, too, with the other excellences. Hence, the mode of a thing's excellence is according to the mode of its being. For a thing is said to be more or less excellent according as its being is limited to a certain greater or lesser mode of excellence. Therefore, if there is something to which the whole power of being belongs, it can lack no excellence that is proper to some thing. But for a thing that is its own being it is proper to be according to the whole power of being. For example, if there were a separately existing whiteness, it could not lack any of the power of whiteness. For a given white thing lacks something of the power of whiteness through a defect in the receiver of the whiteness, which receives it according to its mode and perhaps not according to the whole power of whiteness. God, therefore, Who is His being, as we have proved above,[1] has being according to the whole power of being itself. Hence, He cannot lack any excellence that belongs to any given thing.

[3] But just as every excellence and perfection is found in a thing according as that thing *is*, so every defect is found in it according as in some way it *is not*. Now, just as God has being wholly, so non-being is wholly absent from Him.

1. See above, ch. 22.

For as a thing has being, in that way is it removed from non-being. Hence, all defect is absent from God. He is, therefore, universally perfect.

[4]   Those things that merely exist are not imperfect because of an imperfection in absolute being. For they do not possess being according to its whole power; rather, they participate in it through a certain particular and most imperfect mode.

[5]   Furthermore, everything that is imperfect must be preceded by something perfect. Thus, the seed is from the animal or the plant. The first being must, therefore, be most perfect. But we have shown that God is the first being.[2] He is, therefore, most perfect.

[6]   Again, each thing is perfect according as it is in act, and imperfect according as it is in potency and lacking act. Hence, that which is in no way in potency, but is pure act, must be most perfect. Such, however, is God. God is, therefore, most perfect.

[7]   Nothing, moreover, acts except as it is in act. Hence, action follows the mode of act in the agent. It is therefore impossible that an effect brought forth by an action be of a more excellent act than is the act of the agent. On the other hand, it is possible that the act of the effect be less perfect than the act of the efficient cause, since an action can become weakened through the effect in which it terminates. Now, in the genus of the efficient cause there is a reduction to one cause, called God, as is evident from what we have said;[3] and from this cause, as we shall show later on,[4] all things come. Hence, it is necessary that whatever is found in act in any thing whatever must be found in God in a more eminent way than in that thing itself. But the converse is not true. God, therefore, is most perfect.

2. See above, ch. 13, ¶34.
3. *Ibid.*, ¶33.
4. *SCG*, II, ch. 15.

[8] In every genus, furthermore, there is something that is most perfect for that genus, acting as a measure for all other things in the genus. For each thing is shown to be more or less perfect according as it approaches more or less to the measure of its genus. Thus, *white* is said to be the measure among all colors, and the *virtuous man* among all men. Now, the measure of all beings cannot be other than God, Who is His own being. No perfection, consequently, that is appropriate to this or that thing is lacking to Him; otherwise, He would not be the common measure of all things.

[9] This is why, when Moses asked to see the divine countenance or glory, he received this reply from the Lord: "I will show thee all good," as it is written in Exodus (33:18, 19); by which the Lord gave Moses to understand that the fullness of all goodness was in Him. Dionysius likewise says: "God does not exist in a certain way; He possesses, and this before all others, all being within Himself absolutely and limitlessly."[5]

[10] We must note, however, that *perfection* cannot be attributed to God appropriately if we consider the signification of the name according to its origin; for it does not seem that what is not made [*factum*] can be called perfect [*perfectum*]. But everything that comes to be is brought forth from potency to act and from non-being to being when it has been made. That is why it is rightly said to be perfect, as being completely made, at that moment when the potency is wholly reduced to act, so that it retains no non-being but has a completed being. By a certain extension of the name, consequently, *perfect* is said not only of that which by way of becoming reaches a completed act, but also of that which, without any making whatever, is in complete act. It is thus that, following the words of Matthew (5:48), we say that God is perfect: "Be ye perfect as also your heavenly Father is perfect."

5. Pseudo-Dionysius, *De divinis nominibus*, V, 4 (PG, 3, col. 817C).

Chapter 29.

ON THE LIKENESS OF CREATURES TO GOD

[1]   In the light of what we have said, we are able to consider how a likeness to God is and is not possible in things.

[2]   Effects that fall short of their causes do not agree with them in name and nature. Yet, some likeness must be found between them, since it belongs to the nature of action that an agent produce its like, since each thing acts according as it is in act. The form of an effect, therefore, is certainly found in some measure in a transcending cause, but according to another mode and another way. For this reason the cause is called an *equivocal cause*. Thus, the sun causes heat among these sublunary bodies by acting according as it is in act. Hence, the heat generated by the sun must bear some likeness to the active power of the sun, through which heat is caused in this sublunary world; and because of this heat the sun is said to be hot, even though not in one and the same way. And so the sun is said to be somewhat like those things in which it produces its effects as an efficient cause. Yet the sun is also unlike all these things in so far as such effects do not possess heat and the like in the same way as they are found in the sun. So, too, God gave things all their perfections and thereby is both like and unlike all of them.

[3]   Hence it is that Sacred Scripture recalls the likeness between God and creatures, as when it is said in Genesis (1:26): "Let us make man to our image and likeness." At times the likeness is denied, as in the text of Isaias (40:18): "To whom then have you likened God, and what image will you make for Him?" or in the Psalm (82:1): "O God, who shall be like to Thee?"

[4] Dionysius is in agreement with this argument when he says: "The same things are both like and unlike God. They are like according as they imitate as much as they can Him Who is not perfectly imitable; they are unlike according as effects are lesser than their causes."[1]

[5] In the light of this likeness, nevertheless, it is more fitting to say that a creature is like God rather than the converse. For that is called *like* something which possesses a quality or form of that thing. Since, then, that which is found in God perfectly is found in other things according to a certain diminished participation, the basis on which the likeness is observed belongs to God absolutely, but not to the creature. Thus, the creature has what belongs to God and, consequently, is rightly said to be like God. But we cannot in the same way say that God has what belongs to the creature. Neither, then, can we appropriately say that God is like a creature, just as we do not say that man is like his image, although the image is rightly said to be like him.

[6] All the less proper, moreover, is the expression that God is likened to a creature. For likening expresses a motion towards likeness and thus belongs to the being that receives from another that which makes it like. But a creature receives from God that which makes it like Him. The converse, however, does not hold. God, then, is not likened to a creature; rather, the converse is true.

Chapter 30.

THE NAMES THAT CAN BE PREDICATED OF GOD

[1] From what we have said we can further consider what it is possible to say or not to say of God, what is said

1. Pseudo-Dionysius, *De divinis nominibus*, IX, 7 (*PG*, 3, col. 916).

of Him alone, and also what is said of Him and other things
together.

[2]   Since it is possible to find in God every perfection
of creatures, but in another and more eminent way, whatever names unqualifiedly designate a perfection without
defect are predicated of God and of other things: for example, goodness, wisdom, being, and the like. But when
any name expresses such perfections along with a mode
that is proper to a creature, it can be said of God only
according to likeness and metaphor. According to metaphor, what belongs to one thing is transferred to another,
as when we say that a man is a *stone* because of the hard-
ness of his intellect. Such names are used to designate the
species of a created thing, for example, *man* and *stone*;
for to each species belongs its own mode of perfection and
being. The same is true of whatever names designate the
properties of things, which are caused by the proper principles of their species. Hence, they can be said of God
only metaphorically. But the names that express such perfections along with the mode of supereminence with which
they belong to God are said of God alone. Such names are
the *highest good, the first being,* and the like.

[3]   I have said that some of the aforementioned names
signify a perfection without defect. This is true with reference to that which the name was imposed to signify; for
as to the mode of signification, every name is defective.
For by means of a name we express things in the way in
which the intellect conceives them. For our intellect, taking
the origin of its knowledge from the senses, does not transcend the mode which is found in sensible things, in which
the form and the subject of the form are not identical
owing to the composition of form and matter. Now, a
simple form is indeed found among such things, but one
that is imperfect because it is not subsisting; on the other
hand, though a subsisting subject of a form is found among
sensible things, it is not simple but rather concreted. Whatever our intellect signifies as subsisting, therefore, it signi-

fies in concretion; but what it signifies as simple, it signifies, not as *that which is*, but as *that by which something is*.
As a result, with reference to the mode of signification
there is in every name that we use an imperfection, which
does not befit God, even though the thing signified in some
eminent way does befit God. This is clear in the name
goodness and *good*. For *goodness* has signification as something not subsisting, while *good* has signification as something concreted. And so with reference to the mode of
signification no name is fittingly applied to God; this is
done only with reference to that which the name has been
imposed to signify. Such names, therefore, as Dionysius
teaches,[1] can be both affirmed and denied of God. They
can be affirmed because of the meaning of the name; they
can be denied because of the mode of signification.

[4] Now, the mode of supereminence in which the abovementioned perfections are found in God can be signified
by names used by us only through negation, as when we
say that God is *eternal* or *infinite*, or also through a relation of God to other things, as when He is called the *first
cause* or the *highest good*. For we cannot grasp what God
is, but only what He is not and how other things are related to Him, as is clear from what we said above.

Chapter 31.

THAT THE DIVINE PERFECTION AND THE PLU-
RALITY OF DIVINE NAMES ARE NOT OPPOSED
TO THE DIVINE SIMPLICITY

[1] From what has been said it can likewise be seen that
the divine perfection and the plurality of names said of
God are not opposed to His simplicity.

1. Pseudo-Dionysius, *De divinis nominibus*, I, 5 (PG, 3, col.
593); *De caelesti hierarchia*, II, 3 (PG, 3, coll. 140C–141C).

[2]   We have said that all the perfections found in other things are attributed to God in the same way as effects are found in their equivocal causes.[1] These effects are in their causes virtually, as heat is in the sun. For, unless the power of the sun belonged to some extent to the genus of heat, the sun acting through this power would not generate anything like itself. The sun, then, is said to be hot through this power not only because it produces heat, but also because the power through which it does this has some likeness to heat. But through the same power through which it produces heat, the sun produces also many other effects among sublunary bodies—for example, dryness. And thus heat and dryness, which in fire are diverse qualities, belong to the sun through one and the same power. So, too, the perfections of all things, which belong to the rest of things through diverse forms, must be attributed to God through one and the same power in Him. This power is nothing other than His essence, since, as we have proved, there can be no accident in God.[2] Thus, therefore, God is called wise not only in so far as He produces wisdom, but also because, in so far as we are wise, we imitate to some extent the power by which He makes us wise. On the other hand, God is not called a stone, even though He has made stones, because in the name stone there is understood a determinate mode of being according to which a stone is distinguished from God. But the stone imitates God as its cause in being and goodness, and other such characteristics, as do also the rest of creatures.

[3]   A similar situation obtains among the knowing and operative powers of man. For by its single power the intellect knows all the things that the sensitive part of the soul grasps through a diversity of powers—and many other things as well. So, too, the higher an intellect is, the more it can know more things through one likeness, while a lesser intellect manages to know many things only through

1. See above, ch. 29.
2. See above, ch. 23.

many likenesses. So, too, a ruling power extends to all th things to which diverse powers under it are ordered. In this way, therefore, through His one simple being God possesses every kind of perfection that all other things come to possess, but in a much more diminished way, through diverse principles.

[4]   From this we see the necessity of giving to God many names. For, since we cannot know Him naturally except by arriving at Him from His effects, the names by which we signify His perfection must be diverse, just as the perfections belonging to things are found to be diverse. Were we able to understand the divine essence itself as it is and give to it the name that belongs to it, we would express it by only one name. This is promised to those who will see God through His essence: "In that day there shall be one Lord, and His name shall be one" (Zach. 14:9).

Chapter 32.

THAT NOTHING IS PREDICATED UNIVOCALLY OF GOD AND OTHER THINGS

[1]   It is thereby evident that nothing can be predicated univocally of God and other things.

[2]   An effect that does not receive a form specifically the same as that through which the agent acts cannot receive according to a univocal predication the name arising from that form. Thus, the heat generated by the sun and the sun itself are not called univocally *hot*. Now, the forms of the things God has made do not measure up to a specific likeness of the divine power; for the things that God has made receive in a divided and particular way that which in Him is found in a simple and universal way. It is evident, then, that nothing can be said univocally of God and other things.

more, an effect should measure up to the ... ise, it will not receive the univocal predica- ... ime unless it receives the same specific form ... he same mode of being. For the house that ... the maker is not univocally the same house that is in ... ter, for the form of the house does not have the same being in the two locations. Now, even though the rest of things were to receive a form that is absolutely the same as it is in God, yet they do not receive it according to the same mode of being. For, as is clear from what we have said, there is nothing in God that is not the divine being itself, which is not the case with other things.[1] Nothing, therefore, can be predicated of God and other things univocally.

[4] Moreover, whatever is predicated of many things univocally is either a genus, a species, a difference, an accident, or a property. But, as we have shown, nothing is predicated of God as a genus or a difference; and thus neither is anything predicated as a definition, nor likewise as a species, which is constituted of genus and difference. Nor, as we have shown, can there be any accident in God, and therefore nothing is predicated of Him either as an accident or a property, since property belongs to the genus of accidents.[2] It remains, then, that nothing is predicated univocally of God and other things.

[5] Again, what is predicated of many things univocally is simpler than both of them, at least in concept. Now, there can be nothing simpler than God either in reality or in concept. Nothing, therefore, is predicated univocally of God and other things.

[6] Everything, likewise, that is predicated univocally of many things belongs through participation to each of the things of which it is predicated; for the species is said to participate in the genus and the individual in the species.

1. See above, ch. 23.
2. See above, ch. 23–25.

But nothing is said of God by participation, since whatever is participated is determined to the mode of that which is participated and is thus possessed in a partial way and not according to every mode of perfection. Nothing, therefore, can be predicated univocally of God and other things.

[7] Then, too, what is predicated of some things according to priority and posteriority is certainly not predicated univocally. For the prior is included in the definition of the posterior, as *substance* is included in the definition of accident according as an accident is a being. If, then, being were said univocally of substance and accident, substance would have to be included in the definition of being in so far as being is predicated of substance. But this is clearly impossible. Now nothing is predicated of God and creatures as though they were in the same order, but, rather, according to priority and posteriority. For all things are predicated of God essentially. For God is called being as being entity itself, and He is called good as being goodness itself. But in other beings predications are made by participation, as Socrates is said to be a man, not because he is humanity itself, but because he possesses humanity. It is impossible, therefore, that anything be predicated univocally of God and other things.

Chapter 33.

THAT NOT ALL NAMES ARE SAID OF GOD AND CREATURES IN A PURELY EQUIVOCAL WAY

[1] From what we have said it likewise appears that not everything predicated of God and other things is said in a purely equivocal way, in the manner of equivocals by chance.

[2] For in equivocals by chance there is no order or reference of one to another, but it is entirely accidental that

one name is applied to diverse things: the application of the name to one of them does not signify that it has an order to the other. But this is not the situation with names said of God and creatures, since we note in the community of such names the order of cause and effect, as is clear from what we have said.[1] It is not, therefore, in the manner of pure equivocation that something is predicated of God and other things.

[3]   Furthermore, where there is pure equivocation, there is no likeness in things themselves; there is only the unity of a name. But, as is clear from what we have said, there is a certain mode of likeness of things to God.[2] It remains, then, that names are not said of God in a purely equivocal way.

[4]   Moreover, when one name is predicated of several things in a purely equivocal way, we cannot from one of them be led to the knowledge of another; for the knowledge of things does not depend on words, but on the meaning of names. Now, from what we find in other things, we do arrive at a knowledge of divine things, as is evident from what we have said. Such names, then, are not said of God and other things in a purely equivocal way.

[5]   Again, equivocation in a name impedes the process of reasoning. If, then, nothing was said of God and creatures except in a purely equivocal way, no reasoning proceeding from creatures to God could take place. But, the contrary is evident from all those who have spoken about God.

[6]   It is also a fact that a name is predicated of some being uselessly unless through that name we understand something of the being. But, if names are said of God and creatures in a purely equivocal way, we understand nothing of God through those names; for the meanings of those names are known to us solely to the extent that they are

1. See above, ch. 32.
2. See above, ch. 29.

said of creatures. In vain, therefore, would it be said or proved of God that He is a being, good, or the like.

[7] Should it be replied that through such names we know only what God is not, namely, that God is called *living* because He does not belong to the genus of lifeless things, and so with the other names, it will at least have to be the case that *living* said of God and creatures agrees in the denial of the lifeless. Thus, it will not be said in a purely equivocal way.

Chapter 34.

THAT NAMES SAID OF GOD AND CREATURES ARE SAID ANALOGICALLY

[1] From what we have said, therefore, it remains that the names said of God and creatures are predicated neither univocally nor equivocally but analogically, that is, according to an order or reference to something one.

[2] This can take place in two ways. In one way, according as many things have reference to something one. Thus, with reference to one *health* we say that an animal is healthy as the subject of health, medicine is healthy as its cause, food as its preserver, urine as its sign.

[3] In another way, the analogy can obtain according as the order or reference of two things is not to something else but to one of them. Thus, *being* is said of substance and accident according as an accident has reference to a substance, and not according as substance and accident are referred to a third thing.

[4] Now, the names said of God and things are not said analogically according to the first mode of analogy, since we should then have to posit something prior to God, but according to the second mode.

[5]   In this second mode of analogical predication the order according to the name and according to reality is sometimes found to be the same and sometimes not. For the order of the name follows the order of knowledge, because it is the sign of an intelligible conception. When, therefore, that which is prior in reality is found likewise to be prior in knowledge, the same thing is found to be prior both according to the meaning of the name and according to the nature of the thing. Thus, substance is prior to accident both in nature, in so far as substance is the cause of accident, and in knowledge, in so far as substance is included in the definition of accident. Hence, *being* is said of substance by priority over accident both according to the nature of the thing and according to the meaning of the name. But when that which is prior in nature is subsequent in our knowledge, then there is not the same order in analogicals according to reality and according to the meaning of the name. Thus, the power to heal, which is found in all health-giving things, is by nature prior to the health that is in the animal, as a cause is prior to an effect; but because we know this healing power through an effect, we likewise name it from its effect. Hence it is that the *health-giving* is prior in reality, but animal is by priority called *healthy* according to the meaning of the name.

[6]   Thus, therefore, because we come to a knowledge of God from other things, the reality in the names said of God and other things belongs by priority in God according to His mode of being, but the meaning of the name belongs to God by posteriority. And so He is said to be named from His effects.

Chapter 35.

THAT MANY NAMES SAID OF GOD ARE NOT SYNONYMS

[1] It is likewise shown from what has been said that, although names said of God signify the same reality, they are yet not synonyms because they do not signify the same notion.

[2] For just as diverse things are likened through their diverse forms to the one simple reality that God is, so our intellect through its diverse conceptions is to some extent likened to God in so far as it is led through the diverse perfections of creatures to know Him. Therefore, in forming many conceptions of one thing, our intellect is neither false nor futile, because the simple being of God, as we have shown, is such that things can be likened to it according to the multiplicity of their forms.[1] But in accord with its diverse conceptions our intellect devises diverse names that it attributes to God. Hence, since these names are not attributed to God according to the same notion, it is evident that they are not synonyms, even though they signify a reality that is absolutely one. For the signification of the name is not the same, since a name signifies the conception of the intellect before it signifies the thing itself understood by the intellect.

1. See above, ch. 29 and 31.

Chapter 36.

HOW OUR INTELLECT FORMS A PROPOSITION ABOUT GOD

[1]   From this it is further evident that, although God is absolutely simple, it is not futile for our intellect to form enunciations concerning God in His simplicity by means of composition and division.

[2]   For although, as we have said, our intellect arrives at the knowledge of God through diverse conceptions, it yet understands that what corresponds to all of them is absolutely one. For the intellect does not attribute its mode of understanding to the things that it understands; for example, it does not attribute immateriality to a stone even though it knows the stone immaterially. It therefore sets forth the unity of a thing by a composition of words, which is a mark of identity, when it says, *God is good* or *goodness*. The result is that if there is some diversity in the composition, it is referred to the intellect, whereas the unity is referred to the thing understood by the intellect. On the same basis, our intellect sometimes forms an enunciation about God with a certain mark of diversity in it, through the use of a preposition, as when we say, *there is goodness in God*. Here, too, there is indicated a certain diversity, which belongs to the intellect, and a certain unity, which must be referred to the reality.

Chapter 37.

THAT GOD IS GOOD

[1]   From the divine perfection, which we have shown, we can conclude to the goodness of God.

[2] For that by which each thing is called good is the virtue that belongs to it; for "the virtue of each thing is what makes its possessor and his work good."[1] Now, virtue "is a certain perfection, for each thing is then called perfect when it reaches the virtue belonging to it," as may be seen in *Physics* VII.[2] Hence, each thing is good from the fact that it is perfect. That is why each thing seeks its perfection as the good belonging to it. But we have shown that God is perfect. Therefore, He is good.

[3] Again, it was shown above that there is a certain first unmoved mover, namely, God.[3] This mover moves as a completely unmoved mover, which is as something desired. Therefore, since God is the first unmoved mover, He is the first desired. But something is desired in two ways, namely, either because it is good or because it appears to be good. The first desired is what is good, since the apparent good does not move through itself but according as it has a certain appearance of the good, whereas the good moves through itself. The first desired, therefore, God, is truly good.

[4] Furthermore, "the good is that which all things desire." The Philosopher introduces this remark as a "felicitous saying" in *Ethics* I.[4] But all things, each according to its mode, desire to be in act; this is clear from the fact that each thing according to its nature resists corruption. To be in act, therefore, constitutes the nature of the good. Hence it is that evil, which is opposed to the good, follows when potency is deprived of act, as is clear from the Philosopher in *Metaphysics* IX[5]. But, as we have shown, God

1. Aristotle, *Nicomachean Ethics*, II, 6 (1106a 3).
2. Aristotle, *Physics*, VII, 3 (246a 2–b 1).—On God as perfect, see above, ch. 28.
3. See above, ch. 13, ¶28.—On God moving as something desired, see Aristotle, *Metaphysics*, XII, 7 (1072b 3).
4. Aristotle, *Nicomachean Ethics*, I, 1 (1094a 3).
5. Aristotle, *Metaphysics*, IX, 9 (1051a 4).

is being in act without potency.[6] Therefore, He is truly good.

[5]   Moreover, the communication of being and goodness arises from goodness. This is evident from the very nature and definition of the good. By nature, the good of each thing is its act and perfection. Now, each thing acts in so far as it is in act, and in acting it diffuses being and goodness to other things. Hence, it is a sign of a being's perfection that it "can produce its like," as may be seen from the Philosopher in *Meteorologica* IV. Now, the nature of the good comes from its being something appetible. This is the end, which also moves the agent to act. That is why it is said that the good is diffusive of itself and of being.[7] But this diffusion befits God because, as we have shown above, being through Himself the necessary being, God is the cause of being for other things. God is, therefore, truly good.

[6]   That is why it is written in a Psalm (72:1): "How good is God to Israel, to them that are of a right heart!" And again: "The Lord is good to them that hope in Him, to the soul that seeketh Him" (Lam. 3:25).

Chapter 38.

THAT GOD IS GOODNESS ITSELF

[1]   From this we can conclude that God is His goodness.

[2]   To be in act is for each being its good. But God is not only a being in act; He is His very act of being, as we have shown.[1] God is, therefore, *goodness itself*, and not only good.

6. See above, ch. 15.

7. Aristotle, *Meteorologica*, IV, 3 (380a 13).—Pseudo-Dionysius, *De divinis nominibus*, IV, 4; 20 (PG, 3, coll. 700 and 720).

1. See above, ch. 22.

[3] Again, as we have shown, the perfection of each thing is its goodness.[2] But the perfection of the divine being is not affirmed on the basis of something added to it, but because the divine being, as was shown above, is perfect in itself.[3] The goodness of God, therefore, is not something added to His substance; His substance is His goodness.

[4] Moreover, each good thing that is not its goodness is called good by participation. But that which is named by participation has something prior to it from which it receives the character of goodness. This cannot proceed to infinity, since among final causes there is no regress to infinity, since the infinite is opposed to the end [*finis*]. But the good has the nature of an end. We must, therefore, reach some first good, that is not by participation good through an order toward some other good, but is good through its own essence. This is God. God is, therefore, His own goodness.

[5] Again, that which is can participate in something, but the act of being can participate in nothing. For that which participates is in potency, and being is an act. But God is being itself, as we have proved.[4] He is not, therefore, by participation good; He is good essentially.

[6] Furthermore, in a simple being, being and that which is are the same. For, if one is not the other, the simplicity is then removed. But, as we have shown, God is absolutely simple.[5] Therefore, for God to be good is identical with God. He is, therefore, His goodness.

[7] It is thereby likewise evident that no other good is its goodness. Hence it is said in Matthew (19:17): "One is good, God."

2. See above, ch. 37.
3. See above, ch. 28.
4. See above, ch. 22.
5. See above, ch. 18.

Chapter 39.

THAT THERE CANNOT BE EVIL IN GOD

[1]   From this it is quite evident that there cannot be evil in God.

[2]   For *being* and *goodness*, and all names that are predicated essentially, have nothing extraneous mixed with them, although *that which is* or *good* can have something besides being and goodness. For nothing prevents the subject of one perfection from being the subject of another, just as that which is a body can be white and sweet. Now, each nature is enclosed within the limits of its notion, so that it cannot include anything extraneous within itself. But, as we have proved, God is goodness, and not simply good.[1] There cannot, therefore, be any non-goodness in Him. Thus, there cannot possibly be evil in God.

[3]   Moreover, what is opposed to the essence of a given thing cannot befit that thing so long as its essence remains. Thus, irrationality or insensibility cannot befit man unless he ceases to be a man. But the divine essence is goodness itself, as we have shown. Therefore, evil, which is the opposite of good, could have no place in God—unless He ceased to be God, which is impossible, since He is eternal, as we have shown.[2]

[4]   Furthermore, since God is His own being, nothing can be said of Him by participation, as is evident from the above argument. If, then, evil is said of God, it will not be said by participation, but essentially. But evil cannot be so said of anything as to be its essence, for it would lose its being, which is a good, as we have shown.[3] In evil, how-

1. See above, ch. 38.
2. See above, ch. 15.
3. See above, ch. 37.

ever, there can be nothing extraneous mixed with it, as neither in goodness. Evil, therefore, cannot be said of God.

[5] Again, evil is the opposite of good. But the nature of the good consists in perfection, which means that the nature of evil consists in imperfection. Now, in God, Who is universally perfect, as we have shown above,[4] there cannot be defect or imperfection. Therefore, evil cannot be in God.

[6] Then, too, a thing is perfect according as it is in act. A thing will therefore be imperfect according as it falls short of act. Hence, evil is either a privation or includes privation. But the subject of privation is potency, which cannot be in God. Neither, therefore, can evil.

[7] If, moreover, the good is "that which is sought by all,"[5] it follows that every nature flees evil as such. Now, what is in a thing contrary to the motion of its natural appetite is violent and unnatural. Evil in each thing, consequently, is violent and unnatural, so far as it is an evil for that thing; although, among composite things, evil may be natural to a thing according to something within it. But God is not composite, nor, as we have shown, can there be anything violent or unnatural in Him.[6] Evil, therefore, cannot be in God.

[8] Scripture likewise confirms this. For it is said in the canonic Epistle of John (I, 1:5): "God is light and in Him there is no darkness"; and in Job (34:10) it is written: "Far from God be wickedness; and iniquity from the Almighty."

4. See above, ch. 28.
5. Aristotle, *Nicomachean Ethics*, I, 1 (1094a 3).
6. See above, ch. 18 and 19.

Chapter 40.

THAT GOD IS THE GOOD OF EVERY GOOD

[1]   From the foregoing it is also shown that God is "the good of every good."[1]

[2]   For the goodness of each thing is its perfection, as we have said.[2] But, since God is absolutely perfect, in His perfection He comprehends the perfections of all things, as has been shown.[3] His goodness, therefore, comprehends every goodness. Thus, He is the good of every good.

[3]   Moreover, that which is said to be of a certain sort by participation is said to be such only so far as it has a certain likeness to that which is said to be such by essence. Thus iron is said to be on fire in so far as it participates in a certain likeness of fire. But God is good through His essence, whereas all other things are good by participation, as has been shown.[4] Nothing, then, will be called good except in so far as it has a certain likeness of the divine goodness. Hence, God is the good of every good.

[4]   Since, furthermore, each thing is appetible because of the end, and since the nature of the good consists in its being appetible, each thing must be called good either because it is the end or because it is ordered to the end. It is the last end, then, from which all things receive the nature of good. As will be proved later on, this is God.[5] God is, therefore, the good of every good.

[5]   Hence it is that God, promising to Moses a vision of Himself, says: "I will show thee all good" (Exod. 33:19).

1. St. Augustine, *De Trinitate*, VIII, 3 (*PL*, 42, col. 949).
2. See above, ch. 37.
3. See above, ch. 28.
4. See above, ch. 38.
5. *SCG*, III, ch. 17.

And in Wisdom (7:11), it is said of the divine wisdom: "All good things come to me together with her."

Chapter 41.

THAT GOD IS THE HIGHEST GOOD

[1] From this conclusion we prove that God is the highest good.

[2] For the universal good stands higher than any particular good, just as "the good of the people is better than the good of an individual,"[1] since the goodness and perfection of the whole stand higher than the goodness and perfection of the part. But the divine goodness is compared to all others as the universal good to a particular good, being, as we have shown, the good of every good. God is, therefore, the highest good.

[3] Furthermore, what is said essentially is said more truly than what is said by participation. But God is good essentially, while other things are good by participation, as we have shown.[2] God is, therefore, the highest good.

[4] Again, "what is greatest in any genus is the cause of the rest in that genus,"[3] for a cause ranks higher than an effect. But, as we have shown, it is from God that all things have the nature of good.[4] God is, therefore, the highest good.

[5] Moreover, just as what is not mixed with black is more white, so what is not mixed with evil is more good. But God is most unmixed with evil, because evil can be in God neither in act nor in potency; and this belongs to God

1. Aristotle, *Nicomachean Ethics*, I, 2 (1094b 8).
2. See above, ch. 38.
3. Aristotle, *Metaphysics*, I*a*, 1 (993b 23).
4. See above, ch. 40.

according to His nature, as we have shown.[5] God is, therefore, the highest good.

[6]   Hence what is written in I Kings (2:2): "There is
none holy as the Lord is."

Chapter 42.

THAT GOD IS ONE

[1]   From what has been shown it is evident that God is
one.

[2]   For it is not possible that there be two highest goods,
since that which is said by superabundance is found in only
one being. But God, as we have shown, is the highest good.
God is, therefore, one.

[3]   Again, it has been shown that God is absolutely perfect, lacking no perfection.[1] If, then, there are many gods,
there must be many such perfect beings. But this is impossible. For, if none of these perfect beings lacks some perfection, and does not have any admixture of imperfection,
which is demanded for an absolutely perfect being, nothing
will be given in which to distinguish the perfect beings
from one another. It is impossible, therefore, that there
be many gods.

[4]   Again, that which is accomplished adequately through
one supposition is better done through one than through
many.[2] But the order of things is the best it can be, since
the power of the first cause does not fail the potency in
things for perfection. Now, all things are sufficiently fulfilled by a reduction to one first principle. There is, therefore, no need to posit many principles.

5. See above, ch. 39.
1. See above, ch. 28.
2. Aristotle, *Physics*, VIII, 6 (258b 10ff.).

[5] Moreover, it is impossible that there be one continuous and regular motion from many movers. For, if they move together, none of them is a perfect mover, but all together rather take the place of one perfect mover. This is not befitting in the first mover, for the perfect is prior to the imperfect. If, however, they do not move together, each of them at times moves and at times does not. It follows from this that motion is neither continuous nor regular. For a motion that is continuous and one is from one mover. Furthermore, a mover that is not always moving is found to move irregularly, as is evident among lesser movers among whom a violent motion is stronger in the beginning and weaker at the end, whereas a natural motion proceeds conversely. But, as the philosophers have proved, the first motion is one and continuous.[3] Therefore, its first mover must be one.

[6] Furthermore, a corporeal substance is ordered to a spiritual substance as to its good. For there is in the spiritual substance a fuller goodness to which the corporeal substance seeks to liken itself, since whatever exists desires the best so far as this is possible. But all the motions of the corporeal creature are seen to be reduced to one first motion, beyond which there is no other first motion that is not in some way reduced to it. Therefore, outside the spiritual substance that is the end of the first motion, there is none that is not reduced to it. But this is what we understand by the name of God. Hence, there is only one God.

[7] Among all the things that are ordered to one another, furthermore, their order to one another is for the sake of their order to something one; just as the order of the parts of an army among themselves is for the sake of the order of the whole army to its general. For that some diverse things should be united by some relationship cannot come about from their own natures as diverse things, since on this basis they would rather be distinguished from one another. Nor can this unity come from diverse ordering causes,

3. Aristotle, *Physics*, VIII, 7 (260a 20).

because they could not possibly intend one order in so far as among themselves they are diverse. Thus, either the order of many to one another is accidental, or we must reduce it to some one first ordering cause that orders all other things to the end it intends. Now, we find that all the parts of this world are ordered to one another according as some things help some other things. Thus, lower bodies are moved by higher bodies, and these by incorporeal substances, as appears from what was said above.[4] Nor is this something accidental, since it takes place always or for the most part. Therefore, this whole world has only one ordering cause and governor. But there is no other world beyond this one. Hence, there is only one governor for all things, whom we call God.

[8]   Then, too, if there are two beings of which both are necessary beings, they must agree in the notion of the necessity of being. Hence, they must be distinguished by something added either to one of them only, or to both. This means that one or both of them must be composite. Now, as we have shown, no composite being is through itself a necessary being.[5] It is impossible therefore that there be many beings of which each is a necessary being. Hence, neither can there be many gods.

[9]   Furthermore, given two gods that are posited as agreeing in the necessity of being, either that in which they differ is in some way required for the completion of their necessity of being, or it is not. If it is not, then it is something accidental, because that which accrues to a thing without contributing to its being is an accident. Hence, this accident has a cause, which is, consequently, either the essence of the necessary being or something else. If its essence, then, since the necessity itself of being is its essence, as is evident from what was said above,[6] the necessity of being will be the cause of that accident. But the necessity of being

4. See above, ch. 13 and 20.
5. See above, ch. 18.
6. See above, ch. 22.

is found in both gods. Therefore, both will have that accident, and thus will not be distinguished with reference to it. If, however, the cause of the accident is something else, it follows that, unless that something else existed, this accident would not exist; and unless this accident existed, the aforesaid distinction would not exist. Therefore, unless that something else existed, these two supposed necessary beings would not be two but one. Therefore, the proper being of each depends on the other, and thus neither of them is through itself a necessary being.

[10] If, however, that in which they are distinguished is required to complete the necessity of their being, either this will be because it is included in the nature of this necessity of being, as *animate* is included in the definition of animal, or this will be because their necessity of being is specified by it, as animal is completed by *rational*. If the first is the case, wherever the necessity of being is found there must be present that which is included in its nature, just as *animate* belongs to whatever being to which *animal* belongs. And thus, since the necessity of being is attributed to both the aforementioned beings, they will not thereby be distinguished. If the second is the case, this too is impossible. A difference specifying a genus does not complete the nature of the genus, but rather through it the genus comes to be in act. For the nature of *animal* is complete before the addition of *rational*. Rather, the fact is that there cannot be an animal in act that is not rational or irrational. Thus, therefore, something completes the necessity of being as to being in act, and not as to the notion of the necessity of being. This is impossible on two counts. First, because the quiddity of a necessary being is its being, as was proved above.[7] Second, because, were it true, the necessary being would acquire being through something else, which is impossible.

[11] It is, therefore, not possible to posit many beings of which each is through itself a necessary being.

7. See above, ch. 18.

[12]   What is more, if there are two gods, either the name God is predicated of both univocally, or equivocally. If equivocally, this is outside our present purpose. Nothing prevents any given thing from being equivocally named by any given name, provided we admit the usage of those who express the name. But if it be used univocally, it must be predicated of both according to one notion, which means that, in notion, there must be in both one nature. Either, therefore, this nature is in both according to one being, or according to a being that is other in each case. If according to one, there will not be two gods, but only one, since there cannot be one being for two things that are substantially distinguished. If each has its own being, therefore in neither being will the quiddity be its being. Yet this must be posited in God, as we have proved.[8] Therefore, neither of these two beings is what we understand by the name God. It is, therefore, impossible to posit two gods.

[13]   Again, nothing that belongs to this designated thing as such can belong to another, for the singularity of some thing belongs to none other than to that singular thing. But its necessity of being belongs to the necessary being so far as it is this designated being. Therefore, it cannot belong to another, and therefore there cannot be several beings of which each is a necessary being. It is, consequently, impossible that there be several gods.

[14]   The proof of the minor. If the necessary being is not this designated being as a necessary being, the designation of its being is not necessary through itself but depends on another. But so far as each thing is in act it is distinct from all other things; this is to be this designated thing. Therefore, the necessary being depends on another to be in act; which is against the nature of the necessary being. Therefore, the necessary being must be necessary according as it is this designated being.

8. Ibid.

[15] Furthermore, either the nature signified by the name *God* is individuated through itself in this God, or it is individuated through something else. If through something else, composition must result. If through itself, then it cannot possibly belong to another, since the principle of individuation cannot be common to several. It is impossible, therefore, that there be several gods.

[16] If, again, there are several gods, the nature of the godhead cannot be numerically one in two of them. There must, therefore, be something distinguishing the divine nature in this and in that god. But this is impossible, because, as we have shown above, the divine nature receives the addition neither of essential differences nor of accidents.[9] Nor yet is the divine nature the form of any matter, to be capable of being divided according to the division of matter. It is impossible, therefore, that there be two gods.

[17] Then, too, the proper being of each thing is only one. But God is His being, as we have shown.[10] There can, therefore, be only one God.

[18] Moreover, a thing has being in the manner it possesses unity. Hence, each thing struggles as much as it can against any division of itself, lest thereby it tend to nonbeing. But the divine nature has being most powerfully. There is, therefore, in it the greatest unity, and hence no plurality is in any way distinguished within it.

[19] Furthermore, we notice in each genus that multitude proceeds from some unity. This is why in every genus there is found a prime member that is the measure of all the things found in that genus. In whatever things, therefore, we find that there is an agreement in one respect, it is necessary that this depend upon one source. But all things agree in being. There must, therefore, be only one being that is the source of all things. This is God.

9. See above, ch. 23 and 24.
10. See above, ch. 22.

[20]   Again, in every rulership he who rules desires unity. That is why among the forms of rulership the main one is monarchy or kingship. So, too, for many members there is one head, whereby we see by an evident sign that he to whom rulership belongs should have unity. Hence, we must admit that God, Who is the cause of all things, is absolutely one.

[21]   This confession of the divine unity we can likewise gather from holy Scripture. For it is said in Deuteronomy (6:4): "Hear, O Israel: the Lord our God is one God"; and in Exodus (20:3): "Thou shalt not have strange gods before Me"; and in Ephesians (4:5): "One Lord, one faith, one baptism."

[22]   Now by this truth are refuted those Gentiles who accepted a multitude of gods. However, many of them said that there was one highest God, by whom all the others whom they named gods were according to them caused. For they attributed the name of divinity to all everlasting substances, and this especially because of their wisdom and felicity and the rulership of things. This manner of speaking is found also in Sacred Scripture, in which the holy angels, or even men, or judges, are called gods. Thus, this verse of the Psalms (85:8): "There is none among the gods like unto Thee, O Lord"; and elsewhere: "I have said: You are gods" (Ps. 81:6). Many such expressions are found in different places in Scripture.

[23]   Hence, it is mainly the Manicheans who seem opposed to this truth, in that they posit two first principles of which one is not the cause of the other.

[24]   The Arians likewise attacked this truth by their errors, in confessing that the Father and the Son are not one but several gods; although the authority of Scripture forces them to believe that the Son is true God.

Chapter 43.

THAT GOD IS INFINITE

[1]   Since, as the philosophers teach,[1] "the infinite accompanies quantity," infinity cannot be attributed to God on the ground of multitude. For we have shown that there is only one God and that no composition of parts or accidents is found in Him.[2] Nor, again, according to continuous quantity can God be called infinite, since we have shown that He is incorporeal.[3] It remains, then, to investigate whether according to spiritual magnitude it befits God to be infinite.

[2]   We speak of spiritual magnitude with reference to two points: namely, power and the goodness or completeness of one's own nature. For something is said to be more or less white according to the mode in which its whiteness is completed. The magnitude of its power likewise is measured from the magnitude of its action or its works. Of these magnitudes one follows the other. For, from the fact that something is in act it is active, and hence the mode of the magnitude of its power is according to the mode in which it is completed in its act. Thus, it remains that spiritual beings are called great according to the mode of their completion. Augustine himself says that "in beings that are great but not in bulk, to be greater is the same as to be better."[4]

[3]   We must therefore show that God is infinite according to the mode of this sort of magnitude. The infinite here will not be taken in the sense of privation, as in the

1. Aristotle, *Physics*, II, 10 (185a 34).
2. See above, ch. 18 and 23.
3. See above, ch. 20.
4. St. Augustine, *De Trinitate*, VI, 8 (PL, 42, col. 929).

case of dimensive or numerical quantity. For this quantity is of a nature to have a limit, so that such things are called infinites according as there is removed from them the limits they have by nature; which means that in their case the infinite designates an imperfection. But in God the infinite is understood only in a negative way, because there is no terminus or limit to His perfection: He is supremely perfect. It is thus that the infinite ought to be attributed to God.

[4] For everything that according to its nature is finite is determined to the nature of some genus. God, however, is not in any genus; His perfection, as was shown above, rather contains the perfections of all the genera. God is, therefore, infinite.

[5] Again, every act inhering in another is terminated by that in which it inheres, since what is in another is in it according to the mode of the receiver. Hence, an act that exists in nothing is terminated by nothing. Thus, if whiteness were self-existing, the perfection of whiteness in it would not be terminated so as not to have whatever can be had of the perfection of whiteness. But God is act in no way existing in another, for neither is He a form in matter, as we have proved,[5] nor does His being inhere in some form or nature, since He is His own being, as was proved above.[6] It remains, then, that God is infinite.

[6] Furthermore, in reality we find something that is potency alone, namely, prime matter, something that is act alone, namely, God, as was shown above,[7] and something that is act and potency, namely, the rest of things. But, since potency is said relatively to act, it cannot exceed act either in a particular case or absolutely. Hence, since prime matter is infinite in its potentiality, it remains that God, Who is pure act, is infinite in His actuality.

5. See above, ch. 26 and 27.
6. See above, ch. 22.
7. See above, ch. 16.

[7] Moreover, an act is all the more perfect by as much as it has less of potency mixed with it. Hence, every act with which potency is mixed is terminated in its perfection. But, as was shown above, God is pure act without any potency. He is, therefore, infinite.

[8] Again, considered absolutely, being is infinite, since there are infinite and infinite modes in which it can be participated. If, then, the being of some thing is finite, that being must be limited by something other that is somehow its cause. But there can be no cause of the divine being, for God is a necessary being through Himself. Therefore, His being is infinite, and so is He.

[9] Then, too, what has a certain perfection is the more perfect as it participates in that perfection more fully. But there cannot be a mode of perfection, nor is one thinkable, by which a given perfection is possessed more fully than it is possessed by the being that is perfect through its essence and whose being is its goodness. In no way, therefore, is it possible to think of anything better or more perfect than God. Hence, God is infinite in goodness.

[10] Our intellect, furthermore, extends to the infinite in understanding; and a sign of this is that, given any finite quantity, our intellect can think of a greater one. But this ordination of the intellect would be in vain unless an infinite intelligible reality existed. There must, therefore, be some infinite intelligible reality, which must be the greatest of beings. This we call God. God is, therefore, infinite.

[11] Again, an effect cannot transcend its cause. But our intellect can be only from God, Who is the first cause of all things. Our intellect, therefore, cannot think of anything greater than God. If, then, it can think of something greater than every finite thing, it remains that God is not finite.

[12]   There is also the argument that an infinite power cannot reside in a finite essence. For each thing acts through its form, which is either its essence or a part of the essence, whereas power is the name of a principle of action. But God does not have a finite active power. For He moves in an infinite time, which can be done only by an infinite power, as we have proved above.[8] It remains, then, that God's essence is infinite.

[13]   This argument, however, is according to those who posit the eternity of the world. If we do not posit it, there is all the greater confirmation for the view that the power of God is infinite. For each agent is the more powerful in acting according as it reduces to act a potency more removed from act; just as a greater power is needed to heat water than air. But that which in no way exists is infinitely distant from act, nor is it in any way in potency. If, then, the world was made after previously not being at all, the power of its maker must be infinite.

[14]   This argument holds in proving the infinity of the divine power even according to those who posit the eternity of the world. For they acknowledge that God is the cause of the substance of the world, though they consider this substance to be everlasting. They say that God is the cause of an everlasting world in the same way as a foot would have been the cause of an imprint if it had been pressed on sand from all eternity.[9] If we adopt this position, according to our previous argumentation it still follows that the power of God is infinite. For, whether God produced things in time, as we hold, or from all eternity, according to them, nothing can be in reality that God did not produce; for God is the universal source of being. Thus, God produced the world without the supposition of any pre-

8. See above, ch. 20.—On the connection of this paragraph to the following, see St. Thomas, *In IV Sent.*, d. 5, q. 1, a. 3, ad 3am quaestionem; ed. M. F. Moos, pp. 209–211.

9. See St. Augustine, *De civitate Dei*, X, 31 (PL, 41, col. 31).

existent matter or potency. Now, we must gather the proportion of an active power according to the proportion of a passive potency, for the greater the potency that preexists or is presupposed, by so much the greater active power will it be brought to actual fulfillment. It remains, therefore, that, since a finite power produces a given effect by presupposing the potency of matter, the power of God, which presupposes no potency, is infinite, not finite. Thus, so is His essence infinite.

[15] Each thing, moreover, is more enduring according as its cause is more efficacious. Hence, that being whose duration is infinite must have been from a cause of infinite efficaciousness. But the duration of God is infinite, for we have shown above that He is eternal.[10] Since, then, He has no other cause of His being than Himself, He must be infinite.

[16] The authority of Sacred Scripture is witness to this truth. For the Psalmist says: "Great is the Lord, and greatly to be praised: and of His greatness there is no end" (Ps. 144:3).

[17] The sayings of the most ancient philosophers are likewise a witness to this truth. They all posited an infinite first principle of things, as though compelled by truth itself.[11] Yet they did not recognize their own voice. They judged the infinity of the first principle in terms of discrete quantity, following Democritus, who posited infinite atoms as the principles of things, and also Anaxagoras, who posited infinite similar parts as the principles of things. Or they judged infinity in terms of continuous quantity, following those who posited that the first principle of all things was some element or a confused infinite body. But, since it was shown by the effort of later philosophers that there is no infinite body, given that there must be a first principle that is in some way infinite, we conclude that the infinite

10. See above, ch. 15.
11. Aristotle, *Physics*, III, 4 (203a 1).

which is the first principle is neither a body nor a power in a body.

Chapter 44.

THAT GOD IS INTELLIGENT

[1]   From what has been said we can show that God is intelligent.

[2]   We have shown above that among movers and things moved we cannot proceed to infinity, but must reduce all movable things, as is demonstrable, to one first self-moving being.[1] The self-moving being moves itself only by appetite and knowledge, for only such beings are found to move themselves, because to be moved and not moved lies in their power. The moving part in the first self-moving being must be appetitive and apprehending. Now, in a motion that takes place through appetite and apprehension, he who has the appetite and the apprehension is a moved mover, while the appetible and apprehended is the unmoved mover. Since, therefore, the first mover of all things, whom we call God, is an absolutely unmoved mover, He must be related to the mover that is a part of the self-moving being as the appetible is to the one who has the appetite. Not, however, as something appetible by sensible appetite, since sensible appetite is not of that which is good absolutely but of this particular good, since the apprehension of the sense is likewise particular; whereas that which is good and appetible absolutely is prior to that which is good and appetible here and now. The first mover, then, must be appetible as an object of intellect, and thus the mover that desires it must be intelligent. All the more, therefore, will the first appetible be intelligent, since the one desiring it is intelligent in act by being joined to it as an intelligible. Therefore, making the supposition that the first mover

1. See above, ch. 13, ¶11ff.

moves himself, as the philosophers intended, we must say that God is intelligent.

[3]   Moreover, the same conclusion must follow if the reduction of movable beings is, not to a first self-moving being, but to an absolutely unmoved mover. For the first mover is the universal source of motion. Therefore, since every mover moves through a form at which it aims in moving, the form through which the first mover moves must be a universal form and a universal good. But a form does not have a universal mode except in the intellect. Consequently, the first mover, God, must be intelligent.

[4]   In no order of movers, furthermore, is it the case that an intellectual mover is the instrument of a mover without an intellect. Rather, the converse is true. But all movers in the world are to the first mover, God, as instruments are related to a principal agent. Since, then, there are in the world many movers endowed with intelligence, it is impossible that the first mover move without an intellect. Therefore, God must be intelligent.

[5]   Again, a thing is intelligent because it is without matter. A sign of this is the fact that forms are made understood in act by abstraction from matter. And hence the intellect deals with universals and not singulars, for matter is the principle of individuation. But forms that are understood in act become one with the intellect that understands them in act. Therefore, if forms are understood in act because they are without matter, a thing must be intelligent because it is without matter. But we have shown that God is absolutely immaterial.[2] God is, therefore, intelligent.

[6]   Then, too, as was shown above, no perfection found in any genus of things is lacking to God.[3] Nor on this account does any composition follow in Him.[4] But among the perfections of things the greatest is that something be

2. See above, ch. 17, 20, and 27.
3. See above, ch. 28.
4. See above, ch. 31.

intelligent, for thereby it is in a manner all things, having within itself the perfections of all things.[5] God is, therefore, intelligent.

[7]   Again, that which tends determinately to some end either has set itself that end or the end has been set for it by another. Otherwise, it would tend no more to this end than to that. Now, natural things tend to determinate ends. They do not fulfill their natural needs by chance, since they would not do so always or for the most part, but rarely, which is the domain of chance. Since, then, things do not set for themselves an end, because they have no notion of what an end is, the end must be set for them by another, who is the author of nature. He it is who gives being to all things and is through Himself the necessary being. We call Him God, as is clear from what we have said.[6] But God could not set an end for nature unless He had understanding. God is, therefore, intelligent.

[8]   Furthermore, everything imperfect derives from something perfect; for the perfect is naturally prior to the imperfect, as is act to potency. But the forms found in particular things are imperfect because they are there in a particular way and not according to the community of their natures. They must therefore be derived from some forms that are perfect and not particular. But such forms cannot exist unless by being understood, since no form is found in its universality except in the intellect. Consequently, these forms must be intelligent, if they be subsistent; for only thus do they have operation. God, then, Who is the first subsistent act, from whom all other things are derived, must be intelligent.

[9]   This truth the Catholic faith likewise confesses. For it is said of God in Job (9:4): "He is wise of heart, and mighty in strength"; and later on (12:16): "With Him is strength and wisdom." So, too, in the Psalms (138:6):

5. Aristotle, De anima, III, 8 (431b 21).
6. See above, ch. 13.

"Thy knowledge is become wonderful to me"; and Romans (11:33): "O the depth of the riches of the wisdom and of the knowledge of God!"

[10] The truth of this faith was so strong among men that they named God from the act of understanding. For *theos* [θεός], which among the Greeks signifies God, comes from *theaste* [θεᾶσθαι], which means *to consider* or *to see*.[7]

Chapter 45.

THAT GOD'S ACT OF UNDERSTANDING IS HIS ESSENCE

[1] From the fact that God is intelligent it follows that His act of understanding is His essence.

[2] To understand is the act of one understanding, residing in him, not proceeding to something outside as heating proceeds to the heated thing. For, by being understood, the intelligible suffers nothing; rather, the one understanding is perfected. Now, whatever is in God is the divine essence. God's act of understanding, therefore, is His essence, it is the divine being, God Himself. For God is His essence and His being.

[3] Furthermore, the act of understanding is to the intellect as being [esse] is to essence [essentia]. But, as we have proved, God's being is His essence. Therefore, God's understanding is His intellect. But the divine intellect is God's essence; otherwise, it would be an accident in God. Therefore, the divine understanding is His essence.

[4] Again, second act is more perfect than first act, as consideration is more perfect than knowledge. But the knowledge or intellect of God is His essence, if, as we have

7. This derivation is taken from St. John Damascene, *De fide orthodoxa*, I, 9 (PG, 94, col. 837A).

proved, He is intelligent;[1] for, as is clear from the above,[2] no perfection belongs to Him by participation but rather by essence. If, therefore, His consideration is not His essence, something will be nobler and more perfect than His essence. Thus, God will not be at the summit of perfection and goodness and hence will not be first.

[5]   Moreover, to understand is the act of the one understanding. If, therefore, God in understanding is not His understanding, God must be related to it as potency to act. Thus, there will be potency and act in God, which is impossible, as we proved above.[3]

[6]   Then, too, every substance exists for the sake of its operation. If, then, the operation of God is other than the divine substance, the end of God will be something other than God. Thus, God will not be His goodness, since the good of each thing is its end.

[7]   If, however, God's understanding is His being, His understanding must be simple, eternal and unchangeable, existing only in act, and including all the perfections that have been proved of the divine being. Hence, God is not potentially understanding, nor does He begin to understand something anew, nor still does He have any change or composition in understanding.

Chapter 46.

THAT GOD UNDERSTANDS THROUGH NOTHING
OTHER THAN THROUGH HIS ESSENCE

[1]   From what has been shown above it appears with evidence that the divine intellect understands through no other intelligible species than through His essence.

1. See above, ch. 44.
2. See above, ch. 23.
3. See above, ch. 16.

[2] The intelligible species is the formal principle of intellectual operation, just as the form of any agent is the principle of its own operation. Now, as we have shown, the divine intellectual operation is God's essence.[1] If, then, the divine intellect understood by an intelligible species other than the divine essence, something other would be added to the divine essence as principle and cause. This is opposed to what was shown above.[2]

[3] Furthermore, the intellect becomes understanding in act through an intelligible species, just as the sense becomes sensing in act through a sensible species. The intelligible species is to the intellect, therefore, as act to potency. If, then, the divine intellect understood through some intelligible species other than itself, it would be in potency with respect to something. This is impossible, as we proved above.[3]

[4] Moreover, an intelligible species in the intellect that is other than the intellect's essence has an accidental being, which is why our knowledge is numbered among the accidents. But in God, as we have shown, there can be no accident.[4] Therefore, there is not in the divine intellect any species other than the divine essence itself.

[5] Again, the intelligible species is the likeness of something understood. If, then, there is in the divine intellect an intelligible species other than the divine essence, it will be the likeness of something understood. It will thus be the likeness either of the divine essence or of some other thing. It cannot be the likeness of the divine essence, because then the divine essence would not be intelligible through itself, but that species would make it intelligible. Nor can there be in the divine intellect a species other than the divine intellect that is the likeness of some other being. For that

1. See above, ch. 45.
2. See above, ch. 13, ¶33.
3. See above, ch. 16.
4. See above, ch. 23.

likeness would then be impressed on the divine intellect by some being. Not by itself, since then the same being would be agent and receiver, and also because there would be an agent that impressed, not its own likeness, but that of another on the receiver, and thus it would not be true that every agent produced its like. Nor by another, for there would then be an agent prior to God. It is, therefore, impossible that there be in God an intelligible species other than His essence.

[6]   Furthermore, God's understanding, as we have shown, is His essence. If, therefore, God understood through a species that was not His essence, it would be through something other than His essence. This is impossible. Therefore, God does not understand through a species that is not His essence.

Chapter 47.

THAT GOD UNDERSTANDS HIMSELF PERFECTLY

[1]   From this it further appears that God understands Himself perfectly.

[2]   Since through the intelligible species the intellect is directed to the thing understood, the perfection of intellectual operation depends on two things. One is that the intelligible species be perfectly conformed to the thing understood. The second is that it be perfectly joined to the intellect, which is realized more fully according as the intellect has greater power in understanding. Now, the divine essence, which is the intelligible species by which the divine intellect understands, is absolutely identical with God and it is also absolutely identical with His intellect. Therefore, God understands Himself most perfectly.

[3]   Furthermore, a material thing is made intelligible by being separated from matter and the conditions of matter.

Therefore, that which is through its nature separate from all matter and material conditions is intelligible in its nature. Now every intelligible is understood by being one in act with the one understanding. But, as we have proved, God is intelligent. Therefore, since He is absolutely immaterial, and most one with Himself, He understands Himself perfectly.

[4] Again, a thing is understood in act because the intellect in act and the understood in act are one. But the divine intellect is always an intellect in act, since there is no potency or imperfection in God. On the other hand, the divine essence is through itself perfectly intelligible, as is clear from what we have said. Since, therefore, the divine intellect and the divine essence are one, it is evident from what we have said that God understands Himself perfectly. For God is His intellect and His essence.

[5] Moreover, what is in something in an intelligible way is understood by it. The divine essence is in God in an intelligible way, for the natural being of God and His intelligible being are one and the same, since His being is His understanding. God, therefore, understands His essence, and hence Himself, since He is His essence.

[6] The acts of the intellect, furthermore, like those of the other powers of the soul, are distinguished according to their objects. The operation of the intellect will be more perfect as the intelligible object is more perfect. But the most perfect intelligible object is the divine essence, since it is the most perfect and the first truth. The operation of the divine intellect is likewise the most noble, since, as we have shown, it is the divine being.[1] Therefore, God understands Himself.

[7] Again, the perfections of all things are found supremely in God. Now, among other perfections found in created things the greatest is to understand God. For the

1. See above, ch. 45, for this and the other cross-references in the present chapter.

intellectual nature, whose perfection is understanding, excels all the others; and the most noble intelligible object is God. God, therefore, knows Himself supremely.

[8] This is confirmed by divine authority. For the Apostle says: "The spirit searcheth all things, yea, the deep things of God" (I Cor. 2:10).

Chapter 48.

THAT PRIMARILY AND ESSENTIALLY GOD KNOWS ONLY HIMSELF

[1] Now, it appears from what we have said that primarily and essentially God knows only Himself.

[2] That thing alone is primarily and essentially known by the intellect by whose species the intellect understands; for an operation is proportioned to the form that is the principle of the operation. But, as we have proved, that by which God understands is nothing other than His essence.[1] Therefore, the primary and essential object of His intellect is nothing other than Himself.

[3] It is, furthermore, impossible to understand a multitude primarily and essentially, since one operation cannot be terminated by many. But, as we have proved, God at some time understands Himself.[2] If, therefore, He understands something other than Himself as the primary and essential object of His understanding, His intellect must change from a consideration of Himself to the consideration of this something else. This something else is less noble than God. The divine intellect is thus changed for the worse, which is impossible.

1. See above, ch. 46.
2. See above, ch. 47.

[4]   Moreover, the operations of the intellect are distinguished according to their objects. If, then, God understands Himself and something other than Himself as the principal object, He will have several intellectual operations. Therefore, either His essence will be divided into several parts, or He will have an intellectual operation that is not His substance. Both of these positions have been proved to be impossible.[3] It remains, then, that nothing other than the divine essence is known by God as the primary and essential object of His intellect.

[5]   Again, in so far as the intellect is different from its object, it is in potency to it. If, then, something other than Himself is God's primary and essential object, it will follow that He is in potency to something else. This is impossible, as is clear from what we have said.[4]

[6]   The thing understood, likewise, is the perfection of the one understanding. For the intellect is perfect according as it understands in act, and this obtains through the fact that the intellect is one with what is understood. If, then, something other than Himself is primarily understood by God, something else will be His perfection, and more noble than He. This is impossible.

[7]   Furthermore, the knowledge of the one understanding is comprised of many things understood. If, then, God knows many things as the principal and essential objects of His knowledge, it will follow that the knowledge of God is composed of many things. Thus, either the divine essence will be composite, or knowledge will be an accident in God. From what we have said, it is clear that both of these suppositions are impossible.[5] It remains, therefore, that what is primarily and essentially understood by God is nothing other than His substance.

3. See above, ch. 18, 23, and 45.
4. See above, ch. 16.
5. See above, ch. 18, 23, and 45.

[8]   Again, intellectual operation derives its specification and nobility from that which is essentially and primarily understood by it. If, then, God understood something other than Himself as His essential and primary object, His intellectual operation would have its specification and nobility according to something other than God. This, however, is impossible, since, as we have shown, God's operation is His essence.[6] Thus, it is impossible that what is understood primarily and essentially by God be other than He.

Chapter 49.

THAT GOD UNDERSTANDS THINGS OTHER THAN HIMSELF

[1]   From the fact that God understands Himself primarily and essentially we must posit that He knows in Himself things other than Himself.

[2]   An effect is adequately known when its cause is known. So "we are said to know each thing when we know the cause."[1] But God Himself is through His essence the cause of being for other things. Since He has a most full knowledge of His essence, we must posit that God also knows other things.

[3]   Moreover, the likeness of every effect somehow pre-exists in its cause; for every agent produces its like. But whatever is in something is in it according to the mode of that in which it is. If, then, God is the cause of certain things, since according to His nature He is intellectual, the likeness of what He causes will exist in Him in an intelligible way. But what is in something in an intelligible way is understood by it. God, therefore, understands within Himself things other than Himself.

6. See above, ch. 45.
1. Aristotle, *Posterior Analytics*, I, 2 (71b 3).

[4] Again, whoever knows perfectly a given thing knows whatever can be truly said of it and whatever befits it according to its nature. But it befits God according to His nature to be the cause of other things. Since, then, God knows Himself perfectly, He knows Himself to be a cause. This cannot be unless He somehow knows what He causes. This is other than He, since nothing is the cause of itself. Therefore, God knows things other than Himself.

[5] If we put together these two conclusions, it appears that God knows Himself as primarily and essentially known, whereas He knows other things as seen in His essence.

[6] This truth is expressly taught by Dionysius. He says: "In seeing them, God does not insert Himself in singulars, but He knows them as contained within a single cause."[2] And later on: "the divine wisdom, knowing itself, knows other things."[3]

[7] To this judgment, too, the authority of Sacred Scripture bears witness. For it is said of God in the Psalms (101:20): "He hath looked forth from His high sanctuary"; as though to say that God sees other things from His own height.

Chapter 50.

THAT GOD HAS A PROPER KNOWLEDGE OF ALL THINGS

[1] Some have said that God has only a universal knowledge of other things. He knows them, that is, in so far as they are beings because He knows the nature of being through a knowledge of Himself. For this reason, it remains for us to show that God knows all other things as they are

2. Pseudo-Dionysius, *De divinis nominibus*, VII, 2 (*PG*, 3, col. 869B).
3. *Ibid.*

distinct from one another and from Himself. This is to know things according to their proper natures.

[2]   In order to show this point, let us suppose that God is the cause of every being, as is somewhat evident from what we said above and will be more fully shown later on.[1] Thus, there is consequently nothing in any thing that is not caused by God, mediately or immediately. Now, when the cause is known, the effect is known. Whatever is in each and every thing can be known if we know God and all the causes that are between God and things. But God knows Himself and all the intervening causes between Himself and any given thing. Now, we have already shown that God knows Himself perfectly.[2] By knowing Himself, God knows whatever proceeds from Him immediately. When this is known, God once more knows what proceeds from it immediately; and so on for all intermediate causes down to the last effect. Therefore, God knows whatever is found in reality. But this is to have a proper and complete knowledge of a thing, namely, to know all that there is in that thing, both what is common and what is proper. Therefore, God has a proper knowledge of things, in so far as they are distinct from one another.

[3]   Furthermore, whatever acts through an intellect knows what it does according to the proper nature of its work; for the knowledge of the maker determines the form for the thing made. Now, God causes things through His intellect, since His being is His understanding and each thing acts in so far as it is in act. God, therefore, has a proper knowledge of what He causes, so far as it is distinct from the others.

[4]   Moreover, the distinction of things cannot be from chance, because it has a fixed order. The distinction in things must therefore be from the intention of some cause. It cannot be from the intention of a cause acting through

1. See above, ch. 13, and SCG, II, ch. 15.
2. See above, ch. 47.

a necessity of nature, for nature is determined to one course of action, and thus the intention of no thing acting through the necessity of nature can terminate in many effects in so far as these are distinct. It remains, then, that distinction in things comes from the intention of a knowing cause. But it seems to be proper to the intellect to consider the distinction of things; and so Anaxagoras called the intellect the source of distinction.[3] Now, the universal distinction of things cannot be from the intention of some secondary cause, because all such causes belong to the world of distinct effects. It belongs to the first cause, that is through itself distinguished from all other things, to aim at the distinction of all things. God, therefore, knows things as distinct.

[5]   Again, whatever God knows He knows most perfectly. For, as was shown above, there is all perfection in God as in the absolutely perfect being. Now, what is known only in a general way is not perfectly known, since one does not yet know what is most important in that thing, namely, the ultimate perfections, by which its proper being is completed; so that by such a knowledge a thing is known potentially rather than actually. Since, then, by knowing His own essence God knows things in a universal way, He must also have a proper knowledge of things.

[6]   Then, too, whoever knows a certain nature knows the essential accidents of that nature. The essential accidents of being as being are one and many, as is proved in *Metaphysics* IV.[4] If, then, by knowing His essence, God knows the nature of being in a universal way, it follows that He knows multitude. But multitude cannot be understood without distinction. Therefore, God knows things as they are distinct from one another.

[7]   Whoever, furthermore, perfectly knows a universal nature knows the mode in which that nature can be possessed. In the same way, he who knows whiteness knows

3. Aristotle, *Physics*, VIII, 1 (250b 26); VIII, 9 (265b 23).
4. Aristotle, *Metaphysics*, IV, 3 (1003b 23).

that which receives it more and less. But the grades of beings are established from the diverse mode of being. If, then, by knowing Himself, God knows the universal nature of being, and this not imperfectly, since, as we have shown, every imperfection is remote from Him,[5] God must know all grades of beings. Thus, God will have a proper knowledge of things other than Himself.

[8] Furthermore, he who knows something perfectly knows all that is in it. But God knows Himself perfectly. Therefore, He knows all that is in Him according to His active power. But all things, in their proper forms, are in Him according to His active power, since God is the principle of every being. Therefore, God has a proper knowledge of all things.

[9] Again, he who knows a certain nature knows whether that nature is communicable. He who did not know that the nature of *animal* is communicable to many would not know it perfectly. Now, the divine nature is communicable by likeness. God, therefore, knows in how many modes there can be something like His essence. But the diversities of forms arise from the fact that things imitate the divine essence diversely; and so the Philosopher has called a natural form "something divine."[6] Therefore, God has a knowledge of things in terms of their proper forms.

[10] Moreover, men and other knowing beings know things as distinct from one another in their multitude. If, then, God does not know things in their distinction, it follows that He is the most foolish being of all, as He must have been for those who held that God did not know strife, a thing known to all—an opinion that the Philosopher considers to be untenable in *De anima* I and *Metaphysics* III.[7]

5. See above, ch. 28.
6. Aristotle, *Physics*, I, 9 (192a 17).
7. *De anima*, I, 5 (410b 5); *Metaphysics*, III, 4 (1000b 5).

[11] We likewise receive this teaching from the canonic Scriptures. For it is said in Genesis (1:31): "And God saw all things that He had made, and they were very good." And in Hebrews (4:13): "Neither is there any creature invisible in His sight: but all things are naked and open to His eyes."

Chapters 51–52.

ARGUMENTS INQUIRING HOW A MULTITUDE OF INTELLECTUAL OBJECTS IS IN THE DIVINE INTELLECT

[1] Lest the multitude of intellectual objects, however, introduce a composition into the divine intellect, we must investigate the mode in which these intellectual objects are many.

[2] Now, this multitude cannot be taken to mean that many intellectual objects have a distinct being in God. For either these objects would be the same as the divine essence, and thus a certain multitude would be posited in the essence of God, which we set aside above in many ways;[1] or they would be added to the divine essence, and thus there would be some accident in God, which we have shown above to be impossible.[2]

[3] Nor, again, can such intelligible forms be posited as existing in themselves. This is what Plato, avoiding the above difficulties, seems to have posited by introducing the Ideas. For the forms of natural things cannot exist without matter, since neither are they understood without matter.

[4] And, even if this position were held, it would not enable us to posit that God has understanding of a multitude. For, since the aforementioned forms are outside God's

1. See above, ch. 18, 20, and 42.
2. See above, ch. 23.

essence, if God could not understand the multitude of things without them, as the perfection of His intellect requires, it would follow that His perfection in understanding depended on something else, and consequently so would His perfection in being, since His being is His understanding. The contrary of this was shown above.[3]

[5]   Furthermore, since whatever is outside His essence must be caused by Him, as will be shown later on,[4] it is necessary that, if the aforementioned forms are to be found outside God, they must be caused by Him. But God is the cause of things through His intellect, as will be shown later on.[5] Therefore, so that these intelligibles may have existence, it is required according to the order of nature that God first understand them. Hence, God does not have knowledge of multitude by the fact that many intelligibles are found outside Him.

[6]   Furthermore, the intelligible in act is the intellect in act, just as the sensible in act is the sense in act.[6] According as the intelligible is distinguished from the intellect, both are in potency, as likewise appears in the case of the sense. For neither the sight is seeing in act, nor is the visible object seen in act, except when the sight is informed by the species of the visible object, so that thereby from the sight and the object something one results. If, then, the intelligible objects of God are outside His intellect, it will follow that His intellect is in potency, as are also its intelligible objects. Thus, some cause reducing them to act would be needed, which is impossible, since there is nothing prior to God.

[7]   Then, too, the understood must be in him who understands. Therefore, to posit the forms of things as existing in themselves outside the divine intellect does not suffice

3. See above, ch. 13.
4. SCG, II, ch. 15.
5. SCG, II, ch. 23.
6. Aristotle, De anima, III, 2 (425b 27).

for God to understand a multitude of things; these intelligibles must be in the divine intellect itself.

[8] [Chapter 52] From the same arguments it likewise appears that the multitude of the aforementioned intelligibles cannot reside in any intellect other than the divine intellect—for example, that of a soul or an angel or intelligence. If this were true, the divine intellect would depend on a lower intellect for some operation. But this is impossible.

[9] Then, too, just as self-subsisting things are from God, so is whatever inheres in them. Hence, the divine understanding, by which God is a cause, is a prerequisite for the being of the aforementioned intelligibles in some lower intellect.

[10] It likewise follows that the divine intellect is in potency, since its intelligible objects are not joined to it.

[11] Furthermore, just as each thing has its own being, so it has its own operation. It cannot happen, then, that because some intellect is disposed for operation another intellect will perform an intellectual operation; rather, the very same intellect in which the disposition is present will do this, just as each thing is through its own essence, not through the essence of another. Therefore, by the fact that there are many intelligible objects in some secondary intellect it could not come about that the first intellect knows a multitude.

Chapter 53.

THE SOLUTION OF THE ABOVE DIFFICULTY

[1] We can solve the above difficulty with ease if we examine diligently how the things that are understood by the intellect exist within the intellect.

[2]   So far as it is possible, let us proceed from our intellect to the knowledge that the divine intellect has. Let us consider the fact that an external thing understood by us does not exist in our intellect according to its own nature; rather, it is necessary that its species be in our intellect, and through this species the intellect comes to be in act. Once in act through this species as through its own form, the intellect knows the thing itself. This is not to be understood in the sense that the act itself of understanding is an action proceeding to the thing understood, as heating proceeds to the heated thing. Understanding remains in the one understanding, but it is related to the thing understood because the abovementioned species, which is a principle of intellectual operation as a form, is the likeness of the thing understood.[1]

[3]   We must further consider that the intellect, having been informed by the species of the thing, by an act of understanding forms within itself a certain intention of the thing understood, that is to say, its notion, which the definition signifies. This is a necessary point, because the intellect understands a present and an absent thing indifferently. In this the imagination agrees with the intellect. But the intellect has this characteristic in addition, namely, that it understands a thing as separated from material conditions, without which a thing does not exist in reality. But this could not take place unless the intellect formed the abovementioned intention for itself.

[4]   Now, since this understood intention is, as it were, a terminus of intelligible operation, it is distinct from the intelligible species that actualizes the intellect, and that we must consider the principle of intellectual operation, though both are a likeness of the thing understood. For, by the fact that the intelligible species, which is the form of the intellect and the principle of understanding, is the likeness of the external thing, it follows that the intellect

1. See St. Thomas, *De veritate*, II, 3, and ad 1, 8, 9; III, 2–3.

forms an intention like that thing, since such as a thing is, such are its works. And because the understood intention is like some thing, it follows that the intellect, by forming such an intention, knows that thing.

[5] Now, the divine intellect understands by no species other than the divine essence, as was shown above.[2] Nevertheless, the divine essence is the likeness of all things.[3] Thereby it follows that the conception of the divine intellect as understanding itself, which is its Word, is the likeness not only of God Himself understood, but also of all those things of which the divine essence is the likeness. In this way, therefore, through one intelligible species, which is the divine essence, and through one understood intention, which is the divine Word, God can understand many things.

Chapter 54.

HOW THE DIVINE ESSENCE, BEING ONE AND SIMPLE, IS THE PROPER LIKENESS OF ALL INTELLIGIBLE OBJECTS

[1] But, again, it can seem to someone difficult or impossible that one and the same simple being, the divine essence for example, is the proper model or likeness of diverse things. For, since among diverse things there is a distinction by reason of their proper forms, whatever is like something according to its proper form must turn out to be unlike something else. To be sure, according as diverse things have something in common, nothing prevents them from having one likeness, as do man and a donkey so far as they are animals. But from this it will follow that God does not have a proper knowledge of things, but a common

2. See above, ch. 46.
3. See above, ch. 29.

one; for the operation that knowledge is follows the mode
in which the likeness of the known is in the knower. So, too,
heating is according to the mode of the heat. For the likeness of the known in the knower is as the form by which
the operation takes place. Therefore, if God has a proper
knowledge of many things, He must be the proper model
of singulars. How this may be we must investigate.

[2]   As the Philosopher says in *Metaphysics* VIII, the forms
of things and the definitions that signify them are like
numbers.[1] Among numbers, the addition or subtraction
of unity changes the species of a number, as appears in the
numbers two and three. It is the same among definitions:
the addition or subtraction of one difference changes the
species. For sensible substance, with the difference *rational*
taken away and added, differs in species.

[3]   Now, with reference to things that contain a multitude, the intellect and nature are differently disposed. For
what is required for the being of something the nature
of that thing does not permit to be removed. For the nature
of an animal will not survive if the soul is taken away from
the body. But what is joined in reality the intellect can at
times receive separately, when one of the elements is not
included in the notion of the other. Thus, in the number
three the intellect can consider the number *two* only, and
in the *rational animal* it can consider that which is *sensible*
only. Hence, that which contains several elements the intellect can take as the proper notion of the several elements
by apprehending one of them without the others. It can,
for example, take the number ten as the proper notion
of nine by subtracting unity, and similarly as the proper
notion of each of the numbers included under it. So, too,
it can take in man the proper exemplar of irrational animal
as such, and of each of its species, except that they would
add some positive differences. On this account a certain

1. Aristotle, *Metaphysics*, VIII, 3 (1048b 33).

philosopher, Clement by name, said that the nobler beings in reality are the exemplars of the less noble.[2]

[4] But the divine essence comprehends within itself the nobilities of all beings, not indeed compositely, but, as we have shown above, according to the mode of perfection. Now, every form, both proper and common, considered as positing something, is a certain perfection; it includes imperfection only to the extent that it falls short of true being. The intellect of God, therefore, can comprehend in His essence that which is proper to each thing by understanding wherein the divine essence is being imitated and wherein each thing falls short of its perfection. Thus, by understanding His essence as imitable in the mode of *life* and not of *knowledge*, God has the proper form of a plant; and if He knows His essence as imitable in the mode of knowledge and not of intellect, God has the proper form of animal, and so forth. Thus, it is clear that, being absolutely perfect, the divine essence can be taken as the proper exemplar of singulars. Through it, therefore, God can have a proper knowledge of all things.

[5] Since, however, the proper exemplar of one thing is distinguished from the proper exemplar of another thing, and distinction is the source of plurality, we must observe in the divine intellect a certain distinction and plurality of understood exemplars, according as that which is in the divine intellect is the proper exemplar of diverse things. Hence, since this obtains according as God understands the proper relation of resemblance that each creature has to Him, it remains that the exemplars of things in the divine intellect are many or distinct only according as God knows that things can be made to resemble Him by many and diverse modes. In accord with this, Augustine says that God made man and a horse by distinct exemplars. He also says that the exemplars of things are a plurality in the divine

2. See Pseudo-Dionysius, *De divinis nominibus*, V, 9 (PG, 3, col. 824D).

mind.³ This conclusion likewise saves to some extent the opinion of Plato and his doctrine of Ideas, according to which would be formed everything that is found among material things.⁴

Chapter 55.

THAT GOD UNDERSTANDS ALL THINGS TOGETHER

[1]   From this it is further apparent that God understands all things together.

[2]   Our intellect cannot understand in act many things together. The reason is that, since "the intellect in act is its object in act,"¹ if the intellect did understand many things together, it would follow that the intellect would be at one and the same time many things according to one genus—which is impossible. I say "according to one genus" because nothing prevents the same subject from being informed by diverse forms of diverse genera, just as the same body is figured and colored. Now, the intelligible species, by which the intellect is formed so as to be the objects that are understood in act, all belong to one genus; for they have one manner of being in the order of intelligible being, even though the things whose species they are do not have one manner of being. Hence, the species are not contrary through the contrariety of the things that are outside the soul. It is in this way that, when certain things that are many are considered as in any way united, they are understood together. For the intellect understands a continuous whole all at once, not part after part. So, too, it understands a proposition all at once, not first the subject

3. St. Augustine, *Liber octaginta trium quaestionum*, q. 46 (*PL*, 40, col. 30).
4. See above, ch. 51, ¶3.
1. Aristotle, *De anima*, III, 4 (430a 3).

and then the predicate, since it knows all the parts according to one species of the whole.

[3] From these remarks we can infer that, whenever several things are known through one species, they can be known together. But all that God knows He knows through one species, which is His essence.[2] Therefore, God can understand all things together.

[4] Again, a knowing power does not know anything in act unless the intention be present. Thus, the phantasms preserved in the organ are not always actually imagined because the intention is not directed to them. For among voluntary agents the appetite moves the other powers to act. We do not understand together, therefore, many things to which the intention is not directed at the same time. But things that must fall under one intention must be understood together; for he who is considering a comparison between two things directs his intention to both and sees both together.

[5] Now, all the things that are in the divine knowledge must fall under one intention. For God intends to see His essence perfectly, which is to see it according to its whole power, under which are contained all things. Therefore God, by seeing His essence, sees all things together.

[6] Furthermore, the intellect of one considering successively many things cannot have only one operation. For since operations differ according to their objects, the operation by which the first is considered must be different from the operation by which the second is considered. But the divine intellect has only one operation, namely, the divine essence, as we have proved.[3] Therefore, God considers all that He knows, not successively, but together.

[7] Moreover, succession cannot be understood without time nor time without motion, since time is "the number.

2. See above, ch. 46.

3. See above, ch. 45.

of motion according to before and after."[4] But there can be no motion in God, as may be inferred from what we have said.[5] There is, therefore, no succession in the divine consideration. Thus, all that He knows God considers together.

[8]   Then, too, God's understanding is His being, as is clear from what we have said.[6] But there is no before and after in the divine being; everything is together, as was shown above.[7] Neither, therefore, does the consideration of God contain a before and after, but, rather, understands all things together.

[9]   Every intellect, furthermore, that understands one thing after the other is at one time potentially understanding and at another time actually understanding. For while it understands the first thing actually it understands the second thing potentially. But the divine intellect is never potentially, but always actually, understanding. Therefore, it does not understand things successively but rather understands them together.

[10]   Sacred Scripture bears witness to this truth. For it is written: "With God there is no change nor shadow of alteration" (James 1:17).

Chapter 56.

THAT GOD'S KNOWLEDGE IS NOT HABITUAL

[1]   From this it appears that there is no habitual knowledge in God.

[2]   Where there is habitual knowledge, not all things are known together; some are known actually, and some

4. Aristotle, *Physics*, IV, 11 (219a 2).
5. See above, ch. 13, ¶28.
6. See above, ch. 45.
7. See above, ch. 15.

habitually. But, as we have proved, God has actual understanding of all things together.[1] There is, therefore, no habitual knowledge in Him.

[3]   Furthermore, he who has a habit and is not using it is in a manner in potency, though otherwise than prior to understanding. But we have shown that the divine intellect is in no way in potency.[2] In no way, therefore, is there habitual knowledge in it.

[4]   Moreover, if an intellect knows something habitually, its essence is other than its intellectual operation, which is the consideration itself. For an intellect that knows habitually is lacking its operation, but its essence cannot be lacking to it. In God, however, as we have proved, His essence is His operation.[3] There is, therefore, no habitual knowledge in His intellect.

[5]   Again, an intellect that knows only habitually is not at its highest perfection. That is why happiness, which is something best, is posited in terms of act, not in terms of habit. If, therefore, God is habitually knowing through His substance, considered in His substance He will not be universally perfect. We have shown the contrary of this conclusion.[4]

[6]   It has also been shown that God understands through His essence, but not through any intelligible species added to His essence. Now, every habitual intellect understands through some species. For either a habit confers on the intellect a certain ability to receive the intelligible species by which it becomes understanding in act, or else it is the ordered aggregate of the species themselves existing in the intellect, not according to a complete act, but in a way intermediate between potency and act. There is therefore no habitual knowledge in God.

1. See above, ch. 55.
2. *Ibid.*, ¶9, and ch. 16 and 45.
3. See above, ch. 45.
4. See above, ch. 28.

[7]   Then, again, a habit is a certain quality. But no quality or accident can be added to God, as we have proved.[5] Habitual knowledge, therefore, does not befit God.

[8]   But because the disposition by which one is only habitually considering or willing or doing is likened to the disposition of one sleeping, hence it is that, in order to remove any habitual disposition from God, David says: "Behold He shall neither slumber nor sleep, that keepeth Israel" (Ps. 120:4). Hence, also, what is said in Eccelesiasticus (23:28): "The eyes of the Lord are far brighter than the sun"; for the sun is always shining.

Chapter 57.

THAT GOD'S KNOWLEDGE IS NOT DISCURSIVE

[1]   We thereby further know that the divine consideration is not ratiocinative or discursive.

[2]   Our consideration is ratiocinative when we proceed from the consideration of one thing to another, as when in syllogistic reasoning we proceed from principles to conclusions. For, when someone examines how a conclusion follows from premises and considers both together, he is not on this account reasoning or discoursing, since this takes place, not by arguing, but by judging the arguments. So, too, knowledge is not material because it judges material things. Now, it has been shown that God does not consider one thing after the other as it were in succession, but all together. His knowledge, therefore, is not ratiocinative or discursive, although He knows all discourse and ratiocination.

[3]   Everyone reasoning sees the principle by one consideration and the conclusions by another. There would be

5. See above, ch. 23.

no need to proceed to conclusions after the consideration of the principles if by considering the principles we also considered the conclusions. But God knows all things by one operation, His essence, as we proved above.[1] His knowledge is, therefore, not ratiocinative.

[4]   Again, all ratiocinative knowledge contains some potency and some act, for conclusions are in principles potentially. But in the divine intellect potency has no place, as was proved above.[2] God's intellect, therefore, is not discursive.

[5]   Moreover, in all discursive knowledge there must be something caused, since principles are in a manner the efficient cause of the conclusion. Hence, demonstration is said to be "a syllogism making one to know."[3] But in the divine knowledge there can be nothing caused, since it is God Himself, as is clear from what has preceded. God's knowledge, therefore, cannot be discursive.

[6]   What is naturally known, furthermore, is known to us without ratiocination. But in God there can be only natural knowledge, indeed, only essential knowledge; for, as was proved above, His knowledge is His essence.[4] God's knowledge, therefore, is not ratiocinative.

[7]   Again, every motion must be reduced to a first mover that is only mover and not moved. That from which the first motion originates, therefore, must be an absolutely unmoved mover. This, as was proved above, is the divine intellect.[5] The divine intellect must, therefore, be an absolutely unmoved mover. But ratiocination is a certain motion of the intellect proceeding from one thing to another. Hence, the divine intellect is not ratiocinative.

1. See above, ch. 46.
2. See above, ch. 16.
3. Aristotle, *Posterior Analytics*, I, 2 (71b 18).
4. See above, ch. 45.
5. See above, ch. 44.

[8]   Then, too, what is highest in us is lower than what is in God, for the lower reaches the higher only in its own highest part. But what is highest in our knowledge is, not reason, but intellect, which is the origin of reason. God's knowledge, then, is not ratiocinative but solely intellectual.

[9]   Moreover, since God is absolutely perfect, as we proved above, every defect must be removed from Him.[6] But ratiocinative knowledge arises from an imperfection in intellectual nature. For that which is known through another is less known than what is known through itself; nor is the nature of the knower sufficient for knowing that which is known through another without that through which it is made known. But in ratiocinative knowledge something is made known through another, whereas that which is known intellectually is known through itself, and the nature of the knower is able to know it without an external means. Hence, it is manifest that reason is a certain defective intellect. Therefore, the divine knowledge is not ratiocinative.

[10]   Furthermore, those things whose species are in the knower are comprehended without discursive reasoning. For the sight does not proceed discursively to know the stone whose likeness it possesses. But the divine essence, as was shown above, is the likeness of all things.[7] Hence, it does not proceed to know something through discursive reasoning.

[11]   The solution of those difficulties that seem to introduce discursiveness into the divine knowledge is likewise at hand. First, because God knows other things through His essence. For it was shown that this does not take place discursively, since God's essence is related to other things, not as a principle to conclusions, but as a species to things known. Secondly, because some might think it unbefitting if God were not able to syllogize. For God possesses the

6. See above, ch. 28.
7. See above, ch. 54.

knowledge of syllogizing as one judging, and not as one proceeding by syllogizing.

[12] To this truth, which has been rationally proved, Sacred Scripture likewise gives witness. For it is written: "All things are naked and open to His sight" (Heb. 4:13). For what we know by reasoning is not through itself naked and revealed to us, but is opened and laid bare by reason.

Chapter 58.

THAT GOD DOES NOT UNDERSTAND BY COMPOSING AND DIVIDING

[1] Through the same means we can also show that the divine intellect does not understand in the manner of a composing and dividing intellect.

[2] For the divine intellect knows all things by knowing its own essence.[1] Now it does not know its own essence by composing and dividing, since it knows itself as it is and there is no composition in it. It does not, therefore, know in the manner of a composing and dividing intellect.

[3] Moreover, what is composed and divided by the intellect is of a nature to be considered separately by it. For there would be no need of composition and division if by apprehending the essence of a thing we grasped what belonged in it and what did not. If, then, God understood in the manner of a composing and dividing intellect, it would follow that He did not consider all things by one intuition but each thing separately. We have shown the contrary of this above.[2]

[4] Furthermore, there can be no before and after in God. But composition and division come after the consid-

1. See above, ch. 46.
2. See above, ch. 55.

eration of the essence, which is their principle. Hence, composition and division cannot be found in the operation of the divine intellect.

[5]   Again, the proper object of the intellect is what a thing is. Hence, in relation to what a thing is the intellect suffers no deception except by accident, whereas as concerns composition and division it is deceived. So, too, a sense dealing with its proper sensibles is always true, but in other cases it is deceived. But in the divine intellect there is nothing accidental, but only that which is substantial. In the divine intellect, therefore, there is no composition and division, but only the simple apprehension of a thing.

[6]   Furthermore, in the case of a proposition formed by a composing and dividing intellect, the composition itself exists in the intellect, not in the thing that is outside the soul. If the divine intellect should judge of things in the manner of a composing and dividing intellect, the intellect itself will be composite. This is impossible, as is clear from what has been said.[3]

[7]   Again, the composing and dividing intellect judges diverse things by diverse compositions, for the composition of the intellect does not exceed the terms of the composition. Hence, the intellect does not judge the triangle to be a figure by the same composition by which it judges man to be an animal. Now, composition or division is a certain operation of the intellect. If, then, God considers things by means of composing and dividing, it will follow that His understanding is not solely one but many. And thus His essence, as well, will not be solely one, since His intellectual operation is His essence, as was proved above.[4]

[8]   But it is not on this account necessary for us to say that God does not know enunciables. For His essence, being one and simple, is the exemplar of all manifold and com-

3. See above, ch. 18.
4. See above, ch. 45

posite things. And thus God knows through His essence all multitude and composition both of nature and of reason.

[9] With these conclusions the authority of Sacred Scripture is in harmony. For it is said in Isaias (55:8): "For My thoughts are not your thoughts." Yet it is said in a Psalm (93:11): "The Lord knoweth the thoughts of men," which thoughts evidently proceed through composition and division in the intellect.

[10] Dionysius likewise says: "Therefore, in knowing itself, the divine wisdom knows all things—the material immaterially, the divisible indivisibly, and the many unitedly."[5]

Chapter 59.

THAT THE TRUTH OF ENUNCIABLES IS NOT EXCLUDED FROM GOD

[1] From this it may be seen that, although the knowledge of the divine intellect is not of the sort belonging to an intellect that composes and divides, truth, which according to the Philosopher is found only in the composition and division of the intellect,[1] is yet not excluded from it.

[2] For, since the truth of the intellect is "the adequation of intellect and thing,"[2] inasmuch as the intellect says that what is is and what is not is not, truth belongs to

5. Pseudo-Dionysius, *De divinis nominibus*, VII, 2 (*PG*, 3, col. 869B).

1. Aristotle, *Metaphysics*, V, 4 (1027b 27); *De anima*, III, 6 (430a 26).

2. The source of this definition of truth, considered to be Isaac's tract on definitions, seems rather to be Avicenna via William of Auvergne. Cf. Avicenna, *Metaphysics*, I, 9 (fol. 74rb) and E. Gilson, *History of Christian Philosophy in the Middle Ages* (New York, 1955), p. 646 (note 26).

that in the intellect which the intellect says, not to the operation by which it says it. For the intellect to be true it is not required that its act of understanding be adequated to the thing known, since the thing is sometimes material whereas the act of understanding is immaterial. Rather, what the intellect in understanding says and knows must be adequated to the thing, so that, namely, the thing be such as the intellect says it to be. Now, by His simple understanding, in which there is no composition and division, God knows not only the quiddities of things but also enunciations, as has been shown. Hence, that which the divine intellect says in understanding is composition and division. Therefore, truth is not excluded from the divine intellect by reason of its simplicity.

[3] When the incomplex is said or understood, the incomplex, of itself, is neither equated to a thing nor unequal to it. For equality and inequality are by relation, whereas the incomplex, of itself, does not imply any relation or application to a thing. Hence, of itself, it can be said to be neither true nor false; but the complex can, in which the relation of the incomplex to a thing is designated by a sign of composition or division. Nevertheless, the incomplex intellect in understanding what a thing is apprehends the quiddity of a thing in a certain relation to the thing, because it apprehends it as the quiddity of that thing. Hence, although the incomplex itself, or even a definition, is not in itself true or false, nevertheless the intellect that apprehends what a thing is is always said to be through itself true, as appears in De anima III;[3] although it can be by accident false, in so far as a definition includes some composition either of the parts of a definition with one another or of the whole definition with the thing defined. Hence, according as the definition is understood to be the definition of this or that thing, as it is received by the intellect, it will be called absolutely false if the parts of the definition do not belong together, as if we should say

3. Aristotle, De anima, III, 6 (430b 27).

insensible animal; or it will be called false with reference to a given thing, as when the definition of a circle is taken as that of a triangle. Given, therefore, by an impossible supposition, that the divine intellect knew only incomplexes, it would still be true in knowing its own quiddity as its own.

[4]   Again, the divine simplicity does not exclude perfection, because it possesses in its simple being whatever of perfection is found in other things through a certain aggregation of perfections or forms, as was shown above.[4] But in apprehending incomplexes, our intellect does not yet reach its ultimate perfection, because it is still in potency to composition or division. So, too, among natural things, the simple are in potency with reference to the mixed, and the parts with reference to the whole. According to His simple understanding, therefore, God has that perfection of knowledge that our intellect has through both knowledges, that of complexes and that of incomplexes. But our intellect reaches truth in its perfect knowledge, that is to say, when it already has arrived at composition. Therefore, in the simple understanding of God as well there is truth.

[5]   Again, since God is the good of every good, as having every goodness in Himself, as has been shown above,[5] the goodness of the intellect cannot be lacking to Him. But the true is the good of the intellect, as appears from the Philosopher.[6] Therefore, truth is in God.

[6]   And this is what is said in a Psalm: "But God is true" (Rom. 3:4).

4. See above, ch. 28 and 31.
5. See above, ch. 40.
6. Aristotle, *Nicomachean Ethics*, VI, 2 (1139a 27).

Chapter 60.

THAT GOD IS TRUTH

[1]   From the foregoing it is evident that God Himself is truth.

[2]   Truth is a certain perfection of understanding or of intellectual operation, as has been said.[1] But the understanding of God is His substance. Furthermore, since this understanding is, as we have shown, the divine being, it is not perfected through any superadded perfection; it is perfect through itself, in the same manner as we have shown of the divine being.[2] It remains, therefore, that the divine substance is truth itself.

[3]   Again, according to the Philosopher, truth is a certain goodness of the intellect.[3] But God is His own goodness, as we have shown above.[4] Therefore, He is likewise His own truth.

[4]   Furthermore, nothing can be said of God by participation, since He is His own being, which participates in nothing. But, as was shown above, there is truth in God.[5] If, then, it is not said by participation, it must be said essentially. Therefore, God is His truth.

[5]   Moreover, although, according to the Philosopher, the true is properly not in things but in the mind,[6] a thing is at times said to be true when it reaches in a proper way the act of its own nature. Hence, Avicenna says in his

1. See above, ch. 59.
2. See above, ch. 45 and 28.
3. Aristotle, Nicomachean Ethics, VI, 2 (1139a 27).
4. See above, ch. 38.
5. See above, ch. 59.
6. Aristotle, Metaphysics, V, 4 (1027b 25).

Metaphysics that "the truth of a thing is the property of the being established in each thing."[7] This is so in so far as each thing is of a nature to give a true account of itself and in so far as it imitates the model of itself which is in the divine mind. But God is His essence. Therefore, whether we speak of the truth of the intellect or of the truth of a thing, God is His truth.

[6] This is confirmed by the authority of our Lord, Who says of Himself: "I am the way, and the truth, and the life" (John 14:6).

Chapter 61.

THAT GOD IS THE PUREST TRUTH

[1] It is clear from this demonstration that in God there is pure truth, with which no falsity or deception can be mingled.

[2] For truth is not compatible with falsity, as neither is whiteness with blackness. But God is not only true, He is truth itself. Therefore, there can be no falsity in Him.

[3] Moreover, the intellect is not deceived in knowing what a thing is, just as the sense is not deceived in its proper sensible. But, as we have shown, all the knowledge of the divine intellect is in the manner of an intellect knowing what a thing is.[1] It is impossible, therefore, that there be error or deception or falsity in the divine knowledge.

[4] Furthermore, the intellect does not err in the case of first principles; it errs at times in the case of conclusions at which it arrives by reasoning from first principles. But the divine intellect, as we have shown above, is not ratio-

7. Avicenna, *Metaphysics*, VIII, 6 (fol. 100ra).
1. See above, ch. 58.

cinative or discursive.[2] Therefore, there cannot be falsity or deception in it.

[5]   Again, the higher a knowing power, so much the more universal is its proper object, containing several objects under it. Thus, that which sight knows by accident the common sense or the imagination apprehends as contained under its proper object. But the power of the divine intellect is at the very peak of elevation in knowing. Hence, all knowable objects are related to it as knowable properly and essentially and not by accident. In such cases, however, the knowing power does not err. Therefore, the divine intellect cannot err in the case of any knowable object.

[6]   Moreover, intellectual virtue is a certain perfection of the intellect in knowing. But according to intellectual virtue no intellect expresses what is false, but always what is true; for to speak the true is the good of the act of the intellect, and it belongs to virtue "to make an act good."[3] But the divine intellect, being at the peak of perfection, is more perfect through its nature than the human intellect is through the habit of virtue. It remains, therefore, that there cannot be falsity in the divine intellect.

[7]   Furthermore, the knowledge of the human intellect is in a manner caused by things. Hence it is that knowable things are the measure of human knowledge; for something that is judged to be so by the intellect is true because it is so in reality, and not conversely. But the divine intellect through its knowledge is the cause of things. Hence, its knowledge is the measure of things, in the same way as an art is the measure of artifacts, each one of which is perfect in so far as it agrees with the art. The divine intellect, therefore, is related to things as things are related to the human intellect. But the falsity that is caused by the lack of equality between the human intellect and a thing is not in reality but in the intellect. If, therefore, there were no

2. See above, ch. 57.
3. Aristotle, *Nicomachean Ethics*, II, 6 (1106a 17).

adequation whatever of the divine intellect to things, the falsity would be found in things and not in the divine intellect. Nevertheless, there is no falsity in things, because, so far as each thing has being, to that extent does it have truth. There is, therefore, no inequality between the divine intellect and things, nor can there be any falsity in the divine intellect.

[8] Again, as the true is the good of the intellect, so the false is its evil.[4] For we naturally seek to know the truth and flee from being deceived by the false. But, as we have proved,[5] there can be no evil in God. Hence, there can be no falsity in Him.

[9] Hence it is written: "But God is true" (Rom. 3:4); and in Numbers (23:19): "God is not a man, that He should lie"; and in John (I, 1:5): "God is light, and in Him there is no darkness."

Chapter 62.

THAT THE DIVINE TRUTH IS THE FIRST AND HIGHEST TRUTH

[1] From what we have shown it clearly results that the divine truth is the first and highest truth.

[2] As is clear from the Philosopher, things are disposed in truth as they are disposed in being. The reason for this is that the true and being follow one another; for the true then exists when that which is is said to be and that which is not is said not to be.[1] But the divine being is first and most perfect. Therefore, its truth is the first and highest truth.

4. Aristotle, *Nicomachean Ethics*, VI, 2 (1139a 27).
5. See above, ch. 39.
1. Aristotle, *Metaphysics*, Iα, 1 (993b 30); IV, 7 (1011b 25).

[3] Again, what belongs to a thing essentially belongs to it most perfectly. But, as we have shown, truth is said of God essentially.[2] Therefore, His truth is the highest and first truth.

[4] Furthermore, there is truth in our intellect because it is adequated to the thing that the intellect understands. But, as can be seen in *Metaphysics* v, unity is the cause of equality.[3] Since, then, in the divine intellect the intellect and that which it understands are absolutely one, its truth is the first and highest truth.

[5] Moreover, that which is the measure in any given genus is most perfect in that genus. That is why all colors are measured by white. But the divine truth is the measure of all truth. For the truth of our intellect is measured by the thing outside the soul, since our intellect is said to be true because it is in agreement with the thing that it knows. On the other hand, the truth of a thing is measured by the divine intellect, which is the cause of things, as will later on be proved.[4] In the same way, the truth of artifacts comes from the art of the artisan, for a chest is then true when it agrees with its art. And since God is the first intellect and the first intelligible, the truth of any given intellect must be measured by the truth of His intellect—if, as the Philosopher teaches, each thing is measured by that which is first in its genus.[5] The divine truth, therefore, is the first, highest, and most perfect truth.

2. See above, ch. 60.
3. Aristotle, *Metaphysics*, V, 15 (1021a 10).
4. *SCG*, II, ch. 24.
5. Aristotle, *Metaphysics*, X, 1 (1052b 25).

Chapter 63.

THE ARGUMENTS OF THOSE WHO WISH TO TAKE AWAY THE KNOWLEDGE OF SINGULARS FROM GOD

[1] Now, there are certain persons who are trying to take away the knowledge of singulars from the perfection of the divine knowledge. They use seven ways to confirm their position.[1]

1. At first glance, *SCG*, I, 63–71, forms a surprising development, since St. Thomas has already dealt in *SCG*, I, 49–59, with the problem of God's knowledge of other things, and especially the problem of a proper knowledge of singulars. In reality, *SCG*, I, 63–71, seems to form an elimination of "contrary errors," as announced in *SCG*, I, 2. Furthermore, the whole development hinges on certain texts of Aristotle, and the consequences drawn from them by Averroes and Avicenna. In *Metaphysics*, XII, 9 (1074b 15–30), and *De anima*, III, 6 (430b 21–26), Aristotle seems to say that a pure intellect does not know anything other than itself: it knows only the noblest object, nothing other than it, nothing lesser or lowly, and nothing evil. Applied to God, this would mean that God knows only Himself. Averroes took Aristotle to mean exactly this in his comments on these Aristotelian texts (see Averroes, *In XII Metaphysicorum*, t.c. 51 [fol. 337ra]; *Commentarium magnum in Aristotelis de anima*, III, t.c. 25 [p. 463, lines 43–48]). In the latter text, Averroes wrote that, if there should be an intellect that was act without potency, "such an intellect will not understand privation at all, indeed, it will not understand any thing outside itself." But Averroes did not say that God does not know things. He rather said (in the *Commentary* on the *Metaphysics*) that God knows things by knowing Himself alone, and to that extent. In his own words, "he who knows only the heat of fire is not said not to know the nature of heat in other hot things; he rather knows the nature of heat as heat".

Avicenna, on the other hand, had taken another line of development. He had said that God understands things universally. He used the analogy of the astronomer to argue that, just as the astronomer can know particulars universally and

[2]   The *first* way is based on the very condition of singularity. For the principle of singularity is designated matter, and hence it seems that singulars cannot be known by any immaterial power, given that all knowledge takes place through a certain assimilation. So, too, in our own case only those powers apprehend singulars that make use of material organs, for example, the imagination, the senses, and the like. But because it is immaterial, our intellect does not know singulars. Much less, therefore, does the divine intellect know singulars, being the most removed from matter. Thus, in no way does it seem that God can know singulars.

[3]   The *second* way is based on the fact that singulars do not always exist. Therefore, either they will be known by God always, or they will be known at some time and not at another. The first alternative is impossible, since of that which does not exist there can be no knowledge; knowledge deals only with what is true, and what does not exist cannot be true. Nor is the second alternative possible,

---

predict them, so God knows particulars universally; neither the astronomer predicting an eclipse nor God knows the concrete singular in itself (see Avicenna, *Metaphysics*, VIII, 6 [foll. 100rb–100va]).

We can follow St. Thomas' reading and use of these texts in his *Commentary on the Sentences* (*In I Sent.*, d. 35 q. 1, a. 3; d. 36, q. 1, a. 1; ed. P. Mandonnet, pp. 816–817, 830–832) and, among other places, in the *Summa Theologiae* (I, 14, 6 and 11; 13, 5). The whole development in *SCG*, I, 63–71, can be seen as an effort to show to and against the philosophers the consequences of saying (as *they*, too, said) that God is Pure Act. The knowledge of such a God is a creative source of things, present to them eternally, immediately and without change, and reaching to the least of them in their minutest detail.

Whether Aristotle can be interpreted as St. Thomas does in *SCG*, I, 63–71, is a delicate historical question. Certainly St. Thomas is flatly opposed to the interpretation of Averroes. What is evident is that Aristotle's God, as interpreted by St. Thomas (*SCG*, I, 70, last ¶), is already capable of becoming the creative providence that St. Thomas makes Him to be.

since, as we have shown, the knowledge of the divine intellect is absolutely unchangeable.[2]

[4] The *third* way is based on the fact that not all singulars come to be of necessity but some happen contingently. Hence, there can be a certain knowledge of them only when they exist. Now, that knowledge is certain which cannot be deceived. But all knowledge of the contingent can be deceived when the contingent is future, since the opposite of what is held by knowledge can happen; for, if it could not happen, it would then be necessary. Hence it is that we cannot have any knowledge of future contingents, but only a certain conjectural estimation. Now, we must suppose that all God's knowledge is, as we have shown, most certain and infallible.[3] And because of His immutability, as we have said, it is impossible for God to begin to know something anew.[4] From all this it seems to follow that God does not know contingent singulars.

[5] The *fourth* way is based on the fact that the will is the cause of some singulars. Before it exists, an effect can be known only in its cause, since, before it begins to be, this is the only way for an effect to exist. But the motions of the will can be known with certitude only by the one willing, in whose power they lie. It seems impossible, therefore, that God should have an eternal knowledge of such singulars as are caused by the will.

[6] The *fifth* way is based on the infinity of singulars. The infinite as such is unknown.[5] Everything that is known is in a manner measured by the comprehension of the knower, since this "measure" is nothing other than a certain certification of the measured thing. That is why every art repudiates the infinite. But singulars are infinite, at least

2. See above, ch. 45.
3. See above, ch. 61.
4. See above, ch. 45.
5. Aristotle, *Physics*, I, 4 (187b 7).

potentially. It seems impossible, then, that God knows singulars.

[7]   The *sixth* way is based on the very lowliness of singulars. Since the dignity of a science is in a way determined from the dignity of its object, the lowliness of the knowable object likewise seems to redound to the lowliness of the science. But the divine intellect is most noble. Its nobility, therefore, forbids that it should know certain of the lowliest among singulars.

[8]   The *seventh* way is based on the evil found in some singulars. For, since that which is known is found in the knower in a certain way, and there can be no evil in God, as was shown above,[6] it seems to follow that God has absolutely no knowledge of evil and privation. This is known only by an intellect that is in potency, for privation can exist only in potency. From this it follows that God has no knowledge of the singulars in which there is evil and privation.

Chapter 64.

THE ORDER OF WHAT IS TO BE SAID ON THE DIVINE KNOWLEDGE

[1]   To remove this error, and likewise to show the perfection of the divine knowledge, we must diligently look into the truth of each of the above ways, so that what is opposed to the truth may be refuted. We shall *first* show, then, that the divine intellect knows singulars. *Second*, we shall show that it knows what does not exist in act. *Third*, that it knows future contingents with an infallible knowledge. *Fourth*, that it knows the motions of the will. *Fifth*, that it knows infinite things. *Sixth*, that it knows every lowly and least thing among beings. *Seventh*, that it knows evils and all privations and defects.

6. See above, ch. 39.

Chapter 65.

THAT GOD KNOWS SINGULARS

[1] We shall therefore first show that the knowledge of singulars cannot be lacking to God.

[2] It was shown above that God knows other things in so far as He is their cause. Now, singular things are God's effects. God causes things in so far as He makes them to be in act. Universals, on the other hand, are not subsisting things, but rather have being only in singulars, as is proved in *Metaphysics* VII.[1] God, therefore, knows things other than Himself, not only universally, but also in the singular.

[3] Again, by knowing the principles of which the essence of a thing is composed, we necessarily know that thing itself. Thus, by knowing a rational soul and a certain sort of body, we know man. Now, the singular essence is composed of designated matter and individuated form. Thus, the essence of Socrates is composed of this body and this soul, just as the universal essence of man is composed of soul and body, as may be seen in *Metaphysics* VII.[2] Hence, just as the latter principles fall within the definition of universal man, so the former principles would fall in the definition of Socrates if he could be defined. Hence, whoever has a knowledge of matter and of what designates matter, and also of form individuated in matter, must have a knowledge of the singular. But the knowledge of God extends to matter and to individuating accidents and forms. For, since His understanding is His essence, He must understand all things that in any way are in His essence. Now, within His essence, as within the first source, there are

1. Aristotle, *Metaphysics*, VII, 13 (1038b 15).—See also above, ch. 49.
2. Aristotle, *Metaphysics*, VII, 10 (1035b 30).

virtually present all things that in any way have being, since He is the first and universal principle of being. Matter and accidents are not absent from among these things, since matter is a being in potency and an accident is a being in another. Therefore, the knowledge of singulars is not lacking to God.

[4] Moreover, the nature of a genus cannot be known perfectly unless its first differences and proper attributes are known. The nature of number would not be known perfectly if the even and the odd were not known. But universal and singular are differences or essential attributes of being. If, then, in knowing His essence God knows perfectly the common nature of being, He must know the universal and the singular perfectly. But, just as He would not know the universal perfectly if He knew the intention of universality and did not know the universal reality, for example, *man* or *animal*, so He would not know the singular perfectly if He knew the nature of singularity and did not know this or that singular. Therefore, God must know singular things.

[5] Furthermore, just as God is His being, so, as we have shown, He is His knowing. Now, since He is His being, all the perfections of being must be found in Him as in the first origin of being, as was shown above.[3] Therefore, there must be found in His knowledge, as in the first source of knowledge, the perfection of all knowledge. But this would not be so if the knowledge of singulars were lacking to Him; for the perfection of some knowers consists in this knowledge. Therefore, it is impossible for God not to have a knowledge of singulars.

[6] Furthermore, among all ordered powers it is commonly found that the higher power, though one, extends to several things, whereas a lower power extends to fewer things and is nevertheless multiplied by its relation to them. This happens in the case of the imagination and the sense.

3. See above, ch. 45 and 28.

The one power of the imagination extends to all the things that the five powers of the senses know, and to more besides. But the knowing power in God is higher than it is in man. Therefore, whatever man knows by means of diverse powers, namely, the intellect, the imagination, and the sense, this God considers by His one simple intellect. God, therefore, knows the singulars that we apprehend by the sense and the imagination.

[7] Moreover, the divine intellect does not gather its knowledge from things, as ours does; rather, as will be shown later on,[4] it is through its knowledge the cause of things. The knowledge that the divine intellect has of other things is after the manner of practical knowledge. Now, practical knowledge is not perfect unless it reaches to singulars. For the end of practical knowledge is operation, which belongs to the domain of singulars. Therefore, the knowledge that God has of other things extends to singulars.

[8] Furthermore, as was shown above, the first movable is moved by a mover moving through intellect and appetite.[5] Now, a mover could not cause motion through his intellect unless he moved the movable in so far as it is of a nature to be moved in place. But this is true of the movable in so far as it is here and now, and consequently in so far as it is singular. Therefore, the intellect that is the mover of the first movable knows the first movable in so far as it is singular. Now, this mover is either held to be God, in which case we have made our point, or it is held to be some being below God. But, if the intellect of such a being can by its power know the singular, which our intellect cannot, all the more will the intellect of God be able to do this.

[9] Again, the agent is more noble than the patient or thing acted upon, as act is more noble than potency. Hence, a form of a lower grade cannot by acting extend its likeness

4. *SCG*, II, ch. 24.
5. See above, ch. 44.

to a higher grade; rather, the higher form by acting can extend its likeness to a lower grade. Thus, from the incorruptible powers of the stars there are produced corruptible forms among sublunary things; but a corruptible power cannot produce an incorruptible form. Now, all knowledge takes place through the assimilation of the knower and the known. There is this difference, however, that the assimilation in human knowledge takes place through the action of sensible things on man's knowing powers, whereas in the case of God's knowledge the assimilation takes place contrariwise through the action of the forms of the divine intellect on the things known. Hence, since the form of the sensible thing is individuated through its materiality, it cannot extend the likeness of its singularity so that it be absolutely immaterial. It can extend its likeness to the level of the powers that use material organs; it reaches the intellect only through the power of the agent intellect in so far as it is completely divested of the conditions of matter. Thus, the likeness of the singularity of a sensible form cannot reach up to the human intellect. But the likeness of a form in the divine intellect, by reaching to the least of things to which its causality reaches, extends to the singularity of the sensible and material form. The divine intellect, therefore, can know singulars, but not the human intellect.

[10]   Then, too, if God does not know singulars which even men know, there would follow the difficulty that the Philosopher raises against Empedocles, namely, that God is the most foolish of beings.[6]

[11]   This truth that we have proved is likewise strengthened by the authority of Sacred Scripture. For it is said in Hebrews (4:13): "Neither is there any creature invisible in His sight." The contrary error likewise is removed by Ecclesiasticus (16:16): "Say not: I shall be hidden from God, and who shall remember me from on high?"

6. Aristotle, De anima, I, 5 (410b 4); Metaphysics, III, 4 (1000b 4).

[12]   It is also clear from what has been said how the objection to the contrary does not conclude properly. For, although that by which the divine intellect understands is immaterial, it is nevertheless the likeness of both form and matter, being the first productive principle of both.

Chapter 66.

THAT GOD KNOWS THE THINGS THAT ARE NOT

[1]   We must next show that the knowledge even of the things that are not is not lacking to God.

[2]   As is clear from what we have said above, the relation of the divine knowledge to the things known is the same as the relation of the things that we know to our knowledge. Now, the relation of a thing known to our knowledge is this, namely, that the known thing can exist without our having a knowledge of it, as Aristotle illustrates of the squaring of a circle;[1] but the converse is not true. The relation of the divine knowledge to other things, therefore, will be such that it can be even of non-existing things.

[3]   Again, the knowledge of the divine intellect is to other things as the knowledge of an artisan to artifacts, since through His knowledge God is the cause of things. Now, the artisan knows through his art even those things that have not yet been fashioned, since the forms of his art flow from his knowledge to external matter for the constitution of the artifacts. Hence, nothing forbids that there be in the knowledge of an artisan forms that have not yet come out of it. Thus, nothing forbids God to have knowledge of the things that are not.

[4]   Furthermore, through His essence God knows things other than Himself in so far as His essence is the likeness of the things that proceed from Him. This is clear from

1. Aristotle, *Categories*, VII (7b 31).

what we have said.[2] But since, as was shown above,[3] the essence of God is of an infinite perfection, whereas every other thing has a limited being and perfection, it is impossible that the universe of things other than God equal the perfection of the divine essence. Hence, its power of representation extends to many more things than to those that are. Therefore, if God knows completely the power and perfection of His essence, His knowledge extends not only to the things that are but also to the things that are not.

[5]   Moreover, by that operation through which it knows what a thing is our intellect can know even those things that do not actually exist. It can comprehend the essence of a lion or a horse even though all such animals were to be destroyed. But the divine intellect knows, in the manner of one knowing what a thing is, not only definitions but also enunciables, as is clear from what we have said.[4] Therefore, it can know even the things that are not.

[6]   Furthermore, an effect can be preknown in its cause even before it exists. Thus, an astronomer preknows a future eclipse from a consideration of the order of the heavenly motions. But God knows all things through a cause; for, by knowing Himself, Who is the cause of other things, He knows other things as His effects, as was shown above.[5] Nothing, therefore, prevents God from knowing even the things that are not.

[7]   Moreover, God's understanding has no succession, as neither does His being. He is therefore an ever-abiding simultaneous whole—which belongs to the nature of eternity. On the other hand, the duration of time is stretched out through the succession of the before and after. Hence, the proportion of eternity to the total duration of time is as the proportion of the indivisible to something continu-

2. See above, ch. 49 and 54.
3. See above, ch. 43.
4. See above, ch. 58 and 59.
5. See above, ch. 49.

ous; not, indeed, of that indivisible that is the terminus of a continuum, which is not present to every part of a continuum (the instant of time bears a likeness to such an indivisible), but of that indivisible which is outside a continuum and which nevertheless co-exists with any given part of a continuum or with a determinate point in the continuum. For, since time lies within motion, eternity, which is completely outside motion, in no way belongs to time. Furthermore, since the being of what is eternal does not pass away, eternity is present in its presentiality to any time or instant of time. We may see an example of sorts in the case of a circle. Let us consider a determined point on the circumference of a circle. Although it is indivisible, it does not co-exist simultaneously with any other point as to position, since it is the order of position that produces the continuity of the circumference. On the other hand, the center of the circle, which is no part of the circumference, is directly opposed to any given determinate point on the circumference. Hence, whatever is found in any part of time co-exists with what is eternal as being present to it, although with respect to some other time it be past or future. Something can be present to what is eternal only by being present to the whole of it, since the eternal does not have the duration of succession. The divine intellect, therefore, sees in the whole of its eternity, as being present to it, whatever takes place through the whole course of time. And yet what takes place in a certain part of time was not always existent. It remains, therefore, that God has a knowledge of those things that according to the march of time do not yet exist.

[8] Through these arguments it appears that God has a knowledge of non-being. But not all non-beings have the same relation to His knowledge. For those things that are not, nor will be, nor ever were, are known by God as possible to His power. Hence, God does not know them as in some way existing in themselves, but as existing only in the divine power. These are said by some to be known by God according to a knowledge of simple understanding. The things

that are present, past, or future to us God knows in His power, in their proper causes, and in themselves. The knowledge of such things is said to be a knowledge of vision. For of the things that for us are not yet God sees not only the being that they have in their causes but also the being that they have in themselves, in so far as His eternity is present in its indivisibility to all time.

[9] Nevertheless, whatever being a thing has God knows through His essence. For His essence can be represented by many things that are not, nor will be, nor ever were. His essence is likewise the likeness of the power of every cause, through which effects pre-exist in their causes. And the being that each thing has in itself comes from the divine essence as from its exemplary source.

[10] Thus, therefore, God knows non-beings in so far as in some way they have being, namely, in His power, or in their causes, or in themselves. This is not incompatible with the nature of knowledge.

[11] The authority of Sacred Scripture likewise offers witness to what has preceded. For it is said in Ecclesiasticus (23:29): "For all things were known to the Lord God before they were created: so also after they were perfected He beholdeth all things." And in Jeremias (1:5): "Before I formed thee in the bowels of thy mother I knew thee."

[12] It is also clear from what has preceded that we are not forced to say, as some said,[6] that God knows singulars universally because He knows them only in universal causes, just as one would know a particular eclipse not in itself but as it arises from the position of the stars. For we have shown that the divine knowledge extends to singulars in so far as they are in themselves.

6. The reference is to Avicenna. See above, ch. 63, note 1.

Chapter 67.

THAT GOD KNOWS FUTURE CONTINGENT SINGULARS

[1] From this we can begin to understand somewhat that God had from eternity an infallible knowledge of contingent singulars, and yet they do not cease to be contingent.

[2] The contingent is opposed to the certitude of knowledge only so far as it is future, not so far as it is present. For when the contingent is future, it can not-be. Thus, the knowledge of one conjecturing that it will be can be mistaken: it will be mistaken if what he conjectures as future will not take place. But in so far as the contingent is present, in that time it cannot not-be. It can not-be in the future, but this affects the contingent not so far as it is present but so far as it is future. Thus, nothing is lost to the certitude of sense when someone sees a man running, even though this judgment is contingent. All knowledge, therefore, that bears on something contingent as present can be certain. But the vision of the divine intellect from all eternity is directed to each of the things that take place in the course of time, in so far as it is present, as shown above.[1] It remains, therefore, that nothing prevents God from having from all eternity an infallible knowledge of contingents.

[3] Again, the contingent differs from the necessary according to the way each of them is found in its cause. The contingent is in its cause in such a way that it can both not-be and be from it; but the necessary can only be from its cause. But according to the way both of them are in themselves, they do not differ as to being, upon which the

1. See above, ch. 66.

true is founded. For, according as it is in itself, the contingent cannot be and not-be, it can only be, even though in the future it can not-be. Now, the divine intellect from all eternity knows things not only according to the being that they have in their causes, but also according to the being that they have in themselves. Therefore, nothing prevents the divine intellect from having an eternal and infallible knowledge of contingents.

[4]   Moreover, just as from a necessary cause an effect follows with certitude, so it follows from a complete contingent cause if it be not impeded. But since, as appears from what was said above,[2] God knows all things, He knows not only the causes of contingent things but also those things by which these causes may be impeded. Therefore, He knows with certitude whether contingent things are or are not.

[5]   Furthermore, an effect cannot exceed the perfection of its cause, though sometime it falls short of it. Hence, since our knowledge comes to us from things, it happens at times that we know what is necessary not according to the mode of necessity but according to that of probability. Now, just as in us things are the cause of knowledge, so the divine knowledge is the cause of the things known. Therefore, nothing prevents those things from being contingent in themselves of which God has a necessary knowledge.

[6]   Again, an effect whose cause is contingent cannot be a necessary one; otherwise, the effect could be even though the cause were removed. Now, of the most remote effect there is both a proximate and a remote cause. If, then, the proximate cause were contingent, its effect would have to be contingent even though the remote cause is necessary. Thus, plants do not bear fruit of necessity, even though the motion of the sun is necessary, because the intermediate causes are contingent. But the knowledge of God, though it is the cause of the things known through it, is yet a

2. See above, ch. 50.

remote cause. Therefore, the contingency of the things known is not in conflict with this necessity, since it may be that the intermediate causes are contingent.

[7] The knowledge of God, furthermore, would not be true and perfect if things did not happen in the way in which God knows them to happen. Now, since God knows all being, and is its source, He knows every effect not only in itself but also in its order to each of its causes. But the order of contingent things to their proximate causes is that they come forth from these causes in a contingent way. Hence, God knows that some things are taking place, and this contingently. Thus, therefore, the certitude and truth of the divine knowledge does not remove the contingency of things.

[8] From what has been said, it is therefore clear how the objection impugning a knowledge of contingents in God is to be repulsed. For change in that which comes later does not induce change in that which has preceded; for it is possible that from prime necessary causes there proceed ultimate contingent effects. Now, the things that are known by God are not prior to His knowledge, as is the case with us, but, rather, subsequent to it. It does not therefore follow that, if something known by God can change, His knowledge of it can be deceived or in any way changed. We shall be deceived in the consequent therefore, if, because our knowledge of changeable things is itself changeable, we suppose on this account that such is necessarily the case in all knowledge.

[9] Again, when it is said that *God knows* or *knew this future thing*, a certain intermediate point between the divine knowledge and the thing known is assumed. This is the time when the above words are spoken, in relation to which time that which is known by God is said to be future. But this is not future with reference to the divine knowledge, which, abiding in the moment of eternity, is related to all things as present to them. If with respect to

the divine knowledge we remove from its intermediate position the time when the words are spoken, we cannot say that this is known by God as non-existent, so as to leave room for the question whether it can not-be; rather, it will be said to be known by God in such a way that it is seen by Him already in its own existence. On this basis there is no room for the preceding question. For that which already is cannot, with respect to that moment of time, not-be. We are therefore deceived by the fact that the time in which we are speaking is present to eternity, as is likewise past time (designated by the words *God knew*). Hence, the relation of past or present time to the future is attributed to eternity, to which such a relation does not belong. It is thus that we commit the fallacy of accident.

[10]   There is more. If each thing is known by God as seen by Him in the present, what is known by God will then have to be. Thus, it is necessary that Socrates be seated from the fact that he is seen seated. But this is not absolutely necessary or, as some say, with the *necessity of the consequent*; it is necessary conditionally, or with the *necessity of the consequence*. For this is a necessary conditional proposition: *if he is seen sitting, he is sitting*. Hence, although the conditional proposition may be changed to a categorical one, to read *what is seen sitting must necessarily be sitting*, it is clear that the proposition is true if understood of what is said, and compositely; but it is false if understood of what is meant, and dividedly. Thus, in these and all similar arguments used by those who oppose God's knowledge of contingents, the fallacy of composition and division takes place.

[11]   That God knows future contingents is also shown by the authority of Sacred Scripture. For it is said of the divine wisdom: "She knoweth signs and wonders before they be done, and the events of times and ages" (Wis. 8:8). And in Ecclesiasticus (39:24–25) it is said: "There is nothing hid from His eyes. He seeth from eternity to

eternity." And in Isaias (48:5): "I foretold thee of old, before they came to pass I told thee."

Chapter 68.

THAT GOD KNOWS THE MOTIONS OF THE WILL

[1] We must now show that God knows the thoughts of the mind and the motions of the will.

[2] As was shown above, whatever in any way exists is known by God in so far as He knows His own essence.[1] There is a certain being in the soul and a certain being in things outside the soul. God, therefore, knows all these differences of being and what is contained under them. But the being that is in the soul is that which is in the will or in thought. It remains, therefore, that God knows that which is in thought and in the will.

[3] Moreover, in knowing His essence, God knows other things in the same way as an effect is known through a knowledge of the cause. By knowing His essence, therefore, God knows all things to which His causality extends. But it extends to the operations of the intellect and the will. For, since each thing acts through its form, from which the thing has a certain being, so the fount and source of all being, from which is also every form, must be the source of all operation; for the effects of second causes are grounded more principally in first causes. Therefore, God knows the thoughts and affections of the mind.

[4] Again, just as God's being is prime and for this reason the cause of all being, so His understanding is prime and on this account the cause of all intellectual operation. Hence, just as God, by knowing His being knows the being of each thing, so by knowing His understanding and willing He knows every thought and will.

1. See above, ch. 49 and 50.

[5]   Moreover, as is clear from what was said above,[2] God knows things not only so far as they are in themselves, but also so far as they are in their causes; for He knows the order of a cause to its effect. But artifacts are in artisans through their intellect and will, just as natural things are in their causes through the powers of these causes. For just as natural things through their active powers assimilate their effects to themselves, so an artisan through his intellect induces into the artifact the form through which it is assimilated to his art. The situation is the same for all things that proceed intentionally from an agent. Therefore, God knows the thoughts and affections of the mind.

[6]   Again, God knows intelligible substances no less than He knows or we know sensible substances; for intellectual substances are more knowable, since they are in act. Now, both God and we know how sensible substances are informed and inclined. Since, then, the soul's thinking is a certain information of the soul itself and its affection is a certain inclination of the soul towards something (so, too, we likewise call the inclination of a natural thing a natural appetite), it remains that God knows the thoughts and affections of the mind.

[7]   This is confirmed by the testimony of Sacred Scripture. For it is said in a Psalm (7:10): "The searcher of hearts and reins is God." And in the Proverbs (15:11): "Hell and destruction are before the Lord: how much more the hearts of the children of men?" And John (2:25): "He knew what was in man."

[8]   As for the dominion that the will has over its acts, through which it lies in the power of the will to will or not to will, this excludes the determination of the power to one effect and any violence from a cause acting from the outside; but it does not exclude the influence of a higher cause from which come its being and operation. Thus, the causality in the first cause, which is God, is not removed

2. See above, ch. 66.

with respect to the motions of the will. Hence, God, by knowing Himself, can know such motions.

Chapter 69.

THAT GOD KNOWS INFINITE THINGS

[1] After this we must show that God knows infinite things.

[2] By knowing Himself to be the cause of things God knows things other than Himself, as is clear from the above.[1] But God is the cause of infinite things, if there are infinite things, since He is the cause of all things that are. Therefore, God knows infinite things.

[3] Again, as is clear from what we have said, God knows His own power perfectly.[2] But a power cannot be known perfectly unless all that it can do is known, since this is how the magnitude of a power is in a manner gauged. But since, as was shown above,[3] His power is infinite, it extends to infinite things. Therefore, God knows infinite things.

[4] Moreover, if the knowledge of God extends to all things that in any way are, as was shown,[4] He must know not only that which is actual but also that which is potential. But among natural things there is the infinite in potency, though not in act, as the Philosopher proves in *Physics* III.[5] God, therefore, knows infinite things. So, too, unity, which is the source of number, would know the infinite species of number if it knew whatever was in it potentially; for unity is potentially every number.

1. See above, ch. 49.
2. *Ibid.*
3. See above, ch. 43.
4. See above, ch. 50, ¶2.
5. Aristotle, *Physics*, III, 6 (206b 12).

[5]   Furthermore, God knows other things by His essence as through a certain exemplary means. But, since His essence is of an infinite perfection, as was shown above,[6] an infinite number of things having finite perfections can be derived from it. For no one thing or any number of things copied from the divine essence can equal the perfection of their cause. There thus always remains a new way in which some copy is able to imitate the divine essence. Hence, nothing prevents God from knowing infinite things through His essence.

[6]   Besides, God's being is His understanding. Hence, just as His being is infinite, as we have shown,[7] so His understanding is infinite. But as the finite is to the finite, so the infinite is to the infinite. If, then, we are able to grasp finite things according to our understanding, which is finite, so God according to His understanding can grasp infinite things.

[7]   Moreover, the intellect that knows the greatest intelligible, all the more, rather than less, knows lesser intelligibles, as is clear from the Philosopher in De anima III.[8] This arises because the intellect is not corrupted by an excelling intelligible, as is the sense, but is rather perfected by it. Now, let us take infinite things, whether of the same species (for example, an infinite number of men) or of infinite species, and let us even assume that some or all of them were infinite in quantity, were this possible—the universe of these things would be of a lesser infinity than is God. For each of them, and all of them together, would have a being that is received and limited to a given species or genus and would thus be finite in some respect. Hence, it would fall short of the infinity of God, Who is absolutely infinite, as was shown above.[9] Therefore, since God knows

6. See above, ch. 43.
7. See above, ch. 45 and 43.
8. Aristotle, De anima, III, 4 (429b 3).
9. See above, ch. 43.

Himself perfectly, nothing prevents Him from also knowing that sum of infinite things.

[8] Again, the more an intellect is more efficacious and penetrating in knowing, the more it can know many things through one means. So, too, every power is more united the more strong it is. But the divine intellect, as is clear from the above, is infinite in power or in perfection.[10] Therefore, it can know infinite things through one means, namely, the divine essence.

[9] Moreover, the divine intellect, like the divine essence, is absolutely perfect. Hence, no intelligible perfection is lacking to it. But that to which our own intellect is in potency is its intelligible perfection. Now, our intellect is in potency to all intelligible species. But such species are infinite, since the species of both numbers and figures are infinite. It remains, then, that God knows all such infinites.

[10] Again, since our intellect can know infinite things in potency, being able to multiply the species of numbers infinitely, if the divine intellect did not know infinite things also in act, it would follow either that the human intellect knew more than did the divine intellect, or that the divine intellect did not know in act all the things that it knew in potency. Both alternatives are impossible, as appears from what was said above.[11]

[11] Again, the infinite cannot be known in so far as it cannot be numbered, for it is in itself impossible to number the parts of the infinite, as implying a contradiction. But to know something by the numbering of its parts belongs to an intellect that knows one part after the other; it does not belong to an intellect that comprehends the diverse parts together. Therefore, since the divine intellect knows all things together without succession, it is no more prevented from knowing infinite things than from knowing finite things.

10. See above, ch. 45.
11. See above, ch. 16 and 29.

[12]   Moreover, all quantity consists in a certain multiplication of parts, and this is why number is the first of quantities. Where, therefore, plurality does not bring about any difference, there neither does anything that follows quantity bring about any difference. Now, in the case of God's knowledge, many things are known as one, since they are known not through diverse species but through one species, namely, the divine essence. Hence, many things are also known together by God, so that in this way plurality introduces no difference in the divine knowledge. Neither, therefore, does the infinite that accompanies quantity. Hence, to know infinite and finite objects makes no difference to the divine intellect. Thus, since God knows finite things, nothing prevents Him from also knowing infinite things.

[13]   What is said in a Psalm (146:5) agrees with this: "And of His wisdom there is no number."

[14]   Now, from what has been said it is evident why our intellect does not know the infinite, as does the divine intellect. For our intellect is distinguished from the divine intellect on four points which bring about this difference. The first point is that our intellect is absolutely finite whereas the divine intellect is infinite. The second point is that our intellect knows diverse things through diverse species. This means that it does not extend to infinite things through one act of knowledge as does the divine intellect. The third point follows from the second. Since our intellect knows diverse things through diverse species it cannot know many things at one and the same time. Hence, it can know infinite things only successively by numbering them. This is not the case with the divine intellect which sees many things together as grasped through one species. The fourth point is that the divine intellect knows both the things that are and the things that are not, as has been shown.[12]

12. See above, ch. 66.

[15] It is likewise evident how the statement of Aristotle, who says that the infinite as infinite is unknown, is not opposed to the present conclusion. For, since the nature of the infinite belongs to quantity, as he himself says,[13] the infinite as infinite would be known if it were known through the measurement of its parts, for this is the proper knowledge of quantity. But God does not know in this way. God, therefore, so to speak, does not know the infinite in so far as it is infinite, but, as we have shown, in so far as it is related to His knowledge as though it were something finite.

[16] It must be observed, however, that God does not know infinite things with the *knowledge of vision*, to make use of an expression employed by others. For there neither are nor have been nor will be infinite things in act, since, according to the Catholic faith, generation is not infinite at either end. But God knows the infinite with *the knowledge of simple understanding*. For He knows the infinite things which neither are nor will be nor have been, which yet lie in the potency of the creation. God likewise knows the infinite things that are in His power, which neither are nor will be nor have been.

[17] Hence, as concerns the question of the knowledge of singulars, we may reply by denying the major. There are not infinite singulars. However, if there were, God would still know them.

Chapter 70.

THAT GOD KNOWS LOWLY THINGS

[1] Having achieved this conclusion, we must show that God knows lowly things, and that this is not opposed to the nobility of His knowledge.

13. Aristotle, *Physics*, I, 4 (187b 7).

[2]   The stronger a given active power is, the more does its action extend to more remote effects. This is also evident in the actions of sensible things. Now, the power of the divine intellect in knowing things is like an active power. For God knows things not by receiving anything from them, but, rather, by exercising His causality on them. Hence, since God is of an infinite power in understanding, as is clear from what has preceded,[1] His knowledge must extend even to the most remote things. But the gradation of nobility and lowliness among all things is measured according to their nearness to and distance from God, Who is at the peak of nobility. Therefore, because of the perfect power of His intellect, God knows the lowliest possible among beings.

[3]   Furthermore, everything that is, in that it is or in what it is, is in act and the likeness of the first act, and on this account has nobility. Whatever is in potency likewise participates in nobility from its order to act; for it is thus that it is said to be. It remains, then, that, considered in itself, each thing is noble, but is called lowly with respect to something more noble. Now, the most noble of creatures are no less distant from God than the lowest of creatures are distant from the highest. Hence, if this distance prevented God from knowing them, all the more would the previous distance. It would thus follow that God did not know anything other than Himself. This was disproved above.[2] If, then, God knows something other than Himself, however supreme in nobility it may be, by the same reason He knows anything whatever, however exceedingly lowly it may be called.

[4]   Moreover, the good of the order of the universe is more noble than any part of the universe, since the individual parts are ordered, as to an end, to the good of the order that is in the whole. This is evident from the Philos-

1. See above, ch. 45.
2. See above, ch. 49.

opher in *Metaphysics* XI.[3] Hence, if God knows some other noble nature, He especially knows the order of the universe. But this order cannot be known without a knowledge both of the things that are more noble and of the things that are more lowly, in whose distances and relations the order of the universe consists. It remains, therefore, that God knows not only noble things but also the things that are deemed lowly.

[5] Again, the lowliness of the things known does not of itself redound to the knower. For it belongs to the nature of knowledge that the knower should contain the species of the thing known according to his own manner. Accidentally, however, the lowliness of the things known can redound to the knower. This may be either because, while he is considering lowly things, his mind is turned away from thinking of more noble things; or it may be because, as a result of considering lowly things, he is inclined towards certain unbefitting affections. This, however, is not possible in God, as is clear from what has been said.[4] The knowledge of lowly things, therefore, does not detract from the divine nobility, but rather belongs to the divine perfection according as it precontains all things in itself, as was shown above.[5]

[6] Furthermore, a power is not judged to be small because it can do small things but because it is limited to small things; for a power that can do great things can likewise do small ones. Hence, a knowledge that extends at the same time to both noble and lowly things is not to be judged as being lowly; rather, that knowledge is to be judged lowly which extends only to lowly things, as happens in our own case. For we examine divine and human things by different considerations, and the knowledge of the one is not the knowledge of the other, so that by comparison with the more noble knowledge the lower

3. Aristotle, *Metaphysics*, XII, 10 (1075a 13).
4. See above, ch. 39 and 55.
5. See above, ch. 28 and 29.

knowledge is deemed to be lowlier. But it is not thus in God. By one and the same knowledge and consideration He considers both Himself and all other things. No lowliness, therefore, is ascribed to His knowledge from the fact that He knows any lowly things whatever.

[7]   What is said of the divine wisdom is in harmony with this conclusion. Wisdom "reacheth everywhere by reason of her purity . . . and therefore no defiled thing cometh into her" (Wis. 7:24–25).

[8]   Now, from what has been said it is evident that the argument advanced on the opposite side is not opposed to the truth we have shown. For the nobility of knowledge is measured in terms of those things to which knowledge is principally directed, and not in terms of all the things that fall within knowledge. For in the most noble among the knowledges that we have there are included not only the highest beings but also the lowest. For first philosophy extends its consideration from the first being to being in potency, which is the lowest being. Thus, under divine science are included the lowest of beings as being known along with its principal object. For the divine essence is the principal object known by God and in this object, as was shown above, all others are known.[6]

[9]   It is also evident that this truth is not opposed to what the Philosopher says in *Metaphysics* xi.[7] Aristotle there intends to show that the divine intellect does not know anything other than itself that is its perfection in the sense of being its principal known object. In this sense he says that it is better not to know lowly things than to know them. This is the case, namely, when the knowledge of the lowly is different from the knowledge of the noble and the consideration of lowly things impedes the consideration of noble things.

6. See above, ch. 48 and 49.
7. Aristotle, *Metaphysics*, XII, 9 (1074b 25).

Chapter 71.

THAT GOD KNOWS EVILS

[1]   It now remains to show that God likewise knows evils.

[2]   When a good is known, the opposite evil is known. But God knows all particular goods, to which evils are opposed. Therefore, God knows evils.

[3]   Furthermore, the notions of contraries are themselves not contraries in the soul; otherwise, they would not be in the soul together nor would they be known together. The notion, therefore, by which evil is known is not opposed to the good but belongs, rather, to the notion of the good. Hence, if all the notions of goodness are found in God because of His absolute perfection, as was proved above,[1] it follows that there is in Him the notion by which evil is known. And thus God also knows evils.

[4]   Again, the true is the good of the intellect.[2] For an intellect is said to be good because it knows the true. But it is true not only that the good is good but also that evil is evil; for just as it is true that that which is is, so it is true that that which is not is not. The good of the intellect, therefore, also consists in the knowledge of evil. But, since the divine intellect is perfect in goodness, no intellectual perfection can be lacking to it. Therefore, it has a knowledge of evils.

[5]   Moreover, as was shown above,[3] God knows the distinction of things. But negation is found within the notion of distinction; for those things are distinct of which one is not the other. Hence, the first notions, which are

1. See above, ch. 40.
2. Aristotle, *Nicomachean Ethics*, VI, 2 (1139a 27).
3. See above, ch. 50.

distinguished by themselves, mutually include a negation of one another. That is why the negative propositions among them are immediate: for example, *no quantity is a substance*. God, therefore, knows negation. But privation is a certain negation in a determinate subject, as is shown in *Metaphysics* IV.[4] God, therefore, knows privation. Consequently, He knows evil, which is nothing other than the privation of a due perfection.

[6]   Furthermore, if God knows all the species of things, as was proved above,[5] and is likewise conceded and proved by certain philosophers, He must know contraries. This is so because the species of certain genera are contraries and also because the differences of genera are contraries, as is proved in *Metaphysics* X.[6] But between contraries there is included the opposition of form and privation, as is said in the same reference.[7] Therefore, God must know privation and consequently evil.

[7]   Again, as was shown above,[8] God knows not only form but also matter. But, since matter is a being in potency, it cannot be known perfectly unless those things to which its potency extends are known. This is the case with all other potencies. Now, the potency of matter extends both to form and to privation, since that which can be can also not-be. Therefore, God knows privation, and consequently He knows evil.

[8]   Again, if God knows something other than Himself, He especially knows that which is the best. This is the order of the universe to which, as to the end, all particular goods are ordered. But in the order of the universe certain things exist to ward off dangers that may come about from certain other things. This is clear from what is given to animals

4. Aristotle, *Metaphysics*, IV, 2 (1004a 16).
5. See above, ch. 50.
6. Aristotle, *Metaphysics*, X, 8 (1057b 37).
7. Aristotle, *Metaphysics*, X, 4 (1055a 33).
8. See above, ch. 65.

for their own protection. Therefore, God knows such dangers. Hence, He knows evils.

[9] Furthermore, in our own case the knowledge of evil is not considered blameworthy according to that which essentially belongs to knowledge, namely, the judgment that we have of evil things. But it is considered blameworthy by accident, in so far as through the consideration of evil one is sometimes inclined to evil things. This is not the case in God, because, as was shown above,[9] He is immutable. Nothing, therefore, prevents God from knowing evils.

[10] What is said in Wisdom (7:30) harmonizes with this conclusion: "No evil can overcome" the "wisdom" of God. And in Proverbs (15:11) it is said: "Hell and destruction are before the Lord." And in the Psalm (68:6): "My offenses are not hidden from Thee." And in Job (11:11) it is said: "For He knoweth the vanity of men, and when He seeth iniquity, doth He not consider it?"

[11] We must observe, however, that on the knowledge of evil and privation the divine intellect and our own are differently disposed. For, since our intellect knows singular things through singular species that are proper and diverse, that which it is in act it knows through an intelligible species through which it is made an intellect in act. Hence, it can also know potency in so far as it is sometimes in potency to such a species; so that just as it knows act through act, so likewise it knows potency through potency. And because potency belongs to the nature of privation, since privation is a negation whose subject is a being in potency, it follows that it is suitable to our intellect in a certain manner to know privation in so far as it is of a nature to be in potency. Nevertheless, it can also be said that the knowledge of potency and privation follows from the knowledge of act.

9. See above, ch. 13, ¶28.

[12]   The divine intellect, on the other hand, which is in no way in potency, does not know privation or anything else in the above given way. For, if it knew something through a species that is not itself, it would necessarily follow that its proportion to that species would be as the proportion of potency to act. God must therefore understand solely through the species that is His own essence. It follows, consequently, that He understands only Himself as the first object of His intellect. But in understanding Himself He understands other things, as was proved above.[10] And He knows not only acts, but also potencies and privations.

[13]   This is the meaning of the words that the Philosopher sets down in De anima III, when he says: "How does it apprehend evil or something black? For in a manner it knows contraries. But the knower must be potentially what it knows and this must be in it. But, if no contrary is present to a certain knower"—that is, in potency—"this knower knows itself and is in act and separable."[11] Nor must we adopt the interpretation of Averroes, who takes the position that it follows from this text that the intellect that is solely in act in no way knows privation.[12] Rather, the sense is that it does not know privation by the fact of being in potency to something else; it knows privation because it knows itself and is always in act.

[14]   Moreover, we must observe that, if God knew Himself in such a way that, by knowing Himself, He did not know other beings, which are particular goods, then in no way would He know privation and evil. For to the good that He is there is no contrary privation, since privation and its opposite bear on the same thing, and thus to that which is pure act no privation is opposed. And, consequently,

10. See above, ch. 49.
11. Aristotle, De anima, III, 6 (430b 22).
12. Averroes, Commentarium magnum in Aristotelis de anima, III, t.c. 25 (p. 473, lines 43–48). The following paragraph of the text is likewise against Averroes.

neither is evil. Hence, granted that God knows only Himself, by knowing the good that He is He will not know evil. But because, in knowing Himself, He knows the beings that are by nature subject to privations, He must know the privations and the evils that are opposed to particular goods.

[15] We must likewise observe, as was shown above,[13] that just as God in knowing Himself knows other things without any discursiveness of the intellect, so likewise it is not necessary that His knowledge be discursive if He knows the evil through the good. For the good is as the principle of the knowledge of what is evil. Hence, evils are known through goods as things are known through their definitions, not as conclusions are known through their principles.

[16] Nor, again, does it mean that there is imperfection in the divine knowledge if God knows evils through the privation of goods. For the position says that evil exists only in so far as it is the privation of good. Hence, in this way alone is it knowable, for each thing is knowable to the extent that it has being.

Chapter 72.

THAT GOD HAS WILL

[1] Having dealt with what concerns the knowledge of the divine intellect, it remains for us to deal with God's will.

[2] From the fact that God is endowed with intellect it follows that He is endowed with will. For, since the understood good is the proper object of the will, the understood good is, as such, willed. Now that which is understood is by reference to one who understands. Hence, he who

13. See above, ch. 57.

grasps the good by his intellect is, as such, endowed with
will. But God grasps the good by His intellect. For, since
the activity of His intellect is perfect, as appears from what
has been said,[1] He understands being together with the
qualification of the good. He is, therefore, endowed with
will.

[3] Again, whoever possesses some form is related through
that form to things in reality. For example, white wood
is through its whiteness like some things and unlike
other things. But in one understanding and sensing there
is the form of the understood and sensed thing, since all
knowledge is through some likeness. There must, therefore,
be a relation of the one understanding and sensing to understood and sensed things according as these are in reality.
But this is not because of the fact that these beings understand and sense, since thereby we rather find a relation
of things to the one understanding and sensing; for to
understand and to sense exist according as things are in the
intellect and the sense, following the mode of each. He
who senses and understands has a relation to the thing
outside the soul through his will and appetite. Hence, all
sensing and understanding beings have appetite and will.
Properly speaking, however, the will is in the intellect.
Since, then, God is intelligent, He must be endowed with
will.

[4] Moreover, that which accompanies every being belongs to being inasmuch as it is in being. This accompani-
ment must be found in a supreme way in that which is
the first being. Now, it belongs to every being to seek its
perfection and the conservation of its being, and this in
the case of each being according to its mode: for intellectual beings through will, for animals through sensible appetite, and to those lacking sense through natural appetite.
To seek perfection belongs differently to those that have
it and those that have it not. For those that have it not
tend by desire, through the appetitive power proper to

1. See above, ch. 44 and 45.

them, to acquire what is lacking to their desire, whereas those that have it rest in it. Hence, this cannot be lacking to the first being, which is God. Since, then, God is intelligent, there is in Him a will by which His being and His goodness are pleasing to Him.

[5] Again, the more perfect understanding is, the more delightful it is to the one understanding. But God understands and His understanding is most perfect, as was shown above.[2] Therefore, His understanding is most full of delight. But intelligible delight is through the will, as sensible delight is through the appetite of concupiscence. There is, therefore, will in God.

[6] Furthermore, a form considered by the intellect does not move or cause anything except through the will, whose object is the end and the good, by which someone is moved to act. Hence, the speculative intellect does not move, nor does the imagination alone without an act of the estimative power. But the form of the divine intellect is the cause of motion and being in other things, since God produces things by His intellect, as will be shown later on.[3] Therefore, God must be endowed with will.

[7] Again, among moving powers in beings possessing an intellect, the first is found to be the will. For the will sets every power to its act: we understand because we will, we imagine because we will, and so with the rest. The will has this role because its object is the end; although it is also a fact that the intellect, though not in the manner of an efficient and moving cause, but in that of a final cause, moves the will by proposing to it its object, namely, the end. It therefore belongs supremely to the first mover to have a will.

[8] Furthermore, "that is free which is for its own sake,"[4] and thus the free has the nature of that which is through

2. *Ibid.*
3. *SCG*, II, ch. 24.
4. Aristotle, *Metaphysics*, I, 2 (982b 26).

itself. Now, first and primarily, will has liberty in acting, for according as someone acts voluntarily he is said to perform any given action freely. To act through will, therefore, supremely befits the first agent, whom it supremely befits to act through himself.

[9]   Moreover, the end and the agent to the end are always found to be of one order in reality; and hence the proximate end that is proportioned to an agent falls into the same species as the agent both among natural things and artificial things. For the form of the art through which the artisan works is the species of the form that is in matter, which is the end of the artisan; and the form by which the generating fire acts is of the same species as the form of the generated fire, which is the end of generation. But nothing is co-ordered with God, as within the same order, except Himself; otherwise, there would be several first beings—whose contrary was proved above.[5] He is therefore the first agent because of the end that He is Himself. He is therefore not only the appetible end, but also the seeker of Himself as the end, so to speak. And this He is with an intellectual appetite, since He is intelligent. This is will. There is, therefore, will in God.

[10]   The testimony of Sacred Scripture is witness to the divine will. For it is said in a Psalm (134:6): "Whatsoever the Lord pleased He hath done." And Romans (9:19): "Who resisteth His will?"

Chapter 73.

THAT THE WILL OF GOD IS HIS ESSENCE

[1]   From this it appears that God's will is not other than His essence.

5. See above, ch. 42.

[2]   It belongs to God to be endowed with will in so far as He is intelligent, as has been shown.[1] But God has understanding by His essence, as was proved above.[2] So, therefore, does He have will. God's will, therefore, is His very essence.

[3]   Again, as to understand is the perfection of the one understanding, so to will is the perfection of the one willing; for both are actions remaining in the agent and not going out (as does heat) to some receiving subject. But the understanding of God is His being, as was proved above.[3] For, since the divine being is in itself most perfect, it admits of no superadded perfection, as was proved above.[4] The divine willing also is, therefore, His being; and hence the will of God is His essence.

[4]   Moreover, since every agent acts in so far as it is in act, God, Who is pure act, must act through His essence. Willing, however, is a certain operation of God. Therefore, God must be endowed with will through His essence. Therefore, His will is His essence.

[5]   Furthermore, if will were something added to the divine substance, since the divine substance is something complete in being it would follow that will would be added to it as an accident to a subject, that the divine substance would be related to it as potency to act, and that there would be composition in God. All this was refuted above.[5] Hence, it is not possible that the divine will be something added to the divine substance.

1. See above, ch. 72.
2. See above, ch. 45 and 46.
3. See above, ch. 45.
4. See above, ch. 23 and 28.
5. See above, ch. 16, 18, and 23.

Chapter 74.

THAT THE PRINCIPAL OBJECT OF THE DIVINE WILL IS THE DIVINE ESSENCE

[1]   From this it further appears that the principal object of the divine will is the divine essence.

[2]   The understood good is the object of the will, as has been said.[1] But that which is principally understood by God is the divine essence, as was proved above.[2] The divine essence, therefore, is principally the object of the divine will.

[3]   Again, the appetible is to appetite as the mover to the moved, as was said above.[3] Similar, too, is the relation of the object of the will to the will, since the will belongs to the class of appetitive powers. If, then, the principal object of the divine will be other than the divine essence, it will follow that there is something higher than the divine will moving it. The contrary of this is apparent from what has been said.[4]

[4]   Moreover, the principal object willed is for each one willing the cause of his willing. For when we say, *I will to walk in order to become healed*, we are of the impression that we are assigning a cause. If, then, it be asked, *why do you want to become healed?* causes will be assigned one after the other until we arrive at the ultimate end. This is the principal object of the will, which is through itself the cause of willing. If, then, God should principally will something other than Himself, it will follow that something

1. See above, ch. 72.
2. See above, ch. 48.
3. See above, ch. 44.
4. See above, ch. 73.

other is the cause of His willing. But His willing is His being, as has been shown.[5] Hence, something other will be the cause of His being—which is contrary to the nature of the first being.

[5] Furthermore, for each being endowed with a will the principal object willed is the ultimate end. For the end is willed through itself, and through it other things become objects of will. But the ultimate end is God Himself, since He is the highest good, as has been shown.[6] Therefore, God is the principal object of His will.

[6] Moreover, every power is proportioned with equality to its principal object, for the power of a thing is measured according to its objects, as may be seen through the Philosopher in *De caelo et mundo* 1.[7] But the will is proportioned with equality to its principal object, and similarly the intellect and likewise the sense. Now, nothing is proportioned with equality to the divine will save only God's essence. Therefore, the principal object of the divine will is the divine essence.

[7] But since the divine essence is God's understanding and all else that is said to be in Him, it is further manifest that in the same way He principally wills Himself to understand, to will, to be one, and other such attributes.

Chapter 75.

THAT IN WILLING HIMSELF GOD ALSO WILLS OTHER THINGS

[1] Thereby it can be shown, however, that in willing Himself God also wills other things.

5. *Ibid.*
6. See above, ch. 41.
7. Aristotle, *De caelo et mundo*, I, 11 (281a 15).

[2] For to whom it belongs to will the end principally, to him it belongs to will the things that are ordered to the end for the sake of the end. Now, God Himself is the ultimate end of things, as appears somewhat from what has been said.[1] Hence, because He wills Himself to be, He likewise wills other things, which are ordered to Him as to the end.

[3] 'Again, everyone desires the perfection of that which is willed and loved by him for its own sake. For the things that we love for their own sake we want to be most perfect, and always to become better and be multiplied as much as possible. But God wills and loves His essence for its own sake. Now, the divine essence cannot be increased or multiplied in itself, as is manifest from what has been said;[2] it can be multiplied solely according to its likeness, which is participated by many.[3] God, therefore, wills the multitude of things in willing and loving His own essence and perfection.

[4] Moreover, whoever loves something in itself and for its own sake consequently loves all the things in which it is found: for example, he who loves sweetness for itself must love all sweet things. But God wills and loves His own being in itself and for its own sake, as shown above.[4] Every other being, however, is by way of likeness a certain participation of His being, as appears somewhat from what has been said.[5] It remains, then, that God, in that He wills and loves Himself, wills and loves other things.

[5] Furthermore, in willing Himself God wills all that is in Him. But all things in a certain manner pre-exist in Him through their proper models, as was shown above.[6]

1. See above, ch. 74.
2. See above, ch. 42.
3. See above, ch. 29, ¶2.
4. See above, ch. 74.
5. See above, ch. 29.
6. See above, ch. 54.

God, therefore, in willing Himself likewise wills other things.

[6] Then, again, the more perfect the power of a being, by so much does its causality extend to more, and more remote, things, as was said above.[7] But the causality of the end consists in this, that other things are desired for its sake. The more perfect an end, therefore, and the more willed, by so much does the will of one willing the end extend to more things for the sake of that end. But the divine essence is most perfect as goodness and as end. It will, therefore, supremely diffuse its causality to many, so that many things may be willed for its sake; and especially so by God, Who wills the divine essence perfectly according to its power.

[7] Moreover, will accompanies intellect. But by His intellect God principally understands Himself, and He understands other things in Himself.[8] In the same way, therefore, He principally wills Himself, and wills all other things in willing Himself.

[8] This is confirmed by the authority of Sacred Scripture. For it is said in Wisdom (11:25): "For Thou lovest all things that are, and hatest none of the things which Thou hast made."

Chapter 76.

THAT GOD WILLS HIMSELF AND OTHER THINGS
BY ONE ACT OF WILL

[1] From this result it follows that God wills Himself and other things by one act of will.

7. See above, ch. 70.
8. See above, ch. 49.

[2]   Every power is directed to its object and to the formal notion of the object by one operation or one act. For example, by the same sight we see light and color, which becomes visible in act through light. Now, when we will something solely for the sake of the end, that which is desired for the sake of the end derives the nature of something willed from the end; and thus the end is to it as the formal notion of the object is to the object, for example, as light is to color. Since, then, God wills other things for His own sake as for the sake of the end, as has been shown,[1] He wills Himself and other things by one act of will.

[3]   Moreover, what is perfectly known and desired is known and desired according to its whole power. But the power of the end is measured not only according as it is desired in itself, but also according as other things become desirable for its sake. Hence, whoever desires an end perfectly desires it in both ways. But there is no act of will in God by which He wills Himself and does not do so perfectly, since there is nothing imperfect in Him.[2] Therefore, by whatever act God wills Himself, He wills Himself absolutely and other things for His sake. But He does not will things other than Himself except in so far as He wills Himself, as has been proved.[3] It remains, then, that God does not will Himself and other things by different acts of will, but by one and the same act.

[4]   Furthermore, as appears from what has been said,[4] discursiveness is found in the act of a cognitive power according as we know principles by themselves and from them we arrive at conclusions. For, if we saw conclusions in principles by knowing the principles themselves, there would be no discursiveness, as likewise there is not when we see something in a mirror. But as principles are to con-

1. See above, ch. 75.
2. See above, ch. 28.
3. See above, ch. 75.
4. See above, ch. 57, ¶s 2 and 3.

clusions in speculative matters, so ends are to the things ordered to them in operative and appetitive matters; for just as conclusions are known through principles, so the appetite and doing of the things ordered to the end proceed from the end. If, then, someone wills separately the end and the things ordered to the end, there will be a certain discursiveness in His will. But this cannot be in God, since He is outside all motion. It remains, then, that God wills Himself and other things together and in the same act of will.

[5] Again, since God wills Himself always, if He wills Himself and other things by different acts it will follow that there are at once two acts of will in Him. This is impossible, since one simple power does not have at once two operations.

[6] Furthermore, in every act of the will the object willed is to the one willing as a mover to the moved. If, then, there be some action of the divine will, by which God wills things other than Himself, which is diverse from the action by which He wills Himself, there will be in Him some other mover of the divine will. This is impossible.

[7] Moreover, God's willing is His being, as has been proved.[5] But in God there is only one being. Therefore, there is in Him only one willing.

[8] Again, willing belongs to God according as He is intelligent.[6] Therefore, just as by one act He understands Himself and other things, in so far as His essence is the exemplar of all things,[7] so by one act He wills Himself and other things, in so far as His goodness is the likeness of all goodness.[8]

5. See above, ch. 73.
6. See above, ch. 72.
7. See above, ch. 49.
8. See above, ch. 40.

Chapter 77.

THAT THE MULTITUDE OF THE OBJECTS OF THE WILL IS NOT OPPOSED TO THE DIVINE SIMPLICITY

[1]   From this it follows that the multitude of the objects of the will is not opposed to the unity and simplicity of the divine substance.

[2]   For acts are distinguished according to their objects. If, then, the many objects that God wills caused a multitude in Him, it would follow that there was not in Him solely one operation of the will. This is against what has been proved above.[1]

[3]   Again, it has been shown that God wills other things in so far as He wills His own goodness. Hence, other things are to His will in the manner in which they are comprehended by His goodness. But all things in His goodness are one, since other things are in Him according to His way, namely, "the material immaterially and the many unitedly," as appears from what has been said.[2] It remains, then, that the multitude of the objects of the will does not multiply the divine substance.

[4]   Moreover, the divine intellect and will are of an equal simplicity, for both are the divine substance, as has been proved.[3] But the multitude of intellectual objects does not cause a multitude in the divine essence, nor a composition in the divine intellect. Neither, therefore, does a multitude

1. See above, ch. 76.
2. Pseudo-Dionysius, *De divinis nominibus*, VII, 2 (*PG*, 3, col. 869B).—See above, ch. 75.
3. See above, ch. 45 and 73.

of the objects of the will cause either a diversity in the divine essence or a composition in the divine will.

[5]   Furthermore, there is this difference between knowledge and appetite, that knowledge takes place according as the known is in some way in the knower, whereas appetite does not take place in this way, but rather conversely, according as the appetite is related to the appetible thing, which the one pursuing seeks or in which he rests. And on this account good and evil, which have reference to appetite, are in things, whereas the true and the false, which have reference to knowledge, are in the mind, as the Philosopher says in *Metaphysics* VI.[4] Now, that something be related to many is not opposed to its simplicity, since unity itself is the principle of numerical multitude. Hence, the multitude of the objects willed by God is not opposed to His simplicity.

Chapter 78.

THAT THE DIVINE WILL EXTENDS TO SINGULAR GOODS

[1]   From this it is likewise apparent that, for the purpose of conserving the divine simplicity, we should not say that God wills other goods in a certain general way, in so far as He wills Himself to be the principle of the goods that can come forth from Him, but that He does not will them in the particular.

[2]   For to will implies a relationship of the one willing to the thing willed. But the divine simplicity does not forbid its being related even to many particulars; for God is said to be something best and first in relation to singulars. Therefore, His simplicity does not forbid Him from willing things other than Himself in the concrete or the particular.

4. Aristotle. *Metaphysics*, VI, 4 (1027b 25).

[3]   Again, the will of God is related to other things in so far as they participate in goodness in virtue of their order to the divine goodness, which is for God the reason of His willing.[1] But not only the totality of goods, but even each one of them derives its goodness from the divine goodness, as well as its being. Therefore, the will of God extends to singular goods.

[4]   Moreover, according to the Philosopher, in *Metaphysics* xi, a twofold good of order is found in the universe:[2] one according to which the whole universe is ordered to what is outside the universe, as the army is ordered to its general; the other according as the parts of the universe are ordered to one another, as are the parts of the army. Now, the second order is for the sake of the first. But God, from the fact of willing Himself as the end, wills other things that are ordered to Him as to the end, as has been proved.[3] He therefore wills the good of the order that the whole universe has to Him, as well as the good of the order that the universe has in the mutual relations of its parts. But the good of an order arises from singular goods. Therefore, God also wills singular goods.

[5]   Furthermore, if God does not will the singular goods of which the universe is composed, it follows that in the universe the good that order is is by chance. For it is not possible that some part of the universe should bring together all the particular goods into the order of the universe; only the universal cause of the whole universe, God, Who acts through His will, as will later be shown, can do this.[4] Now, that the order of the universe be by chance is impossible, since it would follow that the consequences of the order would all the more be by chance. It remains, then, that God wills even singulars among goods.

1. See above, ch. 75.
2. Aristotle, *Metaphysics*, XII, 10 (1075a 12).
3. See above, ch. 75.
4. *SCG*, II, ch. 23.

[6] Again, the understood good, as such, is what is willed.[5] But God understands even particular goods, as was proved above.[6] He therefore wills even particular goods.

[7] This is confirmed by the authority of Scripture, which, in the first chapter of Genesis (1:4, 31), shows the pleasure of the divine will with each single work, in the words: "God saw the light that it was good," and similarly of His other works, and then of all the works together: "And God saw all the things that He had made, and they were very good."

Chapter 79.

THAT GOD WILLS EVEN THE THINGS THAT ARE NOT YET

[1] If willing implies a relationship of the one willing to the thing willed, it can possibly seem to someone that God cannot will save only the things that are. For relatives ought to be together, and when one is destroyed so is the other, as the Philosopher teaches.[1] If, then, willing implies the relationship of the one willing to the thing willed, no one can will save the things that are.

[2] Furthermore, *will* is said in relation to the things that are willed, and similarly with *cause* and *creator*. But not even God can be called Creator, or Lord, or Father, save of the things that are. Therefore, neither can He be said to will save the things that are.

[3] From this it could be further concluded that, if the divine willing is unchangeable as is the divine being, and God does not will save the things that are in act, He wills nothing that does not always exist.

5. See above, ch. 72.
6. See above, ch. 65.
1. Aristotle, *Categories*, VII (7b 15).

[4] To these difficulties some answer that the things that are not in themselves are in God and in His intellect. Hence, nothing prevents God from willing the things that do not exist in themselves in so far as they are in Him.

[5] But this does not seem to be a sufficient reply. For someone with a will is said to will something in so far as his will is related to the thing willed. If, then, the divine will is not related to the thing willed save only in so far as it exists in Him or in His intellect, it will follow that God does not will that thing except because He wills it to be in His being or in His intellect. But this is not the intention of those who hold the position; they intend that God wills such not-yet-existents to be even in themselves.

[6] Again, if the will is related to the thing willed through its object, the understood good, and the intellect understands not only that the good exists in it but that it exists in its own nature, the will likewise is related to the thing willed not only as it is in the knower, but likewise as it is in itself.

[7] Let us therefore reply that, since the apprehended good moves the will, the act of will itself must follow the condition of apprehension; just as the motions of the other movers follow the conditions of the mover that is the cause of motion. But the relation of the apprehension to the thing apprehended follows upon the apprehension itself, because one who apprehends is related to the apprehended thing in that he apprehends it. Now, he who apprehends does not apprehend a thing solely as it is in him, but as it is in its own nature; for not only do we know that a thing is understood by us because it is in the intellect, but we know also that it exists or has existed or will exist in its own nature. Therefore, although at that moment the thing does not exist save only in the intellect, the relation following upon the apprehension is to the thing, not as it exists in the knower, but as it is in its own nature, which the one apprehending apprehends.

[8] The relation of the divine will, therefore, is to the non-existing thing according as it exists in its proper nature at a certain time, and not only according as it is in God knowing it. The thing that does not now exist God wills to be at a certain time; He does not will solely the fact that He understands it.

[9] The relations of the one willing to the thing willed, of creator to created, and of maker to thing made, or of Lord to His subject creature, are not similar. For willing is an action remaining in the one willing, and hence does not require that something existing outside the will be understood. But to make, to create, and to govern signify an action terminating in an exterior effect, without whose existence such an action cannot be understood.

Chapter 80.

THAT HIS OWN BEING AND HIS OWN GOODNESS GOD WILLS NECESSARILY

[1] From what was shown above it follows that God wills His own being and His own goodness in a necessary way, and cannot will the contrary.

[2] For it was shown above[1] that God wills His own being and His own goodness as His principal object, which is for Him the reason for willing other things. In everything willed, therefore, God wills His own being and His own goodness, just as the sight in every color sees light. But it is impossible for God not to will something in act, for He would be willing only in potency, which is impossible, since His willing is His being.[2] It is therefore necessary that God will His own being and His own goodness.

1. See above, ch. 74.
2. See above, ch. 16 and 73

[3]   Again, every being endowed with will necessarily wills his own ultimate end: for example, man necessarily wills his own beatitude and cannot will misery. But God wills Himself to be as the ultimate end, as appears from what has been said.[3] Therefore, He necessarily wills Himself to be, nor can He will Himself not to be.

[4]   Moreover, in appetitive and operative matters the end functions as an indemonstrable principle does in speculative matters.[4] For just as in speculative matters the conclusions are reached from principles, so in active and appetitive matters the principle of all the things to be done and sought is taken from the end. But in speculative matters the intellect necessarily assents to the first and indemonstrable principles, and can in no way assent to their contraries. Therefore, the will necessarily inheres to the ultimate end, so as to be unable to will the contrary. Thus, if the divine will has no end other than itself,[5] it necessarily wills itself to be.

[5]   Again, all things in so far as they are, are likened to God Who is primarily and supremely being.[6] But all things, in so far as they are, in their own way naturally love their own being. All the more, then, does God naturally love His own being. But His nature is a being necessary through itself, as was shown above.[7] Therefore, God of necessity wills Himself to be.

[6]   Furthermore, every perfection and goodness found in creatures is proper to God in an essential way, as was proved above.[8] But to love God is the highest perfection of the rational creature, since thereby it is somehow united to

3. See above, ch. 74.
4. Aristotle, *Physics*, II, 9 (200a 19).
5. See above, ch. 74.
6. See above, ch. 29.
7. See above, ch. 13.
8. See above, ch. 28.

God. Therefore, this love is found in God in an essential way. Therefore, of necessity God loves Himself. And thus He wills Himself to be.

Chapter 81.

THAT GOD DOES NOT WILL OTHER THINGS IN A NECESSARY WAY

[1] But, if the divine will of necessity wills the divine goodness and the divine being, it might seem to someone that it wills of necessity other things as well, since God wills all other things in willing His own goodness, as was proved above.[1] Nevertheless, if we consider the matter correctly, it appears that He does not will other things necessarily.

[2] For God wills other things as ordered to the end of His goodness.[2] But the will is not directed to what is for the sake of the end if the end can be without it. For, on the basis of his intention to heal, a doctor does not necessarily have to give to a sick person the medicine without which the sick person can nevertheless be healed. Since, then, the divine goodness can be without other things, and, indeed, is in no way increased by other things, it is under no necessity to will other things from the fact of willing its own goodness.

[3] Furthermore, since the understood good is the object of the will, the will can will anything conceived by the intellect in which the nature of the good is present. Hence, although the being of any given thing is as such a good and its non-being an evil, the non-being of something can fall under the will (though not by necessity) because of

1. See above, ch. 75.
2. *Ibid.*

some adjoined good that is preserved; since it is a good that something be, even though something else does not exist. Therefore, according to its own nature, the will cannot not will that good whose non-existence causes the nature of the good entirely to be lost. But there is no such good apart from God. According to its nature, therefore, the will can will the non-existence of anything whatever apart from God. But in God will is present according to its whole range, since all things in Him are universally perfect.[3] God, therefore, can will the non-existence of anything whatever apart from Himself. Hence, it is not of necessity that things other than Himself exist.

[4]   Moreover, God, in willing His own goodness, wills things other than Himself to be in so far as they participate in His goodness.[4] But, since the divine goodness is infinite, it can be participated in in infinite ways, and in ways other than it is participated in by the creatures that now exist. If, then, as a result of willing His own goodness, God necessarily willed the things that participate in it, it would follow that He would will the existence of an infinity of creatures participating in His goodness in an infinity of ways. This is patently false, because, if He willed them, they would be, since His will is the principle of being for things, as will be shown later on.[5] Therefore, God does not necessarily will even the things that now exist.

[5]   Again, the will of a wise man, by the fact of dealing with a cause, deals also with the effect that necessarily follows from the cause. For it would be foolish to wish the sun to be overhead and yet that it should not be daylight. But, as to an effect that does not follow of necessity from a cause, it is not necessary that someone will it because he wills the cause. Now, other things proceed from God without necessity, as will be shown later on.[6] It is not necessary,

3. See above, ch. 28.
4. See above, ch. 75.
5. SCG, II, ch. 23.
6. Ibid.

therefore, that God will other things from the fact of willing Himself.

[6] Moreover, things proceed from God as artifacts from an artisan, as will be shown later on.[7] But, although the artisan wishes to have the art, he does not necessarily wish to produce the artifacts. Neither, therefore, does God necessarily will that there be things other than Himself.

[7] We must therefore consider why it is that God necessarily knows things other than Himself, but does not necessarily will them, even though from the fact that He understands and wills Himself He understands and wills other things.[8] The reason is as follows. That he who understands should understand something arises from the fact that he is disposed in a certain way, since something is understood in act in so far as its likeness is in the one understanding. But that he who wills should will something arises from the fact that what is willed is disposed in a certain way. For we will something either because it is the end or because it is ordered to the end. Now, that all things be in God, so that they can be understood in Him, is necessarily required by the divine perfection;[9] but the divine goodness does not necessarily require that other things exist, which are ordered to it as to the end. That is why it is necessary that God know other things, but not necessary that He will them. Hence, neither does God will all the things that can have an order to His goodness; but He knows all things that have any order whatever to His essence, by which He understands.

7. SCG, II, ch. 24.
8. See above, ch. 49 and 75.
9. See above, ch. 50.

Chapter 82.

ARGUMENTS LEADING TO AWKWARD CONSE-
QUENCES IF GOD DOES NOT NECESSARILY
WILL THINGS OTHER THAN HIMSELF

[1] Awkward consequences seem to follow if God does not will necessarily the things that He wills.

[2] For, if with respect to certain objects the will of God is not determined to them, it would seem to be disposed to opposites. But every power that is disposed to opposites is in a manner in potency, since "to opposites" is a species of the contingent possible. Therefore, there is potency in the will of God, which will consequently not be the substance of God, in which there is no potency, as was shown above.[1]

[3] If being in potency, as such, is of a nature to be moved, because what can be can not-be, it follows that the divine will is changeable.

[4] Furthermore, if it is natural to God to will something about His effects, it is necessary. Now there can be nothing unnatural in God, since there cannot be anything accidental or violent in Him, as was proved above.[2]

[5] Again, if what is open to opposites, being indifferently disposed, tends no more to one thing than to another unless it be determined by another, it is necessary either that God will none of the things towards which He is disposed to opposites, of which the contrary was proved above,[3] or that

1. See above, ch. 16.
2. See above, ch. 19.
3. See above, ch. 75.

God be determined to one effect by another. Thus, there will be something prior to Him, determining Him to one effect.

[6] But of these conclusions none necessarily follows. For to be open to opposites belongs to a certain power in a twofold way: in one way, from the side of itself; in another way, from the side of its object. From the side of itself, when it has not yet achieved its perfection, through which it is determined to one effect. This openness redounds to the imperfection of a power, and potentiality is shown to be in it; as appears in the case of an intellect in doubt, which has yet not acquired the principles from which to be determined to one alternative. From the side of its object, a certain power is found open to opposites when the perfect operation of the power depends on neither alternative, though both can be. An example is an art which can use diverse instruments to perform the same work equally well. This openness does not pertain to the imperfection of a power, but rather to its eminence, in so far as it dominates both alternatives, and thereby is determined to neither, being open to both. This is how the divine will is disposed in relation to things other than itself. For its end depends on none of the other things, though it itself is most perfectly united to its end. Hence, it is not required that any potentiality be posited in the divine will.

[7] Mutability, similarly, is not required. For, if there is no potentiality in the divine will, God does not thus prefer one of the opposites among His effects as if He should be thought as being in potency to both, so that He first wills both in potency and afterward He wills in act; rather, He wills in act whatever He wills, not only in relation to Himself but also in relation to His effects. The reason rather is because the object willed does not have a necessary order to the divine goodness, which is the proper object of the divine will; just as we call enunciables, not necessary, but possible when there is not a necessary order of the predicate

to the subject. Hence, when it is said, *God wills this effect*, it is manifest that it is not a necessary enunciable but a possible one, not in the sense in which something is said to be possible according to some power, but in the sense in which the possible is that whose existence is neither necessary nor impossible, as the Philosopher teaches in *Metaphysics* v.[4] For example, for a triangle to have two equal sides is a possible enunciable, but not according to some power, since in mathematics there is neither power nor motion. The exclusion of the aforesaid necessity, therefore, does not take away the immutability of the divine will. This Sacred Scripture professes: "But the triumpher in Israel will not spare, and will not be moved to repentance" (I Kings 15:29).

[8]   However, although the divine will is not determined to its effects, we yet cannot say that it wills none of them, or that in order to will one of them it is determined by an exterior agent. For, since the apprehended good determines the will as its proper object, and the divine intellect is not outside God's will, because both are His essence, if God's will is determined to will something through the knowledge of His intellect, this determination of the divine will will not be due to something extraneous. For the divine intellect apprehends not only the divine being, which is God's goodness, but also other goods, as was shown above.[5] These goods it apprehends as certain likenesses of the divine goodness and essence, not as its principles. And thus, the divine will tends to them as befitting its goodness, not as necessary to it. The same thing happens in the case of our own will. When it is inclined to something as absolutely necessary to the end, it is moved to it with a certain necessity; but when it tends to something only because of a certain befittingness, it tends to it without necessity. Hence, neither does the divine will tend to its effects in a necessary way.

4. Aristotle, *Metaphysics*, V, 12 (1019b 30).
5. See above, ch. 49.

[9]   Nor, furthermore, is it necessary because of the foregoing to posit something unnatural in God. For His will wills itself and other things by one and the same act. But its relation to itself is necessary and natural, whereas its relation to other things is according to a certain befittingness, not indeed necessary and natural, nor violent and unnatural, but *voluntary*; for the voluntary need be neither natural nor violent.

Chapter 83.

THAT GOD WILLS SOMETHING OTHER THAN HIMSELF WITH THE NECESSITY OF SUPPOSITION

[1]   From this we may infer that, although among His effects God wills nothing with absolute necessity, yet He does will something with the necessity of supposition.

[2]   For it has been shown that the divine will is immutable.[1] Now, if something is found in any immutable being, it cannot afterwards not be; for we say that a thing has moved if it is otherwise disposed now than it was previously. If, then, the divine will is immutable, assuming that it wills something, God must by supposition will this thing.

[3]   Again, everything eternal is necessary. Now, that God should will some effect to be is eternal, for, like His being, so, too, His willing is measured by eternity,[2] and is therefore necessary. But it is not necessary considered absolutely, because the will of God does not have a necessary relation to this willed object.[3] Therefore, it is necessary by supposition.

1. See above, ch. 82, ¶7.
2. See above, ch. 73.
3. See above, ch. 82, ¶6.

[4]   Furthermore, whatever God could He can, for His power is not decreased, as neither is His essence. But He cannot now not will what He is posited as having willed, because His will cannot be changed. Therefore, at no time could He not will what He has willed. It is therefore necessary by supposition that He willed whatever He willed, and also that He wills it; neither, however, is absolutely necessary, but, rather, possible in the aforementioned way.[4]

[5]   Moreover, whoever wills something, necessarily wills whatever it necessarily required for it, unless there be a defect in him either because of ignorance or because he is led astray through passion from the right choice of that which leads to the intended end. This cannot be said of God. If God, then, in willing Himself wills something other than Himself, it is necessary that He will for this object whatever is necessarily required by it. Thus, it is necessary that God will the rational soul to exist supposing that He wills man to exist.

Chapter 84.

THAT THE WILL OF GOD IS NOT OF WHAT IS IN ITSELF IMPOSSIBLE

[1]   From this it appears that the will of God cannot be of the things that are impossible in themselves.

[2]   For these have a contradiction in themselves, for example, *that man is an ass*, in which the rational and the irrational are included. For what is incompatible with something excludes some of the things that are necessary to it, as to be an ass excludes man's reason. If, then, God necessarily wills the things that are required for what He wills by supposition, it is impossible for Him to will what is in-

4. *Ibid.*

compatible with these things. Thus, it is impossible for God to will the absolutely impossible.

[3] Again, as was shown above,[1] in willing His own being, which is His own goodness, God wills all other things in so far as they bear His likeness. But in so far as a thing is opposed to the nature of being as such, there cannot be preserved in it the likeness of the first being, namely, the divine being, which is the source of being. Hence, God cannot will something that is opposed to the nature of being as such. But just as it is opposed to the nature of man as man to be irrational, so it is opposed to the nature of being as such that something be at once being and non-being. God, therefore, cannot will that affirmation and negation be true together. But this is included in everything that is of itself impossible, which has an opposition with itself as implying a contradiction. The will of God, therefore, cannot be of that which is of itself impossible.

[4] Moreover, the will is only of the understood good. Hence, whatever cannot be the object of the intellect is not an object of the will. But that which is of itself impossible is not an object of the intellect, since it is self-contradictory, except, of course, through the fault of one who does not understand what belongs to things—which cannot be said of God. Therefore, that which is of itself impossible cannot be the object of the will.

[5] Furthermore, as a thing is disposed toward being, so it is disposed toward goodness. But the impossible is that which cannot be. Therefore, it cannot be good, and hence cannot be willed by God, Who does not will save only the things that are or can be good.

1. See above, ch. 75.

Chapter 85.

THAT THE DIVINE WILL DOES NOT REMOVE CONTINGENCY FROM THINGS, NOR DOES IT IMPOSE ABSOLUTE NECESSITY ON THEM

[1]   From what has been said it results that the divine will does not remove contingency from things, nor does it impose absolute necessity on things.

[2]   God wills whatever is required for a thing that He wills, as has been said.[1] But it befits certain things, according to the mode of their nature, that they be contingent and not necessary. Therefore, God wills that some things be contingent. Now, the efficacy of the divine will requires not only that something be that God wills to be, but also that it be as He wills it to be. For, among natural agents as well, when the acting power is strong it assimilates its effect to itself not only as to species but also as to the accidents, which are certain modes of that thing. Therefore, the efficacy of the divine will does not remove contingency.

[3]   Moreover, God wills the good of the universe of His effects more principally than He does any particular good, according as a fuller likeness of His goodness is found in it.[2] But the completeness of the universe requires that there be some contingent things; otherwise, not all grades of beings would be contained in the universe. Therefore, God wills that there be some contingent things.

[4]   Furthermore, the good of the universe is seen in a certain order, as appears in Metaphysics XI.[3] But the order of the universe requires that there be some changeable

1. See above, ch. 83.
2. See above, ch. 78, ¶4.
3. Aristotle, Metaphysics, XII, 10 (1075a 14).

causes, since bodies are part of the perfection of the universe, and they do not move unless they be moved. Now, contingent effects follow from a changeable cause, for an effect cannot have a more stable being than its cause. Hence we see that, even though the remote cause is necessary, provided the proximate cause is contingent, the effect is contingent, as may be seen in the things that happen among sublunary bodies, which are contingent because of the contingency of the proximate causes even though the remote causes, which are the heavenly motions, are necessary. God, therefore, wills something to come to pass contingently.

[5]   The necessity of supposition in the cause, moreover, does not require an absolute necessity in the effect. But God wills something in the creature, not by absolute necessity, but only by a necessity of supposition, as was shown above.[4] From the divine will, therefore, an absolute necessity in created things cannot be inferred. But only this excludes contingency, for even the contingents open to opposites are made necessary by supposition: for example, *that Socrates be moved, if he runs, is necessary.* Therefore, the divine will does not exclude contingency from the things it wills.

[6]   Hence, it does not follow, if God wills something, that it will of necessity take place. But this conditional is true and necessary: *If God wills something, it will be.* But the consequent does not have to be necessary.

Chapter 86.

THAT A REASON CAN BE ASSIGNED TO THE DIVINE WILL

[1]   From what has been said we can infer that a reason can be assigned to the divine will.

4. See above, ch. 81.

[2]   The end is the reason for willing the things that are for the sake of the end. But God wills His own goodness as the end, and other things He wills as things that are for the sake of the end. His goodness, therefore, is the reason why He wills the other things which are different from Himself.

[3]   Again, a particular good is ordered to the good of the whole as to its end, as the imperfect to the perfect. Now, some things fall under the divine will according to their disposition in the order of the good.[1] It remains, then, that the good of the universe is the reason why God wills each particular good in the universe.

[4]   Again, as was shown above,[2] on the supposition that God wills something, it follows necessarily that He wills the things required for it. But that which imposes necessity on another is the reason why that other exists. Therefore, the reason why God wills the things that are required for each thing is that that thing be for which they are required.

[5]   Thus, therefore, can we proceed in assigning the reason of the divine will. God wills man to have a reason in order that man be; He wills man to be so that the universe may be complete; and He wills that the good of the universe be because it befits His goodness.

[6]   However, this threefold reason does not proceed according to the same relationship. For the divine goodness neither depends on the perfection of the universe nor is anything added to it from this perfection. For, although the perfection of the universe necessarily depends on certain particular goods that are its essential parts, yet on some of them it does not depend of necessity, but nevertheless a certain goodness or adornment accrues to the universe from them, as from those things that exist only for the support or adornment of the other parts of the universe. A particular good depends necessarily on the things that

1. See above, ch. 78, ¶s 4 and 5.
2. See above, ch. 83.

are absolutely required for it, even though this too has certain things that are for its embellishment. Hence, at times the reason of the divine will contains only a befitting-ness; at other times, usefulness; at still other times, a necessity of supposition; but a necessity that is absolute only when it wills itself.

Chapter 87.

THAT NOTHING CAN BE THE CAUSE OF THE DIVINE WILL

[1] Now, although a certain reason of the divine will can be assigned, it does not follow that anything is the cause of the divine will.

[2] For to the will the cause of its willing is the end. But the end of the divine will is its goodness. Hence, it is the cause of God's willing, just as it is also His act of will.

[3] As to the other objects willed by God, none is the cause of willing for God. But one of them is the cause for the other to have an order to the divine goodness. And thus God is understood to will one of them for the sake of another.

[4] It is nevertheless manifest that no discursiveness is to be posited in the divine will. For where there is one act that is no discursiveness, as was shown above in connection with the intellect.[1] But by means of one act God wills His goodness and all other things, since His action is His essence.

[5] Through the foregoing is set aside the error of certain persons who said that all things proceed from God according to His simple will, which means that we are not to give an explanation of anything except that God wills it.

1. See above, ch. 73.

[6]   This view is likewise opposed to Sacred Scripture, which proclaims that God made all things according to the order of His wisdom, as is said in the Psalm (103:24): "Thou hast made all things in wisdom." And in Ecclesiasticus (1:10) it is said that God "poured" His wisdom "out upon all His works."

Chapter 88.

THAT IN GOD THERE IS FREE CHOICE

[1]   From what has been said it can be shown that free choice is found in God.

[2]   Free choice is said in relation to the things that one wills, not of necessity, but of his own accord. Thus, there is in us free choice in relation to our willing to run or to walk. But God wills things other than Himself without necessity, as was shown above.[1] Therefore, to have free choice befits God.

[3]   Again, towards the things to which it is not determined by nature the divine will is in a manner inclined through its intellect, as was shown above.[2] But on this account is man said to have free choice as opposed to the other animals because he is inclined to willing by the judgment of the reason and not by the impulse of nature, as are the brutes. Therefore, in God there is free choice.

[4]   Furthermore, according to the Philosopher in *Ethics* III, "will is of the end, but election is of that which is for the sake of the end."[3] Since, then, God wills Himself as the end, and other things as what is for the sake of the end, it follows that with reference to Himself God has

1. See above, ch. 81.
2. See above, ch. 82, ¶8.
3. Aristotle, *Nicomachean Ethics*, III, 5 (1113b 3).

only will, but with reference to other things He has election. But election is made by choice. Therefore, free choice befits God.

[5] Moreover, because he has free choice, man is said to be master of his acts. But this supremely befits the first agent, whose act does not depend on another. Therefore, God has free choice.

[6] This can likewise be gathered from the very meaning of the name. For "that is free which is for its own sake," according to the Philosopher in the beginning of the *Metaphysics*.⁴ But this befits no being more than the first cause, God.

Chapter 89.

THAT IN GOD THERE ARE NOT THE PASSIONS OF THE APPETITES

[1] From what has preceded we can know that the passions of the appetites are not in God.

[2] Now, according to intellective appetite there is no passion, but only according to sensitive appetite, as is proved in *Physics* VII.¹ But no such appetite can be in God, since He does not have sensitive knowledge, as is manifest from what has been said above.² Therefore, there is no passion of the appetite in God.

[3] Moreover, every passion of the appetite takes place through some bodily change, for example, the contraction or distension of the heart, or something of the sort. Now, none of this can take place in God, since He is not a body

4. Aristotle, *Metaphysics*, I, 2 (982b 25).
1. Aristotle, *Physics*, VII, 3 (246b 20).
2. See above, ch. 44.

or a power in a body, as was shown above.[3] There is, therefore, no passion of the appetite in Him.

[4]   Again, in every passion of the appetite the patient is somehow drawn out of his usual, calm, or connatural disposition. A sign of this is that such passions, if intensified, bring death to animals. But it is not possible for God to be somehow drawn outside His natural condition, since He is absolutely immutable, as has been shown.[4] It appears, then, that such passions cannot be found in God.

[5]   Moreover, every affection arising from a passion is directed determinately to one thing according to the manner and measure of the passion. For passion has an impulse to something one, as does nature, and on this account it must be curbed and regulated by reason. But the divine will is not determined in itself to something one among creatures, except out of the order of its wisdom, as was shown above.[5] Therefore, there is no passion of the appetite in God.

[6]   Furthermore, every passion belongs to something existing in potency. But God is completely free from potency, since He is pure act. God, therefore, is solely agent, and in no way does any passion have a place in Him.

[7]   Thus, therefore, by reason of its genus, passion is excluded in God.

[8]   Some passions, however, are excluded from God not only by reason of their genus, but also by reason of their species. For every passion is specified by its object. That passion, therefore, whose subject is absolutely unbefitting to God is removed from God even according to the nature of its proper species.

3. See above, ch. 20.
4. See above, ch. 13, ¶28.
5. See above, ch. 82, ¶6.

[9] Such a passion, however, is *sorrow* or *pain*, for its subject is the already present evil, just as the object of *joy* is the good present and possessed. Sorrow and pain, therefore, of their very nature cannot be found in God.

[10] Furthermore, the notion of the object of a given passion is derived not only from good and evil, but also from the fact that one is disposed in a certain way towards one of them. For it is thus that *hope* and *joy* differ. If, then, the mode itself in which one is disposed toward the object that is included in the notion of passion is not befitting to God, neither can the passion itself befit Him, even through the nature of its proper species. Now, although hope has as its object something good, yet it is not a good already possessed, but one to be possessed. This cannot befit God, because of His perfection, which is so great that nothing can be added to it.[6] *Hope*, therefore, cannot be found in God, even by reason of its species. And likewise, neither can the *desire* of something not possessed.

[11] Moreover, just as the divine perfection excludes from God the potency of the addition of some good to be obtained, so likewise, and all the more, does it exclude the potency to evil. *Fear* has reference to the evil that can threaten, as hope has reference to a good to be obtained. By a twofold reason of its species, therefore, is fear excluded from God: both because it belongs only to one existing in potency and because it has for its object a threatening evil.

[12] Again, *repentance* implies a change of affection. Therefore, the nature of repentance likewise is repugnant to God, not only because it is a species of sadness, but also because it implies a change of will.

[13] Furthermore, without an error of the cognitive power it is impossible that what is good be apprehended as evil.

6. See above, ch. 28.

Nor is it possible that the evil of one be the good of another, except among particular goods in which "the corruption of one is the generation of another."[7] But the universal good does not lose anything because of the existence of some particular good, but is rather mirrored by each one. God, however, is the universal good, and by participating in His likeness all things are called good.[8] The evil of no thing, therefore, can be His good. Nor is it possible that what is absolutely good, and is not evil to itself, He should apprehend as something evil; for His knowledge is without error, as has been shown.[9] Envy, therefore, cannot be found in God, even according to the nature of its species, not only because it is a species of sadness, but also because it is saddened by the good of another and thus takes his good as its own evil.

[14]   Moreover, to be saddened over a good and to seek evil are of the same nature, for the first arises because the good is judged to be evil, while the second arises because evil is judged to be good. *Anger* is the appetite of another's evil for the sake of revenge. Anger, therefore, is far from God according to the nature of its species, not only because it is an effect of sadness, but likewise because it is an appetite for revenge arising from sadness due to an injury received.

[15]   Again, whatever other passions are species of these or are caused by them, are for the same reason removed from God.

7. Aristotle, *Physics*, III, 8 (208a 10).
8. See above, ch. 29.
9. See above, ch. 61.

Chapter 90.

THAT IN GOD THERE ARE DELIGHT AND JOY,
BUT THEY ARE NOT OPPOSED TO THE
DIVINE PERFECTION

[1] There are certain passions which, though they do not befit God as passions, do not signify anything by the nature of their species that is repugnant to the divine perfection.

[2] Among these passions are *joy* and *delight*. Delight is of a present good. Neither, therefore, by reason of its object, which is a good, nor by reason of its disposition towards its object, which is possessed in act, is joy, according to the nature of its species, repugnant to the divine perfection.

[3] From this it is manifest that joy or delight is properly in God. For just as the apprehended good and evil are the object of sensible appetite, so, too, are they of intellective appetite. It belongs to both to seek good and avoid evil, whether truly or by estimation. There is the difference that the object of intellective appetite is more common than that of the sensitive appetite, because intellective appetite has reference to good and evil absolutely, whereas sensitive appetite has reference to good or evil according to the sense. So, too, the object of the intellect is more common than that of the sense. But the operations of appetite derive their species from their objects. Hence, there are found in intellective appetite, which is the will, operations that in the nature of their species are similar to the operations of the sensitive appetite, differing in that in the sensitive appetite there are passions because of its union to a bodily organ, whereas in the intellective appetite there are simple operations; for just as through the passion of fear, which resides in the sensitive appetite, someone flees a future evil,

so without passion the intellective appetite does the same thing. Since, then, joy and delight are not repugnant to God according to their species, but only in so far as they are passions, and since they are found in the will according to their species but not as passions, it remains that they are not lacking even to the divine will.

[4]   Again, joy and delight are a certain resting of the will in its object. But God, Who is His own principal object willed,[1] is supremely at rest in Himself, as containing all abundance in Himself. God, therefore, through His will supremely rejoices in Himself.

[5]   Furthermore, delight is a certain perfection of operation, as appears from the Philosopher in *Ethics* x;[2] "for it perfects operation, as does beauty youth." But God has the most perfect operation in understanding, as appears from what has been said.[3] If, then, our understanding is delightful because of its perfection, the divine understanding will be most full of delight.

[6]   Moreover, each thing takes joy in its like as in something agreeable, except by accident in so far as it may interfere with one's own advantage: for example, "potters quarrel among themselves"[4] because one interferes with the profit of the other. Now, every good is a likeness of the divine good, as was said above,[5] nor does God lose any good because of some good. It remains, then, that God takes joy in every good.

[7]   Joy and delight, then, are properly in God. Now, joy and delight differ in notion. For delight arises from a really conjoined good, whereas joy does not require this, but the resting of the will in the object willed suffices for the nature of joy. Hence, delight is only of the conjoined

1. See above, ch. 74.
2. Aristotle, *Nicomachean Ethics*, X, 4 (1174b 33).
3. See above, ch. 45.
4. Aristotle, *Rhetoric*, II, 10 (1388a 16).
5. See above, ch. 40, ¶3.

good if it be taken properly, whereas joy is of a non-conjoined good. From this it is apparent that God properly delights in Himself, but He takes joy both in Himself and in other things.

Chapter 91.

THAT IN GOD THERE IS LOVE

[1] In the same way, there must be love in God according to the act of His will.

[2] For this belongs properly to the nature of love, that the lover will the good of the one he loves. Now, God wills His own good and that of others, as appears from what has been said.[1] This means, therefore, that God loves Himself and other things.

[3] Again, for true love it is required that we will someone's good as his good. For if we will someone's good only in so far as it leads to the good of another, we love this someone by accident; just as he who wishes to store wine in order to drink it or loves a man so that this man may be useful or enjoyable to him, loves the wine or the man by accident, but essentially he loves himself. But God wills the good of each thing according as it is the good of each thing; for He wills each thing to be according as it is in itself good (although He likewise orders one thing to another's use). God, then, truly loves Himself and other things.

[4] Moreover, since each thing in its own way wills and seeks its proper good, if it is the nature of love that the lover will and seek the good of the one he loves, it follows that the lover is to the loved as to that which in some way is one with him. From this the proper nature of love is

1. See above, ch. 74 and 75.

seen to consist in this, that the affection of the one tends to the other as to someone who is somehow one with him. On this account it is said by Dionysius that love is a "unitive power."[2] Therefore, the more that through which the lover is one with the one he loves is greater, the more is the love intense. For we love those whom the origin of birth joins to us, or the way of life, or something of the sort, more than those whom the community of human nature alone joins to us. Again, the more the source of the union is intimate to the lover, by so much the stronger becomes the love. Hence, at times, the love arising from some passion becomes more intense than the love that is of natural origin or from some habit; but it passes more easily. But the source whence all things are joined to God, namely, His goodness, which all things imitate, is what is supreme and most intimate in God, since it is His goodness.[3] There is, therefore, in God not only a true love, but also a most perfect and a most enduring love.

[5]   Again, from the side of its object love does not signify anything repugnant to God, since its object is the good; neither does it from the mode of its disposition towards its object. For we love some thing, not less, but more when we have it, because a good is closer to us when we have it. So, too, a motion to an end among natural things becomes intensified from the nearness of the end. (The contrary sometimes happens by accident, namely, when in the one we love we experience something repugnant to love; then the object loved is loved less when it is gained.) Hence, love is not repugnant to the divine perfection according to the nature of its species. Therefore, it is found in God.

[6]   Moreover, it belongs to love to move towards union, as Dionysius says.[4] For since, because of a likeness or con-

2. Pseudo-Dionysius, *De divinis nominibus*, IV, 13 (PG, 3, col. 713).
3. See above, ch. 38.
4. Pseudo-Dionysius, *ibid.*

geniality between the lover and the one he loves, the affection of the lover is in a manner united to the one loved, his appetite tends to the perfection of the union, so that, namely, the union that has already begun in affection may be completed in act. Hence, it is also the privilege of friends to take joy in one another's presence, in living together, and in conversation.[5] But God moves all things to union, for, in so far as He gives them being and other perfections, He joins them to Himself in the manner in which this is possible. God, therefore, loves Himself and other things.

[7] Again, the principle of every affection is love. For joy and desire are only of a good that is loved, and fear and sadness are only of an evil that is opposed to the good that is loved; and from these all the other affections take their origin. But in God there is joy and delight, as was shown above.[6] Therefore, in God there is love.

[8] Now, it might seem to someone that God does not love this thing more than that. For, if increase or decrease in intensity properly belongs to a changeable nature, it cannot befit God, from whom all mutability is absent.

[9] Again, none of the other things that are said of God in terms of operation are said of Him according to more and less; for neither does He know one thing more than another, nor does He take more joy over this thing than over that.

[10] We must therefore observe that, although the other operations of the soul deal with only one object, love alone seems to be directed to two objects. For by the fact that we understand and rejoice, we must be somehow related to some object. Love, however, wills something for someone, for we are said to love the thing to which we wish some good, as explained above. Hence, the things that we *want*, absolutely and properly we are said to *desire*, but not to love; rather, we love ourselves for whom we *want* those

5. Aristotle, *Nicomachean Ethics*, IX, 12 (1171b 32).
6. See above, ch. 90.

things: whence it is by accident and improperly that such things are said to be loved. Now, then, the other operations are susceptible of more and less only according to the vigor of the action. This cannot take place in God. For the vigor of an action is measured according to the power by which it is done, and every divine action belongs to one and the same power. On the other hand, love is said according to more and less in a twofold way. In one way, from the good that we will to someone, and according to this we are said to love him more to whom we will the greater good. In a second way, from the vigor of the action, and in this way we are said to love him more to whom we will with greater fervor and efficacity, though not a greater good, yet an equal good.

[11]   In the first way, nothing prevents us from saying that God loves one thing more than another, according as He wills it a greater good. In the second way, this cannot be said, for the same reason that was given in the case of the other operations.

[12]   It is therefore apparent from what has been said that, from among our affections, there is none that can properly exist in God save only joy and love; although even these are not in God as passions, as they are in us.

[13]   That there are joy and delight in God is confirmed by the authority of Sacred Scripture. For it is said in a Psalm (15:11): "At Thy right hand there are delights even to the ends." In the Proverbs (8:30), divine Wisdom, which is God, as we have shown,[7] says: "I . . . was delighted every day playing before Him at all times." And Luke (15:10): "There is joy in heaven before the angels of God upon one sinner doing penance." The Philosopher likewise says in *Ethics* VII that "God ever rejoices with one simple delight."[8]

7. See above, ch. 45 and 60.
8. Aristotle, *Nicomachean Ethics*, VII, 14 (1154b 26).

[14] Sacred Scripture likewise records the love of God: "He hath loved the people" (Deut. 33:3); "I have loved thee with an everlasting love" (Jer. 31:3); "For the Father Himself loveth you" (John 16:27). Certain philosophers likewise made God's love to be the principle of things. With this view the words of Dionysius agree when he says that "the divine love did not allow Him to be without offspring."[9]

[15] It must be noted, however, that the other affections, which in their species are repugnant to the divine perfection, are also said of God in Sacred Scripture, not indeed properly, as has been proved,[10] but metaphorically, because of a likeness either in effects or in some preceding affection.

[16] I say of *effects* because the will at times, following the order of wisdom, tends to that effect to which someone is inclined because of a defective passion; for a judge punishes from justice, as the angry man punishes from anger. Hence, God is at times called *angry* in so far as, following the order of His wisdom, He wills to punish someone, according to a Psalm (2:13): "When His wrath shall be kindled in a short time." On the other hand, God is called *merciful* in so far as out of His loving-kindness He takes away the miseries of men, just as we do the same thing through the passion of mercy. Hence the Psalm (102:8): "The Lord is compassionate and merciful: longsuffering and plenteous in mercy." Sometimes, too, God is said to *repent* in so far as according to the eternal and immutable order of His providence He makes what He previously had destroyed, or destroys what He had previously had made—as those who are moved by repentance are found doing. Hence Genesis (6:7): "It repenteth Me that I have made man." That this cannot be taken at the letter appears from what is said in I Kings (15:29): "But the triumpher in Israel will not spare, and will not be moved to repentance."

9. Pseudo-Dionysius, *De divinis nominibus*, IV, 11 (*PG*, 3, col. 708B).
10. See above, ch. 89 and 30.

[17]   And I say *in some preceding affection* since love and
joy, which are properly in God, are the principles of the
other affections, love in the manner of a moving principle
and joy in the manner of an end. Hence, those likewise
who punish in anger rejoice as having gained their end.
God, then, is said to be saddened in so far as certain things
take place that are contrary to what He loves and approves;
just as we experience sadness over things that have taken
place against our will. This is apparent in Isaias (59:15–16):
God "saw, and it appeared evil in His eyes, because there
is no judgment. And He saw that there is not a man, and
He stood astonished, because there is none to oppose Himself."

[18]   Now, what we have said sets aside the error of certain Jews who attributed anger, sadness, repentance, and
all such passions in their proper sense to God, failing to
distinguish what in Sacred Scripture is said properly and
what metaphorically.

Chapter 92.

HOW VIRTUES MAY BE HELD TO BE IN GOD

[1]   Following what has been said, it remains to show how
virtues may be posited in God. For just as God's being is
universally perfect, containing in itself the perfections of
all beings,[1] so His goodness must in a manner contain the
goodness in each and every thing.[2] Now, virtue is a certain
goodness in the virtuous, for "according to it is one called
good, and his work good."[3] Therefore, the divine goodness
must contain in its way all the virtues.

[2]   As a consequence, none of them is posited as a habit
in God, as happens in our case. For it does not befit God

1. See above, ch. 28.
2. See above, ch. 40.
3. Aristotle, *Nicomachean Ethics*, II, 6 (1106a 22).

to be good through something else superadded to Him, but through His essence, since He is absolutely simple.[4] Nor, likewise, does He act through something added to His essence, since His action is His being, as has been shown.[5] Hence, His virtue is not some habit, but His essence.

[3]   Again, a habit is an imperfect act, as being intermediate between potency and act; hence, those possessing a habit are compared to those who are asleep. But in God there is most perfect act. Act, therefore, is not in Him as a habit, for example, *science*, but as the *act of considering*, which is an ultimate and perfect act.

[4]   Further, habit is perfective of a power. But in God there is nothing in potency, but only in act. A habit, therefore, cannot be found in Him.

[5]   Moreover, a habit is in the genus of accident, which in no way is found in God, as was shown above.[6] Neither, therefore, is any virtue said of God as a habit, but only according to His essence.

[6]   Now, since human virtues are those by which human life is directed, and human life is twofold, contemplative and active, the virtues belonging to the active life, so far as they perfect this life, cannot befit God.

[7]   For man's active life consists in the use of bodily goods, and hence the active life is directed by the virtues by which we make a right use of these goods. Such goods, however, cannot befit God, nor, therefore, can such virtues so far as they direct this life.

[8]   Furthermore, such virtues perfect the ways of men in the domain of political life. Hence, for those who do not take part in such a life the active virtues do not seem very suitable. Much less, therefore, can they suit God,

4. See above, ch. 18 and 38.
5. See above, ch. 45 and 73.
6. See above, ch. 23.

whose conduct and life is far removed from the manner of human life.

[9]   Of the virtues that deal with the active life some, likewise, direct the passions. These we cannot posit in God. For the virtues that deal with the passions take their species from the passions as from their proper objects; and so temperance differs from fortitude so far as it deals with desires, whereas the latter with fear and daring. But in God there are no passions, as has been shown,[7] and therefore neither can such virtues be found in Him.

[10]   Again, such virtues are not found in the intellective part of the soul but in the sensitive part, in which alone passions can be found, as is proved in *Physics* VII.[8] In God, however, there is no sensitive part, but only intellect. It remains, then, that such virtues cannot be in God even according to their proper natures.

[11]   Of the passions, with which the virtues deal, some exist according to the inclination of the appetite to some corporeal good that is delightful to the sense, for example, food, drink, and sex. For the desires of these passions there are *sobriety* and *chastity*, and, in general, *temperance* and *continence*. Hence, because bodily delights are absolutely foreign to God, the aforesaid virtues neither befit God properly, since they deal with passions, nor are they said of God even metaphorically in Scripture, because there is no available likeness of them in God in terms of a likeness of some effect.

[12]   Some passions, however, follow the inclination of the appetite to some spiritual good, such as honor, power, victory, revenge, and the like; and concerned with their hopes, their darings, and in general their desires there are *fortitude, magnanimity, gentleness,* and other like virtues. These, properly speaking, cannot be found in God, since they deal with passions, but in Scripture they are said meta-

7. See above, ch. 87.
8. Aristotle, *Physics,* VII, 3 (246b 20).

phorically of God, because of a likeness in effects. For example, what is said in I Kings (2:2): "There is none strong like our God"; and Micheas [rather, Sophonias 2:3]: "Seek the just, seek the meek."

Chapter 93.

THAT IN GOD THERE ARE THE MORAL VIRTUES
THAT DEAL WITH ACTIONS

[1] Now, there are some virtues directing the active life of man that do not deal with passions, but with actions: for example, *truth, justice, liberality, magnificence, prudence,* and *art.*

[2] Since, however, virtue derives its species from its object or its matter, and since the actions that are the matter or the objects of such virtues are not repugnant to the divine perfection, neither do these virtues, according to their proper species, have anything on whose account they are excluded from the divine perfection.

[3] Again, these virtues are certain perfections of the intellect and the will, which are principles of operation without passion. But in God there are intellect and will, lacking no perfection. Therefore, these virtues cannot be absent from God.

[4] Moroever, of the things that come into being from God the proper model is in the divine intellect, as was shown above.[1] Now, the model in the mind of the maker of the thing to be made is *art.* Hence, the Philosopher says in *Ethics* VI that "art is the true model of things to be made."[2] Art, then, is properly in God. And therefore

1. See above, ch. 54.
2. Aristotle, *Nicomachean Ethics*, VI, 4 (1140a 9, 20).

it is said in Wisdom (7:21): "the artisan of all things has taught me wisdom."[3]

[5]   Again, the divine will, with reference to things other than God, is determined to one effect by His knowledge, as was shown above.[4] But the knowledge directing the will to act is prudence; for, according to the Philosopher in *Ethics* VI, "prudence is the true notion of the things to be done."[5] There is, therefore, *prudence* in God. And this is what is said in Job (12:13): "With Him is prudence [Douay, wisdom] and strength."

[6]   Furthermore, it was shown above that because God wills something He also wills those things that are necessary to it.[6] But that which is necessary to the perfection of each thing is due to it. Therefore, there is *justice* in God, to which it belongs to give to each one what belongs to him. Hence it is said in a Psalm (10:8): "The Lord is just and hath loved justice."

[7]   Moreover, as was shown above,[7] the ultimate end for which God wills all things in no way depends on the things that exist for the sake of the end, and this either as to being or as to some perfection. Hence, He does not will to give to someone His goodness so that thereby something may accrue to Himself, but because for Him to make such a gift befits Him as the fount of goodness. But to give something not for the sake of some benefit expected from the giving, but because of the goodness and befittingness of the giving, is an act of liberality, as appears from the Philosopher in *Ethics* IV. God, therefore, is supremely *liberal*; and, as Avicenna says, He alone can truly be called

3. This translates Wisdom 7:21, as found in St. Thomas' text, with *sapientiam* for *sapientia*. The Vulgate has: "*Omnium Artifex docuit me sapientia*," which in the Douay version reads: "For Wisdom, which is the worker of all things, taught me."

4. See above, ch. 82.

5. Aristotle, *Nicomachean Ethics*, VI, 5 (1140b 20).

6. See above, ch. 83.

7. See above, ch. 81.

liberal, for every agent other than God acquires some good from his action, which is the intended end.[8] Scripture sets forth this liberality of God, saying in a Psalm (103:28): "When Thou openest Thy hand, they shall all be filled with good"; and in James (1:5): "Who giveth to all men abundantly and upbraideth not."

[8] Again, all things that receive being from God must bear His likeness in so far as they are, are good, and have their proper models in the divine intellect, as was shown above.[9] But it belongs to the virtue of truth, as appears from the Philosopher in *Ethics* IV,[10] for someone in his deeds and words to show himself such as he is. Therefore, there is in God the virtue of *truth*. Hence, Romans (3:4): "But God is true"; and the Psalm (118:151): "All Thy ways are truth."

[9] But, if there are any virtues that deal with notions belonging to subordinates in relation to their superiors, such cannot befit God: for example, obedience, worship, or something of the sort that is due a superior.

[10] If, furthermore, some of the aforementioned virtues have certain imperfect acts, the virtues in question cannot be attributed to God according to those acts. Thus, prudence, according to the act of taking good counsel, does not befit God. For, since counsel is "a certain inquiry," as is said in *Ethics* VI,[11] and the divine knowledge is not inquiring, as was shown above,[12] to take counsel cannot befit God. Hence Job (26:3): "To whom hast thou given counsel? Perhaps to him that hath no understanding" [Douay, wisdom]; and Isaias (40:14): "With whom hath He consulted: and who hath instructed Him?" But as to the act

8. Aristotle, *Nicomachean Ethics*, IV, 1 (1120b 8); Avicenna, *Metaphysics*, VI, 5 (fol. 95ra).

9. See above, ch. 40 and 54.

10. Aristotle, *Nicomachean Ethics*, IV, 7 (1127a 26).

11. Aristotle, *Nicomachean Ethics*, VI, 9 (1142a 33).

12. See above, ch. 57.

that consists in judging the matter of counsel and choosing what has been approved, nothing prevents prudence from being said of God. Nevertheless, *counsel* is at times said of God. This is either because of the likeness in privacy, since counsels take place in private, so that what is hidden in the divine wisdom is called by likeness counsel, as appears in Isaias in the other version: "May Thy ancient counsel be verified" (25:1, Septuagint); or in so far as He gives satisfaction to those who seek His counsel, since one who has understanding can, even without any discursiveness, instruct the inquiring.

[11]   In the same way, justice, as concerns the act of commutative justice, cannot befit God, since He does not receive anything from anyone. Hence Romans (11:35): "Who hath first given to Him and recompense shall be made him?" And Job (41:2): "Who hath given me before that I should repay him?" Through a likeness, however, we are said to give some things to God in so far as God looks with favor upon our gifts. Commutative justice, therefore, does not befit God, but only distributive. Hence, Dionysius says that "God is praised for His justice as giving to all according to their worth."[13] And in the words of Matthew (25:15): "He gave . . . to every one according to his proper ability."

[12]   We must observe, however, that the actions with which the above virtues deal, do not according to their natures depend on man; for to judge of the things that are to be done, or to give or distribute something, does not belong to man alone but to any being possessing an intellect. Yet, in so far as these are narrowed to the human sphere, in a manner they receive their species from them, as the curvature in a nose produces the species of the snub. The aforementioned virtues, therefore, according as they order man's active life, are ordered to these actions in so far as they are narrowed to human affairs and take their

13. Pseudo-Dionysius, *De divinis nominibus*, VIII, 3 (PG, 3, col. 896A).

species from them. In this manner they cannot befit God. But in so far as the aforementioned actions are taken in their generality, they can be attributed even to divine things. For just as man is a distributor of human goods, such as money and honor, so too God is the distributor of all the goods of the universe. The aforementioned virtues, therefore, are of a more universal extension in God than in man; for as the justice of man is to the community or the household, so the justice of God is to the whole universe. Hence, the divine virtues are said to be the exemplar virtues of ours; for the things that are contracted and particularized are the likenesses of certain absolute beings, just as the light of a candle is to the light of the sun. As for the other virtues, which do not properly befit God, they do not have an exemplar in the divine nature, but only in the divine wisdom, which contains the proper likenesses of all beings:[14] this is the case with other corporeal beings.

Chapter 94.

THAT IN GOD THERE ARE CONTEMPLATIVE VIRTUES

[1] Concerning the contemplative virtues there can be no doubt that they supremely befit God.

[2] For if wisdom consists in the knowledge of the highest causes, according to the Philosopher in the beginning of the *Metaphysics*,[1] and if God especially knows Himself, and does not know anything, as has been proved,[2] except by knowing Himself Who is the first cause of all things, it is manifest that *wisdom* must most especially be attributed to Him. Hence Job (9:4): "He is wise in heart"; and

14. See above, ch. 54.
1. Aristotle, *Metaphysics*, I, 2 (982b 2).
2. See above, ch. 47.

Ecclesiasticus (1:1): "All wisdom is from the Lord God, and hath been always with Him." The Philosopher also says in the beginning of the *Metaphysics* that wisdom is a divine possession, not a human one.[3]

[3]   Again, if science is the knowledge of a thing through its cause,[4] and if God knows the order of all causes and effects, and thereby knows the proper causes of singulars, as was shown above,[5] it is manifest that in a proper sense there is *science* in Him. Nevertheless, this is not the science caused by ratiocination,[6] as our science is caused by demonstration. Hence I Kings (2:3): "For the Lord is the God of all knowledge [*scientiarum*]."

[4]   Furthermore, if the immaterial knowledge of some things without discursiveness is intellect, and God has such knowledge of all things, as was shown above,[7] there is therefore *intellect* in God. Hence Job (12:13): "He hath counsel and understanding."

[5]   These virtues, likewise, are in God the exemplars of ours, as the perfect of the imperfect.

Chapter 95.

THAT GOD CANNOT WILL EVIL

[1]   From what has been said it can be shown that God cannot will evil.

[2]   For the virtue of a being is that by which he operates well. Now every operation of God is an operation of virtue,

3. Aristotle, *Metaphysics*, I, 2 (982b 28).
4. Aristotle, *Posterior Analytics*, I, 2 (71b 10).
5. See above, ch. 64.
6. See above, ch. 57.
7. *Ibid.*

since His virtue is His essence, as was shown above.[1] Therefore, God cannot will evil.

[3] Again, the will never aims at evil without some error existing in the reason, at least with respect to a particular object of choice. For, since the object of the will is the apprehended good, the will cannot aim at evil unless in some way it is proposed to it as a good; and this cannot take place without error. But in the divine knowledge there cannot be error, as was shown above.[2] God's will cannot, therefore, tend towards evil.

[4] Moreover, God is the highest good, as has been shown.[3] But the highest good cannot bear any mingling with evil, as neither can the highest hot thing bear any mingling with the cold. The divine will, therefore, cannot be turned to evil.

[5] Furthermore, since the good has the nature of an end, evil cannot enter the will except by turning away from the end. But the divine will cannot be turned from the end, since it can will nothing except by willing itself.[4] Therefore, it cannot will evil.

[6] And thus it appears that free choice in God naturally stands abiding in the good.

[7] This is what is said in Deuteronomy (32:4): "God is faithful and without any iniquity"; and Habacuc (1:13): "Thy eyes are too pure to behold evil, and Thou canst not look on iniquity."

[8] By this is refuted the error of the Jews, who say in the *Talmud* that at times God sins and is cleansed from sin; and of the Luciferians, who say that God sinned in ejecting Lucifer.

1. See above, ch. 92.
2. See above, ch. 61.
3. See above, ch. 41.
4. See above, ch. 74ff.

Chapter 96.

THAT GOD HATES NOTHING, AND THE HATRED OF NO THING BEFITS HIM

[1]   From this it appears that the hatred of something does not befit God.

[2]   For as love is to the good, so hatred is to evil; for to those we love we will good, and to those we hate, evil. If, then, the will of God cannot be inclined to evil, as has been shown,[1] it is impossible that He should hate anything.

[3]   Again, the will of God is directed to things other than Himself, as has been shown,[2] in so far as, by willing and loving His own being and His own goodness, God wills it to be diffused as much as possible through the communication of likeness. This, then, is what God wills in other things, that there be in them the likeness of His goodness. But this is the good of each thing, namely, to participate in the likeness of God; for every other goodness is nothing other than a certain likeness of the first goodness.[3] Therefore, God wills good to each thing. Hence, He hates nothing.

[4]   Furthermore, from the first being all the others take the origin of their being. If, then, God hates anything among the things that are, He wills it not to be, since to be is each thing's good. He wills, therefore, the non-existence of His own action by which that thing is brought into being either mediately or immediately. For it was shown above that, if God wills something, He must will the things that are necessary for it.[4] Now, this is impos-

1. See above, ch. 95.
2. See above, ch. 75.
3. See above, ch. 40, ¶3.
4. See above, ch. 83.

sible. This is apparent if things come into being through His will, for then the action by which things are produced must be voluntary. The same is the case if God is by nature the cause of things, for, just as His nature is pleasing to Him, so whatever His nature requires is pleasing to Him. God, therefore, does not hate anything.

[5] Moreover, that which is found in all naturally active causes must be especially found in the first cause. But all agents in their own way love their effects as such: thus, parents love their children, poets their poetry, and artists their works. All the more, then, does God not hate anything, since He is the cause of all things.

[6] This is what is said in Wisdom (11:25): "For Thou lovest all the things that are, and hatest none of the things which Thou hast made."

[7] However, God is said by similitude to hate some things, and this in a twofold way. In the first way, because God, in loving things and by willing the existence of their good, wills the non-existence of the contrary evil. Hence, He is said to have a hatred of evils, for we are said to hate what we will not to exist. In the words of Zacharias (8:17): "And let none of you imagine evil in your hearts against his friend and love not a false oath. For all these are the things that I hate, saith the Lord." These, however, are not effects in the manner of subsisting things, to which properly love and hate refer.

[8] The second way arises from the fact that God wills some greater good that cannot be without the loss of some lesser good. And thus He is said to hate, although this is rather to love. For thus, inasmuch as He wills the good of justice or of the order of the universe, which cannot exist without the punishment or corruption of some things, God is said to hate the things whose punishment or corruption He wills. In the words of Malachias (1:3): "I have hated Esau"; and the Psalms (5:7): "Thou hatest all workers of

iniquity: Thou wilt destroy all that speaks a lie. The bloody and the deceitful man the Lord will abhor."

Chapter 97.

THAT GOD IS LIVING

[1]   From what has already been proved it necessarily follows that God is living.

[2]   For it has been shown that God is understanding and willing,[1] and the acts of understanding and willing belong only to a living being. Therefore, God is living.

[3]   Again, to live is attributed to some beings because they are seen to move themselves, but not to be moved by another. And on this account the things that seem to be moved by themselves, whose movers people in general do not perceive, we call by similitude living: for example, the living water of a flowing spring, but not the water of a cistern or a stagnant pool; or quicksilver, which appears to have a certain movement. For, in a proper sense, those things move through themselves that move themselves, being composed of a mover and something moved, for example, animate things. These alone we properly say are living, while all other things are moved by some exterior agent, be it a generating cause, or one removing an obstacle, or an impelling cause. And because all sensible operations involve motion, everything that moves itself to its own operations is further said to live, though this be not with motion; and so understanding, appetition, and sensing are actions of life. But it is supremely true of God that He does not act from another, but through Himself, since He is the first agent. Therefore, to live belongs to Him in a supreme way.

1. See above, ch. 44 and 72.

[4]   Again, the divine being comprehends every perfection of being, as has been shown.[2] But to live is a certain perfection, which is why living things in the order of being are higher than non-living things. Hence, the divine being is living. Therefore, God is living.

[5]   This is likewise confirmed by the authority of the divine Scripture. For it is said in Deuteronomy (32:40) in the person of the Lord: "I will say: I live forever"; and in a Psalm (83:3): "My heart and my flesh have rejoiced in the living God."

Chapter 98.

THAT GOD IS HIS LIFE

[1]   From this it further appears that God is His life.

[2]   For the *life* of the living being is the very act of living signified in an abstract manner, as *running* is in reality nothing other than *to run*. Now, "to live is for the living their very being," as appears from the Philosopher in *De anima* II.[1] For, since an animal is said to be living because it has a soul, through which it has being as through its proper form, it follows that *to live* is nothing other than such a being arising from such a form. But God is His own being, as was proved above.[2] Therefore, He is His own act of living and His own life.

[3]   Again, understanding is a certain way of living, as appears from the Philosopher in *De anima* II;[3] for to live is the act of a living being. But God is His own understand-

2. See above, ch. 28.
1. Aristotle, *De anima*, II, 4 (415b 12).
2. See above, ch. 22.
3. Aristotle, *De anima*, II, 2 (413a 23).

ing, as was shown above,[4] and therefore He is His own act of living and His own life.

[4]   Moreover, if God were not His life, since He is living, as has been shown,[5] it would follow that He would be living through the participation of life. But everything that is through participation is reduced to that which is through itself. Therefore, God would be reduced to something prior, through which He would be living. This is impossible, as is apparent from what has been said.[6]

[5]   Furthermore, if God is living, as has been shown,[7] there must be life in Him. If, then, He is not His own life, there will be something in Him that is not He. Thus, He will be composite, which has been disproved.[8] Therefore, God is His life.

[6]   This is what is said in John (14:6): "I am . . . the life."

Chapter 99.

THAT THE LIFE OF GOD IS EVERLASTING

[1]   From this it appears that God's life is everlasting.

[2]   Nothing ceases to live except through separation from life. But nothing can be separated from God, since every separation takes place through the division of something from something. It is therefore impossible that God cease to live, since He is His life, as has been shown.[1]

4. See above, ch. 45.
5. See above, ch. 97.
6. See above, ch. 13.
7. See above, ch. 97.
8. See above, ch. 18.
1. See above, ch. 98.

[3]   Again, everything that at times is and at times is not is through some cause, for nothing leads itself from non-being to being, since that which does not yet exist does not act. But the divine life has no cause, as neither does the divine being. Hence, God is not at times living and at times not-living, but He always lives. Therefore, His life is everlasting.

[4]   Furthermore, in every operation the agent abides, even though at times the operation passes through succession. Hence, in motion likewise, the movable remains the same in subject during the whole motion, although not in situation. Where, therefore, the action is the agent itself, of necessity nothing there passes through succession, but the whole remains all together. But the understanding and living of God are God Himself, as has been shown.[2] Therefore, His life has no succession, but is life all together. Therefore, it is everlasting.

[5]   Moreover, God is absolutely immobile, as was shown above.[3] But what begins to live and ceases to live, or in living suffers succession, is mutable. For one's life begins through generation, it ceases through corruption, and as to succession, it exists because of some motion. But God neither began to live, nor will He cease to live, nor in living does He suffer any succession. Therefore, His life is everlasting.

[6]   Hence what is said in Deuteronomy (32:40) in the person of the Lord: "I live forever"; and in I John (5:20): "This is true God and life eternal."

2. See above, ch. 45 and 98.
3. See above, ch. 13, ¶28.

Chapter 100.

THAT GOD IS BLESSED

[1]   It remains from the foregoing to show that God is blessed.

[2]   The proper good of every intellectual nature is blessedness. Since, then, God is intelligent, His proper good will be blessedness. But He is not related to His proper good as is something that tends to a good not yet possessed, since this belongs to a nature that is movable and existing in potency; He is related rather as that which already possesses its proper good. Therefore, He not only desires blessedness, as we do, but enjoys it. Therefore, He is blessed.

[3]   Moreover, that is supremely desired or willed by an intellectual nature which is most perfect in it; and this is its blessedness. But the most perfect thing in each being is its most perfect operation. For potency and habit are perfected by operation, and so the Philosopher says that "felicity is perfect operation."[1] But the perfection of operation depends on four things. *First*, on its genus, namely, that it be abiding in its operating cause. By an operation that abides in its cause I mean one through which nothing takes place but the operation itself: for example, to see and to hear. For these are the perfections of the beings whose operations they are, and can be ultimate because they are not ordered to something made as to their end. On the other hand, the operation or the action from which there follows some result beyond the action itself is the perfection of the thing produced, and not of the operating cause, and is related to it as to an end. Hence, such an operation of an intellectual nature is not blessedness or felicity. *Second*, it depends on the principle of operation, namely, that it be

1. Aristotle, *Nicomachean Ethics*, X, 7 (1177a 19).

the operation of the highest power. Hence, there is not felicity in us according to the operation of sense, but according to the operation of the intellect, and one perfected by a habit. *Third,* it depends on the object of operation. On this account, the highest felicity in us consists in understanding the highest intelligible. *Fourth,* it depends on the form of the operation, namely, that it be done perfectly, easily, firmly, and with delight. Such, however, is the operation of God, since He is intelligent, and His intellect is the highest power, nor does He need any perfecting habit, because He is perfect in Himself, as was shown above.[2] Furthermore, He understands Himself, being the highest intelligible, and this perfectly, without any difficulty, and with delight. God is, therefore, blessed.

[4]   Furthermore, through blessedness every desire is given rest, because, when blessedness is possessed, nothing else remains to be desired, since it is the ultimate end. He must, therefore, be blessed who is perfect in relation to all the things that He can desire. Hence, Boethius says that blessedness is "a state made perfect by the accumulation of all goods."[3] But such is the divine perfection, because it comprehends all perfection in a certain simplicity, as was shown above.[4] Therefore, God is truly blessed.

[5]   Again, as long as someone is missing something that he needs, he is not yet blessed, for his desire is not yet at rest. Whoever, therefore, is self-sufficient, needing nothing, he is blessed. But it has been shown above that God does not need other things,[5] since His perfection depends on nothing outside Himself, nor does God will other things for His own sake as though He needed them, but solely because this befits His goodness. Therefore, He is blessed.

2. See above, ch. 45.
3. Boethius, *De consolatione philosophiae,* III, prosa 2 (*PL,* 63, col. 724).
4. See above, ch. 28 and 31.
5. See above, ch. 81 and 82.

[6]   Furthermore, it was shown above that God cannot will something impossible.[6] But it is impossible that God should receive what He does not already have, since He is in no way in potency, as has been shown.[7] Therefore, He cannot will to have anything that He does not have. Hence, whatever He wills, He has. Nor does He will anything evil, as was shown above.[8] He is therefore blessed, in the manner in which some proclaim the blessed man to be "he who has whatever He wills and who wills nothing evil."[9]

[7]   Sacred Scripture, furthermore, proclaims the blessedness of God: "Which in His times He shall show Who is the Blessed and only Mighty" (I Tim. 6:15).

Chapter 101.

THAT GOD IS HIS BLESSEDNESS

[1]   From this it is apparent that God is His blessedness.

[2]   For His blessedness is a certain intellectual operation, as has been shown.[1] But it was shown above that His understanding is His substance.[2] Therefore, He is His blessedness.

[3]   Again, blessedness, since it is the ultimate end, is that which he who can have it, or has it, principally wills. But it was shown above that God principally wills His essence.[3] Therefore, His essence is His blessedness.

[4]   Furthermore, everyone relates to his blessedness whatever he wills. For it is what is not desired for the sake of

6. See above, ch. 84.
7. See above, ch. 16.
8. See above, ch. 95.
9. St. Augustine, De Trinitate, XIII, 5 (PL, 42, col. 1020).
1. See above, ch. 100.
2. See above, ch. 45.
3. See above, ch. 74.

something else, and that in which terminates the motion of the desire of someone desiring one thing for the sake of another—so that the motion may not be infinite. Since, then, God wills all other things for the sake of His goodness,[4] which is His essence, it is necessary that, just as He is His essence and His goodness, He be His blessedness.

[5] Moreover, that there be two highest goods is impossible. For, if one lacked something that the other had, neither would be highest and perfect. But God was shown above to be the highest good.[5] Blessedness will also be shown to be the highest good because it is the ultimate end. Therefore, blessedness and God are identical. Therefore, God is His blessedness.

Chapter 102.

THAT THE PERFECT AND UNIQUE BLESSEDNESS
OF GOD EXCELS EVERY OTHER BLESSEDNESS

[1] From what has preceded we may further examine the excellence of the divine blessedness.

[2] The nearer something is to blessedness, the more blessed it is. Hence, although a man may be called blessed because he hopes to obtain blessedness, in no way does his blessedness compare with the blessedness of the one who already possesses it in act. But the thing nearest to blessedness is blessedness itself. This has been shown of God.[1] Therefore, God is in a unique way perfectly blessed.

[3] Again, since delight is caused by love, as has been shown,[2] where the love is greater, there is greater delight in

4. See above, ch. 75.
5. See above, ch. 41.
1. See above, ch. 101.
2. See above, ch. 90.

the possession of what is loved. But, other things being equal, each thing loves itself more than another, and a sign of this is that the nearer a thing is to something else the more it is naturally loved. God, therefore, delights more in His blessedness, which He Himself is, than do other blessed ones in the blessedness which is not they themselves. The desire has therefore all the more repose, and the blessedness is all the more perfect.

[4] Furthermore, that which is through its essence is more excellent than what is said by participation: for example, the nature of fire is found more perfectly in fire itself than in things that are on fire. But God is blessed through His essence, and this befits no other being, since no being other than He can be the highest good, as can be seen from what has been said.[3] And thus, whoever other than God is blessed, must be called blessed by participation. The divine blessedness, therefore, excels every other blessedness.

[5] Moreover, blessedness consists in the perfect operation of the intellect, as has been shown.[4] But no other intellectual operation can compare with God's operation. This is evident not only because it is a subsistent operation but also because by one operation God knows Himself as perfectly as He is perfect, as well as all other things, those that are and those that are not, the good and the evil. But in all other beings with an intellect, the operation of the intellect is not itself subsistent, but the act of something subsistent. Nor, again, is God Himself, Who is the highest intelligible, understood by anyone as perfectly as He is perfect, since the being of no thing is as perfect as the divine being, nor can the operation of any being be more perfect than its substance. Nor, still, is there another intellect that knows also all the things that God can make, for then it would comprehend the divine power. And even as to the things that another intellect knows, it does not know them all by

3. See above, ch. 41.
4. See above, ch. 100.

one and the same operation. God, therefore, is blessed above all things beyond compare.

[6] Again, the more something is united, by so much the more are its power and goodness more perfect. But a successive operation is divided according to the diverse parts of time. Its perfection, therefore, can in no way be compared to the perfection of an operation that is all at once without succession, and this especially if it does not pass away in a moment but abides for eternity. Now, in God, to understand exists eternally all at once and without succession,[5] whereas in us to understand implies succession because continuity and time are by accident joined to it. Hence, the divine blessedness infinitely excels human blessedness, as the duration of eternity excels the flowing now of time.

[7] Furthermore, weariness and the various cares with which perforce our contemplation in this life is mingled (in this contemplation human felicity especially consists, if by chance there is such in the present life), and the errors, doubts and hazards to which the present life is exposed show that human felicity, especially that of the present life, cannot at all compare with the divine blessedness.

[8] Moreover, the perfection of the divine blessedness can be observed from the fact that it includes within itself every blessedness in a most perfect way. For contemplative felicity God has the most perfect and everlasting consideration of Himself and other things. For active felicity He has the government, not of the life of one man, or of a household, a city, or a kingdom, but of the whole universe.

[9] As for false and earthly felicity, it contains no more than a shadow of that most perfect felicity. For it consists in five things, according to Boethius; namely, in pleasure,

5. See above, ch. 55.

riches, power, honor, and fame.[6] But God enjoys a most excelling delight in Himself, as well as a universal joy in all things, without the admixture of any contrary.[7] For wealth, He has the all-abundant sufficiency of all good things within Himself, as was shown above.[8] For power, He has His infinite strength.[9] For honor, He has the primacy and rule over all beings.[10] For fame, He has the admiration of every intellect that knows Him however little.

To Him, then, Who is singularly blessed, be honor and glory unto the ages of ages. Amen.

6. Boethius, *De consolatione philosophiae*, III, Prosa 2 (*PL*, 63, coll. 726–728).

7. See above, ch. 90.

8. See above, ch. 100.

9. See above, ch. 43.

10. See above, ch. 13.

INDEX OF PROPER NAMES

—— that the first motion is continuous and regular, 114, 159

—— that to live is for the living their being, 295

—— that being cannot be a genus, 127; the accidents of being as being, 183

—— that the first in a genus is a measure, 208

—— that the true is the good of the intellect, 203, 204

—— that we are said to know each thing when we know the cause, 180

—— the different and the diverse, 102

—— on forms as numbers, 190

III. Some definitions:

—— art, 285; demonstration, 198; felicity, 298; prudence, 286; science, 290; virtue, 151, 282; wisdom, 289

IV. Aristotle as a historical source:

101–102, 115, 169, 183, 184, 216

Augustine, St.,

—— that God is the good of every good, 156

—— that God made man and a horse by distinct exemplars, 191–192

—— that, in spiritual beings, to be greater is to be better, 165

—— that he is blessed who has whatever he wills and who wills nothing evil, 300

—— that there is no accident in God, 123

—— that truth and the sacred books cannot be opposed, 75

—— as a historical source, 168

Averroes (the Commentator)

—— that God does not know singulars, 209–210

—— that the first cause is distinguished from the rest by the purity of its goodness[?], 132

—— that the intellect that is solely in act does not know privation, 238

—— that the order of the world proves the existence of a providence, 96

—— that what can be and not-be moved can acquire perpetuity from another, 112

—— that what is in potency to non-being cannot naturally acquire perpetuity from another, 113